Horoscope Reading

Made Easy and Self Learning

By
U.C. Mahajan

PUSTAK MAHAL®
Delhi • Bangalore • Mumbai • Patna • Hyderabad

Publishers
Pustak Mahal®, Delhi

J-3/16, Daryaganj, New Delhi-110002
☎ 23276539, 23272783, 23272784 • *Fax:* 011-23260518
E-mail: info@pustakmahal.com • *Website:* www.pustakmahal.com

Branch Offices
Bangalore: ☎ 22234025
E-mail: pmblr@sancharnet.in • pustak@sancharnet.in
Mumbai: ☎ 22010941
E-mail: rapidex@bom5.vsnl.net.in
Patna: ☎ 309419 • *Telefax:* 0612-2302719
E-mail: rapidexptn@rediffmail.com
Hyderabad: *Telefax:* 040-24737290
E-mail: pustakmahalhyd@yahoo.co.in

© **Pustak Mahal, 6686, Khari Baoli, Delhi-110006**

ISBN 81-223-0639-X

Edition : 2005

Printed at : Unique Colour Carton, Mayapuri, Delhi-110064

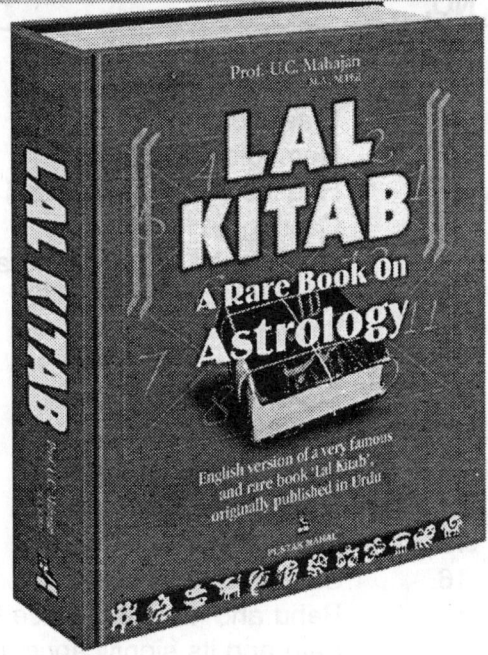

OVERVIEW

Humble Dedication

At the feet of ancient sages and seers and the Master astrologer, who wrote the 'Ancient texts' in Urdu and inspired me to write this book and other visionaries who gave us the science of Astrology, I bow my head in reverence to them.

Dedicated to the sacred memory of my revered parents, Late Shrimati Maya Devi and Late Shri Ghamir Chand, who blessed me in my dreams.

—Uttam Chand

With Love and Affection

To my wife, Shrimati Sudershan, my brother Dr. Sant K. Bhatnagar and my children Rajiv, Nirupma, Sanjeev, Manisha, Sandeep, Shivali, Karan, Apoorva & Neha who all exhorted me to write down my experiences in the form of a book in English. But for my eldest son, Rajiv, I would not have completed this book.

—Uttam Chand

TABLE OF CONTENTS

INTRODUCTION

Human mind is always curious to comprehend the movements of the planets and their influence on human life. 'Stars do govern our condition and there is a divinity that shapes our ends'. Every man or woman, however, educated is anxious to pierce through the veil of future and to unravel the mysteries of science of Astrology.

Miracles do happen and one such miracle happened in my life a few years ago. I was a skeptic and always regarded Astrology as simply humbug and trash. One fine morning, while rummaging through the old books in my ancestral home, I was fortunate enough to lay my hands upon few old books on astrology in Urdu and English. I read and re-read them & they changed my concept about Astrology. It was indeed a very rewarding and fruitful experience. I am now a strong advocate of this ancient science as it gave a new direction to my life.

I, therefore, thought of writing a comprehensive book on Astrology in English based on Ancient texts on the Hindu system of Astrology and my own research and experience on the subject spanning to more than a decade. This book in fact is the quintessence of all the finest points in Astrology garnered from various old texts on the subject in Urdu and English.

I do not claim originality and perfection, but being an humble student of this ancient science, I have based all my predictions, calculations, remedies etc. not only on the old books in Urdu and English, but also on other known texts and my varied experience; that is why I have added chapters on casting a horoscope, Nakshtras, Raashi, Mahadasha, Antardasha etc. to make it a complete and comprehensive book on the subject. It may be remembered that no human being is perfect and infallible and the Astrologer should not be blamed if a few predictions go wrong. Only God is perfect.

I take this opportunity of thanking all those known and unknown authors and their works without whose cooperation it would have been well-nigh impossible for me to write this book. I also express my debt of gratitude to all the wise men and seers and immortal Astrologer of the past who could see through the veils of future by studying the movements of the planets and their influence on human life. What a tremendous task they did ! They were indeed the 'Men of God' who could prophesy.

I express my special feeling of love for my son Rajiv who wrote & revised some of the chapters and gave a special format to the book. I am also grateful to all my well-wishers, my brothers - Romesh and Sant Kumar Bhatnagar and my favourite student Usha Barowalia, for their encouragement.

I am also thankful to my publishers for their magnanimity in accepting this manuscript for publication.

U.C. MAHAJAN

BASICS OF ASTROLOGY

Man has been looking at the heavens with wonder and awe. Our ancient sages in their wisdom, ascribed certain functions and virtues to the planets. They believed that " the stars above us governs our condition," and obviously gave us the science of Astrology.

ZODIAC & SOLAR SYSTEM

Hindu Astrology is sidereal. Zodiac is a diagram used by astrologers to represent the circular movement of the planets & stars and their positions in space at particular times. It is the belt of the heavens limited by lines about 8° from the ecliptic on each side, including all apparent positions of the Sun, Moon and planets as known to the ancient. It is divided into twelve equal sections or signs (e.g., Aries, Taurus, Gemini, Cancer, Leo, Virgo, Libra, Scorpio, Sagittarius, Capricorn, Aquarius & Pisces). Zodiac is used by astrologers to calculate the influence of the planets on people's lives.

INFORMATION ABOUT THE RAASHIS OF THE ZODIAC AND THEIR NAMES

The ancient Hindus and Egyptians divided the year into spring, summer, autumn and winter and assigned to each season three constellations through which the Sun passed. They gave amusing but apt names to the various signs of the Zodiac.

RAASHI	NAME	DATE ON WHICH SUN ENTERS THE CONSTELLATION	REASON FOR ASSIGNING THE NAME
Aries	Ram	March 21-April 20	At this time the sheep produce their young
Taurus	Bull	April 21-May 20	Agriculture depended on the bull as it tilled the land.
Gemini	Twins	May 22-June 21	Domestic goats usually produce two young ones during this month.
Cancer	Crab	June 22-July 22	Sun turns back towards equator i.e., the crab crawls backwards.

Leo	Lion	July 23-august 23	Sun is at its zenith and powerful like a lion.
Virgo	Virgin	Aug 24-Sept 23	In the harvest season girl gleans the ears of corn.
Libra	Scales	Sept 24-Oct 23	Day and night of equal strength i.e., like the two scales having equal weight.
Scorpio	Scorpion	Oct 24-Nov 22	Sun retreats and gives rise to diseases; hence poisonous.
Sagittarius	Archer	Nov 23-Dec 22	It is the hunting time.
Capricorn	Crocodile or goat	Dec 23-Jan 20	Sun begins to rise higher under the sign of ibex (wild goat) or capricornous.
Aquarius	Water carrier	Jan 21-Feb 19	Rainy season; hence pitcher full of water.
Pisces	Fish	Feb 20- March 20	Time for fishing as the fish enjoy gliding downwards.

HINDI EQUIVALENTS OF PLANETS

ENGLISH NAMES OF PLANETS	EQUIVALENT IN HINDI	EQUIVALENT IN URDU	COLOUR
JUPITER	GURU, BRIHSPATI	MUSHTRI	YELLOW
SUN	RAVI	SHAMSH	COPPER RED
MOON	CHANDER	QAMAR	WHITE(MILK)
VENUS	SHUKRA,BHRIGU	ZOHRA	WHITE(CURD)
MARS(BENEFICIAL)	MANGAL,BHAUM	MARIAKH	RED BLOOD
MARS(MALEFIC)	MANGAL,BHAUM	MARIAKH	RED BLOOD
MERCURY	BUDH	ATTAROO	GREEN
SATURN	SHANI	ZUHAL	BLACK
RAHU(NODE) DRAGON'S HEAD	RAHU	RAAS	BLUE
KETU(NODE) DRAGON'S TAIL	KETU	ZUNAB	BLACK & WHITE

HINDI EQUIVALENTS OF RAASHIS

S.NO	ENGLISH NAME	HINDI EQUIVALENT
1.	ARIES	MESH
2.	TAURUS	VRISH
3.	GEMINI	MITHUN
4.	CANCER	KARK
5.	LEO	SINGH
6.	VIRGO	KANYA

7.	LIBRA	TULA
8.	SCORPIO	VRISHCHAK
9.	SAGITTARIUS	DHANU
10.	CAPRICORN	MAKAR
11.	AQUARIUS	KUMBH
12.	PISCES	MEEN

☞ Heavenly sphere being of 360°, each of the above signs (Raashis) covers 30° of the Zodiac, e.g., Aries (first 30°), Taurus (30°- 60°), Gemini (60°-90°), Cancer (90°-120°) - so on and so forth.

In some of the ancient texts, the author has done away with the Raashis (Signs) Nakshatra (Asterisms) etc. and the Houses are the most important. It may however, be noted that Planets are exalted or debilitating according to their signs and placement in the houses. This is based on my personal experience and research.

Raashis (Signs) are equally important and their significance cannot be under-estimated. Exaltation & debilitation of a planet depends entirely upon its sign e.g., Jupiter in the 4th house is exalted provided it is in Cancer sign or its own Rashi or in a friend's Rashi. If it is in Capricorn (10th sign) or in enemy's Rashi, even in the 4th house it is debilitating. Similarly Saturn is in the 7th house is exalted or benefic only if it is in its own sign or in friend's Rashi, but if it is in Aries or in enemy's Rashi, it is debilitating and malefic. Sign means the foundation of the house and the planet indicates the house built on it, e.g., Saturn is the Lord of Aquarius (11th sign), but Jupiter is the Lord of 11th house. It means that the foundation of the house is controlled by Saturn & Jupiter is the tenant dwelling in that house.

EXAMPLE: According to Astrology the following horoscope has been prepared :

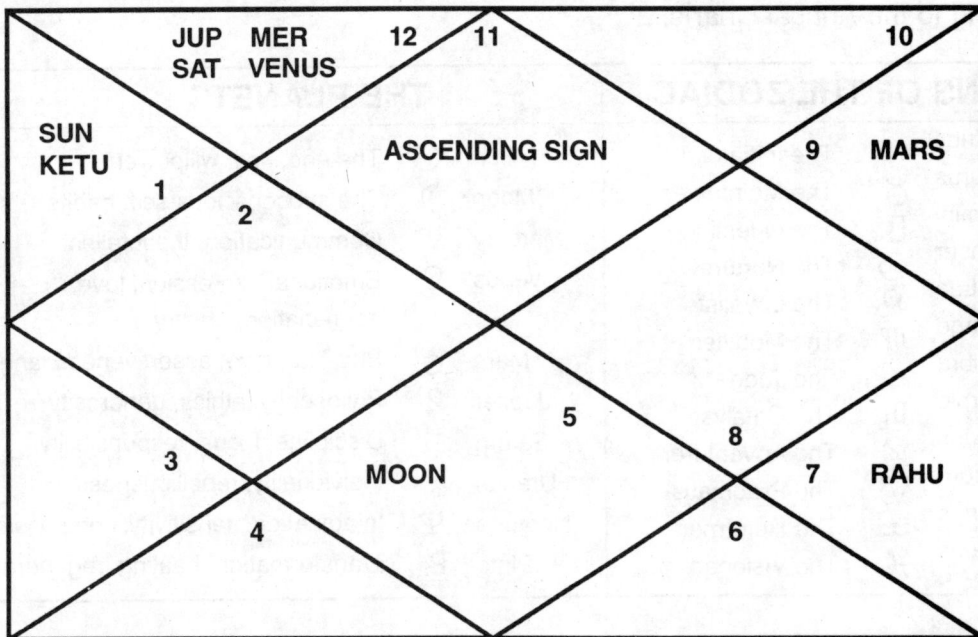

We have changed the above horoscope as under, taking the Ascendant or lagana as the first house :

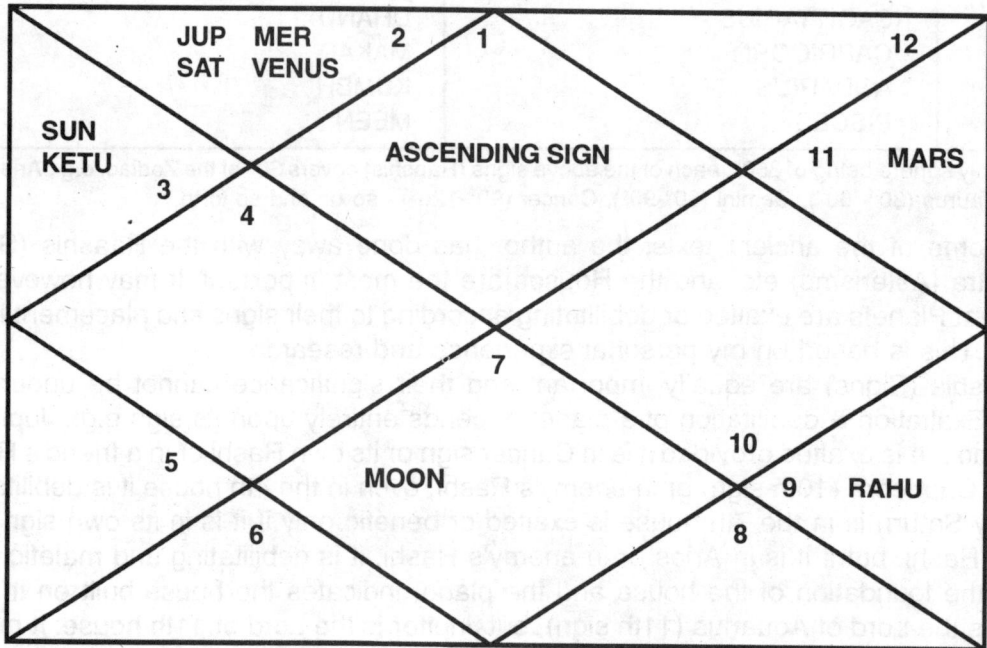

```
        JUP   MER    2  /  1                       12
        SAT   VENUS

  SUN
  KETU                    ASCENDING SIGN      11    MARS
        3
           4

                              7

                                                10
        5                                      9    RAHU
           6                              8
```

For general predictions see 2,3,7,9 & 11th houses, but Raashi results should also be taken into account, while making predictions. Similarly, annual predictions should be made according to the Annual Charts.

SIGNS OF THE ZODIAC			THE PLANETS		
Aries	♈	The Initiator	Sun	☉	The ego, self, willpower
Taurus	♉	The Maintainer	Moon	☽	The subconscious self, habits
Gemini	♊	The Questioner	Mercury	☿	Communication, the intellect
Cancer	♋	The Nurturer	Venus	♀	Emotional expression, love,
Leo	♌	The Loyalist			appreciation, artistry
Virgo	♍	The Modifier	Mars	♂	Physical drive, assertiveness, anger
Libra	♎	The Judge			
Scorpio	♏	The Catalyst	Jupiter	♃	Philosophy, ethics, generosity
Sagittarius	♐	The Adventurer	Saturn	♄	Discipline, focus, responsibility
Capricorn	♑	The Pragmatist	Uranus	♅	Individuality, rebelliousness
Aquarius	♒	The Reformer	Neptune	♆	Imagination, sensitivity, compassion
Pisces	♓	The Visionary	Pluto	♇	Transformation, healing, regeneration

CHAPTER 2

HOUSES

PERMANENT 1ST HOUSE (LAGNA)

KING'S THRONE, BODY, FAME ETC.

LORD : SUN

First house is like the throne of Solomon. It is the king Lagna or Ascendant. It is the most important house. If an exalted planet occupies this house, it becomes the planet of fate, encouraging promotion, health and prosperity. Conversely, if a malefic planet occupies this house it spells doom, disaster and misfortune.

Body, constitution, appearance, knowledge, complexion, strength or weakness, fame, dignity, dreams, happiness etc. are also to be judged from the first house or Lagna.

PERMANENT 2ND HOUSE

GOD'S TEMPLE, OLD AGE, PERSONAL FATE, WEALTH.

LORD : JUPITER

This is the house and temple of god. It confers honours, wealth, prosperity and domestic happiness. An exalted planet in this house makes a man great and eminent. It is the house of personal fate where goddess Lakshmi resides. Even the malefic planets shun their bad and wicked ways in this house and pay their respect to Jupiter, the great guru. This house also denotes speech, family, precious metals, jewels, face, the mouth and the tongue.

EXPLANATORY NOTES :

- House no.2 is always the foundation of all the nine planets or house no.9 which is regarded as boundless ocean. But house no. 4 is the foundation of house no. 2.
- House no. 8 aspects House no. 2, and house no. 2 aspects house no. 6. In other words, House no. 8 and 6 are mutually aspected by each other. If no. 8 is vacant, no.2 confers good results. In the case of Jupiter in no. 2, with house no. 8 vacant, Jupiter remains

dormant and gives bad results and man incurs loses. If house no. 9 is the ocean laden with Monsoons, house no. 2 is like the series of hills where the Monsoons strike and bless the hills and the plains with rains.

PERMANENT 3RD HOUSE

ROAD TO THE OTHER WORLD; ILLNESS, BROTHERS, ETC.

LORD : MARS

This house is reserved for relatives e.g. Brothers, Sisters, Parents etc. A malefic planet in this house spells disaster. If a feminine planet such as Moon occupies this house, it confers life and it saves the household from thefts etc. Even malefic Mars is no longer malefic. Such a person is protected by Lord Shiva and the women in the household are braver than men.

Valour, relatives, servants, courage, travelling, ears, legs, neck, throat and upper parts of the chest etc are also to be judged from this house.

EXPLANATORY NOTES :

- When the third house is occupied by wicked planets and no.8 and 6 are also malefic, death may knock at the door. But the planet in no. 12, whether friend or foe of no. 3, will act as a saving grace. For example, Mars in no.12 will financially help Ketu in no.3, though both of them are enemies.
- If Mercury is in no. 12 and Jupiter is in no. 3, man will gain a lot. It is like a receptacle filled with nectar.
- If Venus and Rahu are in no. 12 and Saturn is in no.3, Rahu will have no adverse effect on Venus.

PERMANENT 4TH HOUSE

MOTHERS' LAP AND BLESSINGS, COMFORTS.

LORD : MOON

This house gives the cool refreshing and silvery light of the moon. It confers all the comforts and amenities of life, such as abundance of Rice, Milk, horses, mothers' blessings, advantageous travel etc. It fills man's house with the ocean of milk. Even Rahu and Ketu take the solemn oath to shun their wicked ways. Such a man is noble and pious.

This house also determines mother, happiness, treasure, immovable property, dwelling houses, position attained through education, good name, maternal relations, generosity, comforts, piety, moral virtues, clothes, perfumes etc.

EXPLANATORY NOTES :

- In the house Saturn is like a poisonous snake and Mars is the most malefic, but Rahu and Ketu shun their wickedness and become noble and pious.
- If Moon is outside the four Kendras (1, 4, 7, 10) and house no. 4 is vacant, Moon exercises good influence on all planets including itself, even if Moon is debilitating.
- If no. 4 is occupied by any planet alone and Moon is debilitating in a house outside the four Kendras, the planet in no. 4 will bestow good results, whether Moon's enemy or friend. For example, house no 4 is occupied by Ketu and Moon is in no. 8 or 11, Ketu will no longer be bad.
- If house no. 4 is vacant, it will give good results till the end of life.
- If houses no. 3, 6 and 8 are malefic in the horoscope, 4th house becomes the excuse for death.
- A planet occupying 4th house imbibes the characteristics of Moon.

PERMANENT 5TH HOUSE

PROGENY; FUTURE OF CHILDREN, KNOWLEDGE.

LORD : SUN & JUPITER

This house is the repository of knowledge bright progeny, sons, Grandsons, eminence goodness, wisdom, and longevity of life. This house also denotes children, their age; health, knowledge, intelligence, scholarship, discretion, authorship, name and fame, happiness from children etc.

EXPLANATORY NOTES :

- If no. 3, 4 or 9 are malefic, they exercise bad influence on no.5.
- If Sun or Jupiter occupies no. 10, they will poison house no. 5, even if no. 5 is occupied by a friend.
- Even if the friend occupies the 6th or 10th house, it will act as a sworn enemy and will destroy the planet of no. 5.
- If Ketu is exalted everything is fine, but if Rahu is malefic everything will become topsy-turvy.
- In order to save the planet occupying this house from the poisonous arrows of no.6 or 10, bury the articles pertaining to its enemies in the earth or in the foundation of the ancestral house. If no. 8 is malefic, then bury such articles in the earth only.
- As long as Jupiter is exalted in the horoscope, children remain happy and prosperous.
- If Saturn and Venus are malefic, they will exercise bad effect; but if Moon is exalted, the malefic effect of Saturn and Venus will be nullified and everything turns out to be fine.
- When Sun-Venus OR Sun or Jupiter are in house no. 5, a malefic planet or Venus occupying the 1st house will cause ill-health.

PERMANENT 6TH HOUSE

UNDERWORLD SECRET HELP; COMPASSION, ENEMIES, LITIGATION ETC.

LORD : KETU AND MERCURY

Ketu and Mercury occupy the 6th house i.e. The underworld. It is the house for enemies. If they are alone it is good and benefic. If they jointly occupy this house, Ketu (Son) becomes malefic whereas, Mercury (daughter) is benefic. Ketu is debilitating and Rahu is exalted in this house. This house also governs maternal uncles, mental worries, god of death, fear of misfortunes, enemies, wounds, hostilities, etc.

EXPLANATORY NOTES :

- If house no. 6 is vacant, it is good. Planet in no. 2 aspects in a friendly manner in no. 6.
- All the planets (except Sun, Jupiter and Moon) in this house give the effect of the permanent house. Sun, Moon and Jupiter will give the Rashi result i.e., their effect is to be judged according to their Rashis (signs).
- Saturn in no.6 is retrograde and adversely aspects the 2nd house.
- Mars in no. 4 is no longer malefic, if Sun or Moon occupies the 6th house.
- Mercury and Rahu, considered exalted in no. 6, will never be malefic nor they will adversely affect the no.2 and the kendras i.e., no. 1, 4, 7 & 10.

PERMANENT 7TH HOUSE

HOUSEHOLD AND SPOUSE

LORD : VENUS

Marriage, wealth, spouse & love are the hallmarks of this house. It is the house of Laxmi. Mercury, Venus and Saturn are exalted in this house and confer all material & conjugal blessings, Sun in this house and sign is debilitating.

Marriage, sexual intercourse including extra marital affairs, passion, domestic harmony, urinary troubles, partnership, sex organs etc. can also be judged from this house.

PERMANENT 8TH HOUSE

DEATH, POETIC JUSTICE

LORD : MARS (MALEFIC)

It is the house of death and Mars - its lord is totally malefic. When this house is out to harm, the 2nd and 6th houses also join it to destroy the man. In that case, 12th house is the arbitrator. If Moon, Saturn and Mars are placed individually in the horoscope, the results are beneficial, otherwise bad. If any Male planets (Sun, Jupiter, Mars) either individually or together, are placed in this house, it will then not be the house of death. Scorpio is the emblem of death, which no body can conquer except Sun or Jupiter. Even Moon in Scorpio becomes debilitating and leads to hysteric epilepsy and ailments of the heart. It also denotes longevity, death, cause and place of death, violence, accidents, genitals, anus, impediments, mutilation of a limb, ailments etc.

EXPLANATORY NOTES :

- By poetic justice we mean that the evil doer will definitely be punished. No element of mercy or compassion will be involved. It is sheer tit for tat. If you kill some one's child, your child must also be killed.
- If no. 8 is occupied by Sun, Jupiter or Moon individually or jointly (whether any two of them or all the three), house no. 8 will not aspect no. 2 and 12. In other words it will be confined to no.8 only and death will be conquered by Sun, Jupiter and Moon.
- Saturn, Mars or Moon, if alone in this house always brings good results; but if they are jointly placed - whether all the three or any two of them - the results are bad. Saturn is the cause of death; Moon destroys health and money; and Malefic Mars in conjunction with no. 2-6 spells doom and disaster. Mercury no. 8 is always malefic; Mars no. 8 is usually malefic, but both Mars and Mercury in no.8 are good, provided no. 2 is not occupied by Saturn; otherwise Mars will be totally malefic.
- If the planet occupying no. 11 in the birth chart occupies no. 8 or 11 in the annual chart, one must not buy new materials pertaining to planet in no. 11, otherwise it will bring about loss of money and health. If one has to purchase such goods he must also buy toys and sports material for children. That will off-set the bad effect and will change it into good luck.

PERMANENT 9TH HOUSE

BEGINNING OF FATE

LORD : JUPITER

It is the house of inherited fate, ancestral property, Malefic Mars and Venus or Mercury are bad and debilitating in this house. Saturn, Ketu or any Masculine planet is beneficial. Jupiter is the Kingpin. It also governs religious piety, good morals, righteous conduct, purity of mind, auspicious happenings, charity, visit to holy places, ancestral houses, present life and life in the previous birth, blessings of parents and grand parents and their long span of life.

If exalted Jupiter is alone in this house, it is like a phoenix (Huma in Urdu - a legendary bird) or swan which confers royal and exalted status on him.

EXPLANATORY NOTES :

- No. 9 marks the foundation and beginning of fate.
- When no. 3 and 5 are vacant, no. 9 fate is awakened by no. 2.
- When a dormant planet of the birth chart occupies no. 9, it becomes awake and active and it gives good results from that year to the end of its life span. Examples are :
- ➢ Sun in no. 8 in the horoscope occupies no. 9 during 22nd year in the annual chart, its good effects will be visible for 22 years i.e. upto 44th years.
- ➢ Mars no. 2 in the horoscope occupies the 9th house during 28th year in the annual chart, its good effects will be visible from 28th year to 56th year i.e., for 28 years.
- ➢ Jupiter no. 2 in the horoscope occupies the 9th house during 16th year in the annual chart, its good effects will be visible from 16th year to 32tndyear i.e., for 16 years.
- ➢ Moon no. 10 in the horoscope occupies the 9th house during 24th year in the annual chart, its good effects will be visible from 24th year to 48th year i.e., for 24 years.
- ➢ Saturn no. 8 in the horoscope occupies the 9th house during 36th year in the annual chart, its good effects will be visible from 36th year to 72nd year i.e., for 36 years.
- ➢ Ketu no. 8 in the horoscope occupies the 9th house during 48th year in the annual chart, its good effects will be visible from 48th year to 96th year i.e., for 48 years.
- ➢ Rahu no. 4 in the horoscope occupies the 9th house during 42nd year in the annual chart, its good effects will be visible from 42nd year to 84th year i.e., for 42 years.
- ➢ Venus no. 12 in the horoscope will occupy the 9th house in the 25th year and will give bad results only during the 25th year if it is adversely aspected by no. 3 or 5. Otherwise it will confer good results.
- ➢ Mercury if malefic in no. 3 will give bad effect from 17th year to 34th year i.e., 17 years. It will occupy house no. 9 in the 17th year.

PERMANENT 10TH HOUSE

FIELD FOR FOUNDATION OF FATE, ACTION.

LORD : SATURN

If the 10th house is adversely affected by malefic stars the whole horoscope is full of blind stars. All stars become malefic even though Saturn may be exalted. It is the field of action, if good and benefic, man gets all the pleasures such as Fathers' blessings, house, property, and if debilitated he is cunning sly, mean and deceitful like a wounded snake. Mars in this house is exalted.

It governs kingdom, status, rank, position of authority, means of livelihood, field of action, reputation, general success in life, distinction, thighs, trade and commerce.

EXPLANATORY NOTES :

- The planet occupying house no. 10 in the annual chart is the planet of deception, which can both be good or bad. If no. 8 is malefic, it will be doubly bad and if no. 2 is benefic, it will be doubly benefic. If no.8 and 2 are vacant, the planets of 3, 5, 11 will be helpful and if all these are also vacant the final verdict will be with Saturn - good or bad.

- If no. 10 is occupied by mutually opposed planets, such a horoscope is a blind horoscope i.e., like a blind man feeling its way with a stick. In that event Moon will be the deciding factor. If Moon is benefic the results are good, otherwise bad.
- If no. 10 is vacant no. 4 will be dormant and asleep. Such a man must get the blessings of his parents and donate articles of food to blind persons.
- The results of Rahu, Ketu or Mercury are doubtful in this house. In that case, if Saturn is benefic, results are doubly benefic; otherwise doubly bad.

PERMANENT 11TH HOUSE

FOUNDATION FOR FATE; PLACE OF JUSTICE AND HOUSE OF INCOME

LORD : JUPITER

It is the house for Income and not expenditure. Income flows from this house and leaves from 3rd house. Aquarius (11th sign) cannot be dominated by any other planet. If Moon or Jupiter occupies this house then Ketu or Rahu are destroyed. The reverse is also true i.e. Rahu or Ketu occupying this house destroys Jupiter and Moon.

This house also denotes acquisition of gold, jewels, all kinds of gains of money, income, mercantile speculations, paternal property etc.

EXPLANATORY NOTES :

- If a wicked planet Saturn, Rahu or Ketu is alone in this house, its good results are visible singly; but if mighty Saturn joins another wicked planet (Rahu or Ketu) benefic results multiply by eleven times. When such a planet occupies house no. 1 in the annual chart (11, 23, 36, 48, 57, 72, 84, 94 etc), it becomes the planet of fate.
- If no. 3 is occupied by Sun, Moon, Mars (friends of Jupiter), no. 11 will always give good results.
- No. 11 is aspected by no. 3. If there are planets in both the houses, no. 11 will be awake and perfect.
- If Ketu occupies this house, Moon is destroyed and vice-versa. Jupiter in this house destroys Rahu and vice-versa.
- Only the wicked planets in this house give good results in this house; others will not be dependable. If no. 3 is vacant, benefic results are visible when it occupies the 1st house in the annual chart and malefic results when it occupies the 8th house in the annual chart (i.e., 7, 20, 34, 45, 53, 67, 79, 92, 97). He must not bring articles pertaining to that planet. Suppose Saturn in no. 11 of the horoscope occupies no. 8 in the annual chart, one must not bring home machinery and leather goods. If he has to buy then he must also buy toys and sports material for children (articles pertaining to Ketu). This will result in changing bad luck to good luck. Remedy lies in Jupiter.

THE EFFECT OF PLANETS IN NO. 11

Name of Planet in no. 11	Benefic or Exalted	Malefic or debilitating
Jupiter	As long as the person lives in a joint family and father is alive, even Saturn (snake) will pay obeisance i.e., best results.	Worst results, if separated from father and of loose character.
Sun	As long as the person remain pious and noble, he will live a noble and glorious life and will have noble children.	Must not take meat and wine. In that case he may be issue-less.
Moon	If Jupiter and Ketu are exalted, man will be blessed with wealth and son during the life span of mother.	Mother may not live to see the son.
Venus	Rich if Mars is exalted in the horoscope.	Simpleton, Coward, impotent and devoid of wealth.
Mars	Like a tiger, who will have heart's desire fulfilled through courage and valour.	Will wander from pillar to post in search of livelihood and wealth.
Mercury	Will come out victorious from all obstacles and sufferings.	Worst results - because of short-sightedness.
Saturn	Must have a son although all other planets may be conspiring otherwise. Saturn will protect him from all storms of life. Such a man is noble and religious minded.	Very bad results. May desert even children in the mid stream.
Rahu	Proud; will not demand even a paisa from parents; will not accept any obligation; will be self made rich; gold received from parents will turn into dust, but will earn gold himself.	Will destroy his parents.
Ketu	Most exalted results regarding sons and income, provided Moon and Jupiter are not in 5th house.	Worst results regarding sons. Saturn and Moon will be malefic.

PERMANENT 12TH HOUSE

CHART SHOWING LORDS OF VARIOUS HOUSES AND SIGNIFICANCE OF HOUSES

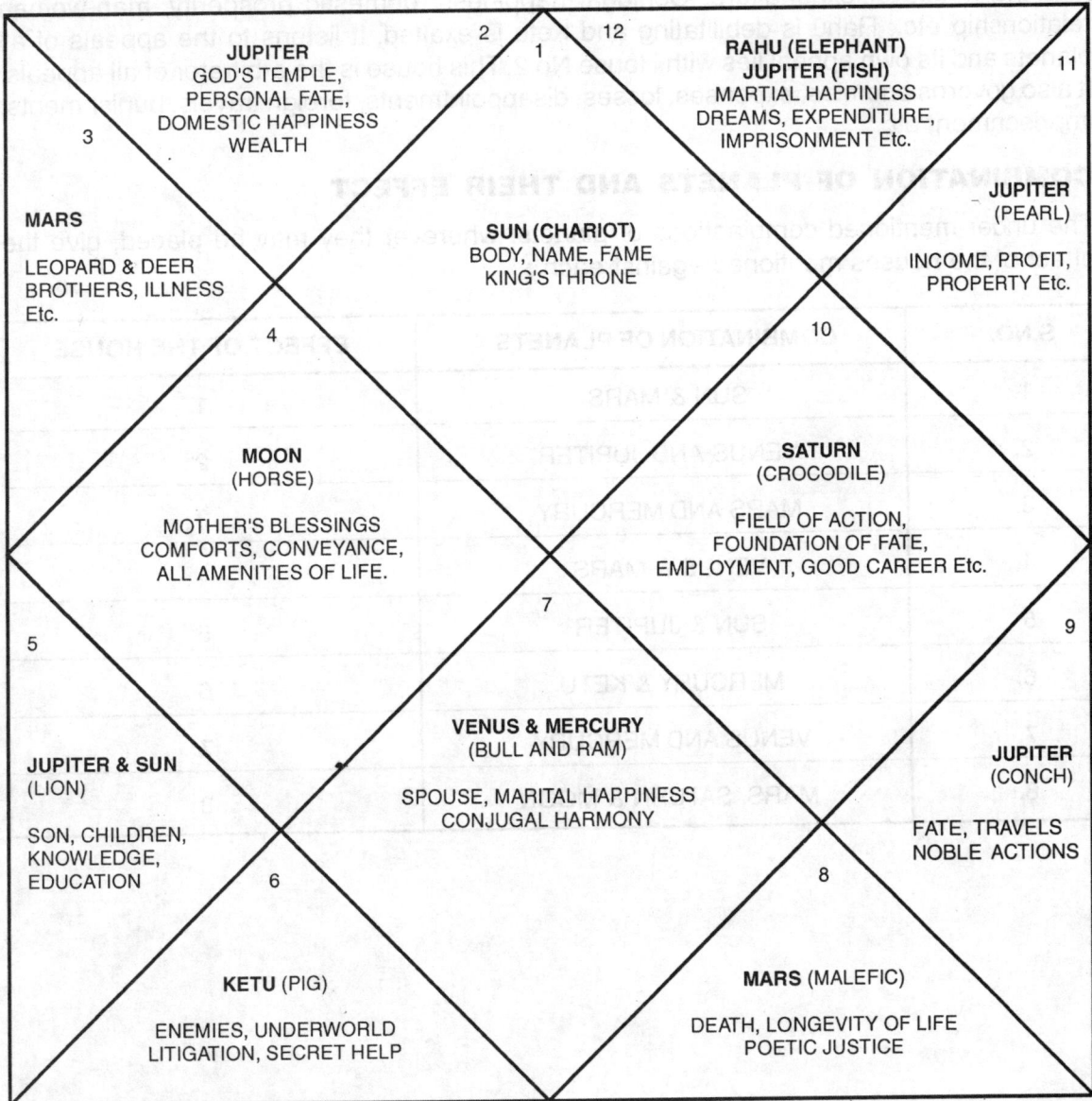

2 1 12

3

JUPITER
GOD'S TEMPLE,
PERSONAL FATE,
DOMESTIC HAPPINESS
WEALTH

RAHU (ELEPHANT)
JUPITER (FISH)
MARTIAL HAPPINESS
DREAMS, EXPENDITURE,
IMPRISONMENT Etc.

11

MARS

LEOPARD & DEER
BROTHERS, ILLNESS
Etc.

SUN (CHARIOT)
BODY, NAME, FAME
KING'S THRONE

JUPITER
(PEARL)

INCOME, PROFIT,
PROPERTY Etc.

4 10

MOON
(HORSE)

MOTHER'S BLESSINGS
COMFORTS, CONVEYANCE,
ALL AMENITIES OF LIFE.

SATURN
(CROCODILE)

FIELD OF ACTION,
FOUNDATION OF FATE,
EMPLOYMENT, GOOD CAREER Etc.

7

5 9

VENUS & MERCURY
(BULL AND RAM)

SPOUSE, MARITAL HAPPINESS
CONJUGAL HARMONY

JUPITER & SUN
(LION)

SON, CHILDREN,
KNOWLEDGE,
EDUCATION

JUPITER
(CONCH)

FATE, TRAVELS
NOBLE ACTIONS

6 8

KETU (PIG)

ENEMIES, UNDERWORLD
LITIGATION, SECRET HELP

MARS (MALEFIC)

DEATH, LONGEVITY OF LIFE
POETIC JUSTICE

MARITAL HAPPINESS, EXPENDITURE, IMPRISONMENT, DREAMS ETC.

LORD : JUPITER AND RAHU

It is the house of expenditure, Conjugal happiness, domestic prosperity, man-woman relationship etc., Rahu is debilitating and Ketu is exalted. It listens to the appeals of all planets and its own appeal lies with House No.2. This house is the arbitrator of all appeals. It also governs enemies, expenses, losses, disappointments, foreign travels, punishments, imprisonment etc.

COMBINATION OF PLANETS AND THEIR EFFECT

The under-mentioned combinations of planets, wherever they may be placed, give the effect of the houses mentioned against each :

S.NO.	COMBINATION OF PLANETS	EFFECT OF THE HOUSE
1.	SUN & MARS	1
2.	VENUS AND JUPITER	2
3.	MARS AND MERCURY	3
4.	VENUS & MARS	4
5.	SUN & JUPITER	5
6.	MERCURY & KETU	6
7.	VENUS AND MERCURY	7
8.	MARS, SATURN & MOON	8

BIRTH CHART (JANAM KUNDALI)

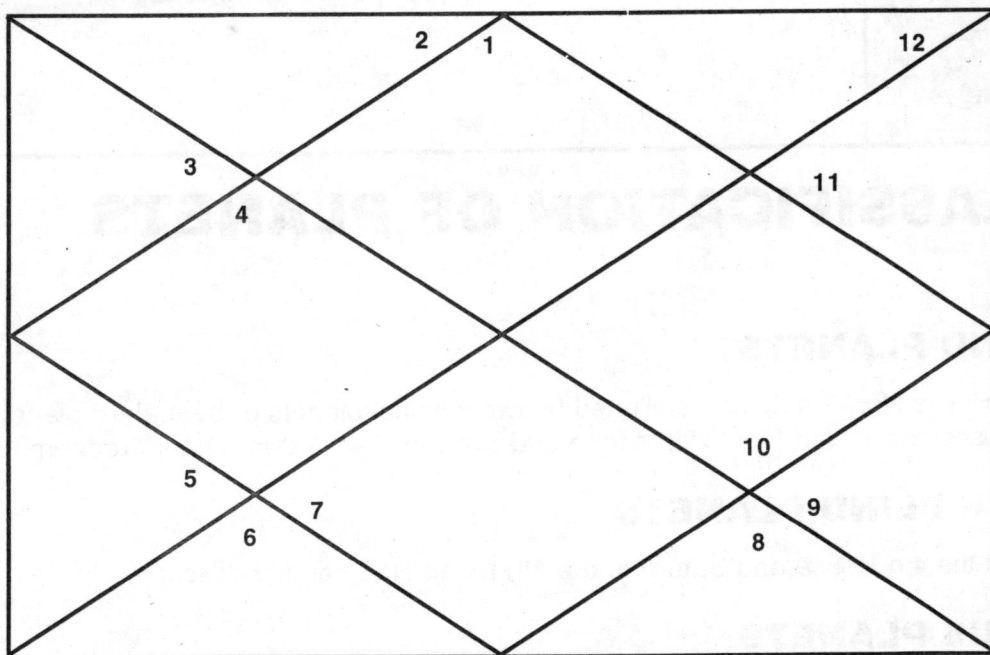

First six houses are on the right side and the remaining from 7 to 12 are on the left side.

☞
- *If there is no planet on the right side, the planets on the left side are ASLEEP.*
- *Jupiter awakens 9th and 11th houses. Moon awakens 2nd, 4th and 8th houses; sun 5th, Venus 7th, Saturn 10th, Rahu 6th, Mercury 3rd, Mars 1st and Ketu 12th.*

HOUSES AND THEIR AGES :

AGE OF THE HOUSE	100	75	90	85	CHILDREN	80	85	DEATH	ANCESTORS	90	TEMPLE OF GOD	90
HOUSE NO.	1	2	3	4	5	6	7	8	9	10	11	12

When Sun and Moon are eclipsed, three years may be deducted.

CLASSIFICATION OF PLANETS

BLIND PLANETS

If the House No.10 is being debilitated by two inimical planets or by malefic planet, such a horoscope is called Blind Horoscope and even exalted Saturn cannot redeem it.

HALF BLIND PLANETS

Sun in the 4th House and Saturn in the 7th mean Half Blind Horoscope.

PIOUS PLANETS

Rahu and Ketu in the 4th house or with Moon in any house and Saturn in 11th or with Jupiter in any house make the subject Pious and noble.

ENEMIES BECOME FRIENDS

For example if Sun whose permanent house is 5th and Saturn whose permanent house is 10th exchange places they become friends. It is a marriage of convenience. It is called Sambandh Yoga.

EXALTED AND PERFECT PLANETS

A planet which occupies its own house and is in its own Raashi (Sign) and is not aspected by enemies is called a perfect and exalted planet.

PLANET'S OWN HOUSE

A planet which occupies its own Raashi (Sign) is called planet in its own house e.g. Mercury in 3rd and 6th Raashi.

ENEMIES

A Planet in debilitating form and is placed in enemy's house is really bad and spells doom and disaster.

WICKED PLANETS

Rahu, Ketu and Saturn are sinful and wicked.

EXALTED AND DEBILITATING PLANETS
(See Pages 12,20,21)

When a planet is in a Raashi (Sign) which is set apart as exalted or debilitating, it is called exalted/debilitating planet.

PLANETS OF EQUAL POWERS

Please refer to the list below.

MASCULINE PLANETS

Jupiter (effect on Soul and Mind)
Sun (effect on Body)
Mars (effect on Blood)
Saturn(effect on minerals and machines etc.)

FEMININE PLANETS

Moon (Mother)
Venus (Wife)

EUNUCHS

Mercury (effect on earth, vegetation etc)
Rahu and Ketu are nodes and not planets. They affect the head and the feet.

FRIENDSHIP AND ENMITY OF PLANETS

S.NO.	PLANET	EQUAL POWERS	FRIENDS	ENEMIES
1.	JUPITER	SATURN, RAHU, KETU	SUN, MOON, MARS	VENUS, MER.
2.	SUN	MER (COMBUST) KETU (DIMS SUN)	JUPITER, MOON, MARS	VENUS, SAT RAHU (SOLAR ECLIPSE)
3.	MOON	SAT, VENUS, MARS, JUPITER	SUN, MER.,	KETU (LUNAR ECLIPSE) RAHU (DIMS MOON)
4.	VENUS	MARS, JUPITER	SAT., MER,KETU	SUN, MOON, RAHU

5.	MARS	SAT, VENUS RAHU(DISAPPEARS)	SUN, MOON, JUPITER	MER, KETU
6.	MERCURY	SAT., KETU, MARS, JUPITER	SUN, VENUS, RAHU	MOON
7.	SATURN	KETU, JUPITER	MER, VENUS, RAHU	MOON, SUN, MARS
8.	RAHU	JUPITER, MOON (DIMMED)	MERCURY, SATURN, KETU	VENUS, SUN(SOLAR ECLIPSE), MARS
9.	KETU	JUPITER, SAT., MER., SUN (DIMMED)	VENUS, RAHU	MOON (LUNAR ECLIPSE), MARS

☞
- *Moon & Venus are of equal strength but Moon opposes Venus.*
- *Jupiter & Venus are of equal strength but Venus opposes Jupiter.*
- *Mars & Saturn are of equal strength but Mars opposes Saturn.*
- *Moon & Mercury are friends but Moon opposes Mercury.*
- *When Rahu and Jupiter are together Jupiter may remain meek but will not disappear.*
- *In the 2nd house, if Rahu & Jupiter are together, Jupiter dominates Rahu.*
- *Although Mercury is Jupiter's enemy and Moon is Mercury's enemy, yet in 2nd & 4th houses, Mercury and Moon will shed their enmity and will monetarily help the enemies.*

SACRIFICIAL LAMBS (PLANETS)

Saturn: Saturn employs Rahu and Ketu as his agents to ward off enemy's attack. Wherever there is a clash between Sun(Father) and Saturn(Son) - Venus (the woman) is sacrificed. For example if Sun is in 6th house and Saturn in 12th house, wife dies.

Mercury: It sacrifices Venus whenever in trouble.

Mars: Mars malefic (Brother) makes Ketu (Son) a scapegoat; for example if Sun is in 6th house and Mars in 10th house, Son dies.

Venus: Venus (Woman) makes Moon (subject's Mother) the scapegoat. If Venus and Moon are opposite each other, mother becomes, blind.

Jupiter: Ketu is sacrificed when Jupiter is in trouble.

Sun: Sacrifices Ketu when in trouble.

Moon: Sacrifices Jupiter, Sun and Mars when in trouble.

INFORMATION ABOUT PLANETS AND SIGNS:

S. NO.	SIGN (RAASHI)	FEATURES SPEED	COLOUR	EFFECT	NATURE	LORD	EXALTED RESULTS	DEBILI-TATING
1.	ARIES	RAM	RED	HOT AND DRY	FIERY	MARS	SUN	SATURN
2.	TAURUS	BULL	WHITE (CURD)	COOL	EARTHLY	VENUS	MOON	NIL
3.	GEMINI	COUPLE (MAN & WOMAN)	GREEN	HOT AND WET	WINDY	MERCURY	RAHU	KETU
4.	CANCER	CRAB	MILKY WHITE	COOL	WATERY	MOON	JUPITER	MARS
5.	LEO	LION	COPPER RED	HOT AND DRY	FIERY	SUN	NIL	NIL
6.	VIRGO	GIRL	GREEN AND COL-OURED	COLD AND DRY	EARTHLY	MER-CURY, AND KETU	MER-CURY, RAHU	KETU
7.	LIBRA	SCALES	WHITE (CURD)	HOT & WET	WINDY	VENUS	SATURN	SUN
8.	SCORPIO	SCORPION	RED	COLD & WET	FIERY	MARS	NIL	MOON
9.	SAGI-TTARIUS	COW & ARCHERS	YELLOW	HOT & WET	FIERY	JUPITER	KETU	RAHU
10.	CAPRI-CORN	CROCODILE	BLACK	COLD & DRY	EARTHLY	SATURN	MARS	JUPITER
11.	AQUARIUS	PITCHER FULL OF WATER	BLACK	HOT & WET	WINDY	SATURN	NIL	NIL
12.	PISCES	FISH	BLUE AND YELLOW	COLD & WET	WATERY	JUPITER AND RAHU	VENUS AND KETU	MER. AND RAHU

PLANETS AND THEIR LIFE PERIODS

S.NO	PLANET	MAHADASHA PERIOD	EFFECT	SPEED
1.	JUPITER	16 YRS	IN THE MIDDLE	TIGER
2.	SUN	6 YRS	IN THE BEGINNING	CHARIOT
3.	MOON	10 YRS	IN THE END	HORSE
4.	VENUS	20 YRS	IN THE MIDDLE	BULL
5.	MERCURY	17 YRS	ALWAYS SAME	RAM
6.	SATURN	19 YRS	IN THE END	FISH
7.	MARS(MALEFIC) MARS(EXALTED)	4 YRS 3 YRS	IN THE BEGINNING; WITHOUT SUN, MARS IS MALEFIC.	LEOPARD, STAG
8.	RAHU	18 YRS	IN THE END	ELEPHANT
9.	KETU	7 YRS	IN THE END	PIG

PLANETS OWN RAASHI (SIGN)

RAASHI NO.	LORD PLANET OF THE RAASHI	PERMANENT HOUSE AND ITS LORD	EXALTED PLANET
2	VENUS	JUPITER	VENUS BENEFICIAL
3	MERCURY	MARS	MER. BENEFICIAL, PROVIDED MARS IS NOT MALEFIC.
5	SUN	SUN & JUPITER	SUN BENEFICIAL
6	MER - KETU	KETU	MERCURY BENEFICIAL, BUT KETU IS DEBILITATING
7	VENUS	VENUS & MER.	VENUS BENEFICIAL, BUT MERCURY HELPS OTHERS
8	MARS	MARS, SAT MOON-LIFE	IF ALONE, GOOD RESULTS, OTHERWISE BAD.
11	SATURN	JUPITER	SATURN BENEFICIAL, OTHERS OUT- WARDLY GOOD BUT NOT OTHERWISE

EFFECTS OF PLANETS ON OTHERS

HOUSE NO (IF ALONE)	NAME OF PLANET	EFFECT ON OTHER PLANETS
1	KETU	Sun will be exalted.
1	RAHU	Solar eclipse; will eclipse the Sun in whatever house it may be placed.
2	MERCURY	Jupiter will be destroyed.
4	MERCURY	Moon will be destroyed.
6	MARS	Sun will be exalted, but Ketu will be destroyed.
11	RAHU	Jupiter will be destroyed.
11	KETU	Moon will be destroyed, if Mercury is in no.9.
11	JUPITER	Rahu will be destroyed, if Mercury is malefic.
12	MOON	Ketu will be destroyed.

EFFECTS OF PLANETS IN VARIOUS HOUSES

S.NO.	PLANET, IF ALONE & NOT ASPECTED BY OTHERS*	HOUSE IN WHICH IT IS BAD**	HOUSE IN WHICH IT IS GOOD***
1	JUPITER	6,7,10,11 (Ketu will help debilitating Jupiter)	1,2,3,4,5,8,9,12
2	SUN	6,7,10	1,2,3,4,5,8,9,11,12
3	MOON	6,8,10,11,12	1,2,3,4,5,7,9
4	VENUS	1,6,9	2,3,4,5,7,8,10,11,12
5	MARS	4,8	1,2,3,5,6,7,9,10,11,12
6	MERCURY	3,8,9,10,11,12 (Mercury is not always bad in 9 & 11)	1,2,4,5,6,7
7	SATURN	1,4,5,6	2,3,7,8,9,10,11,12
8	RAHU	1,2,5,7,8,9,10,11,12	3,4,6
9	KETU	3,4,5,6,8	1,2,7,9,10,11,12

*   The planet is not aspected by any other planet and is alone for all intents and purposes.

**   When the planet occupies the house in which it is considered debilitating or is placed in the enemy house and is malefic according to Raashi (sign).

*** When it occupies its own house or a friendly house and is considered exalted or benefic according to Raashi (sign).

LUNAR MANSIONS

According to ancient astrological system, the Zodiac is divided into 27 lunar mansions each extending to 13 degree and 20 minutes of arc. They are called Nakshtras or Asterisms or simply stars. The mansions are grouped into triads (group of three) and a planet rules each of them:

	CONSTELLATION		PLANET	
ASHWINI	MAGHA	MOOLAM	KETU	7 YRS
BHARANI	P.PHALGUNI	P.SHADHA	VENUS	20 YRS
KRITTIKA	U.PHALGUNI	U.SHADHA	SUN	6 YRS
ROHINI	HASTHA	SHRAVANA	MOON	10 YRS
MRIGASHIRA	CHITRA	DHANISHTA	MARS	7 YRS
ARDRA	SWATHI	SHATABHISHA	RAHU	18 YRS
PUNARVASU	VISAKHA	P.BHADRA	JUPITER	16 YRS
PUSHYA	ANURADHA	U.BHADRA	SATURN	19 YRS
ASHLESHA	JYESHTA	REVATHI	MERCURY	17 YRS

35 - YEAR CYCLE OF PLANETS

All planets complete their cycle after 35 years. Planets which show bad results during the first 35 years, will lose their sting in the next cycle i.e., their effect will no longer be adverse. The following chart indicates the years each planet will have its duration :

S.NO	NAME OF PLANET	YEARS OF CYCLE OF 35 YEARS	PERIOD OF MAHADASHA	YEAR OF PLANET'S PERSONAL INFLUENCE IN MAHADASHA	REMARKS
1.	JUPITER	6	16	10th year of Mahadasha	This is in addition to 1st year (Guru Dakshina), 2nd, 8th and 14th years of Mahadasha.
2.	SUN	2	6	Odd years of Mahadasha	1st, 3rd & 5th years.

3.	MOON	1	10	Even years of Mahadasha	2nd, 4th, 6th, 8th & 10th years.
4.	VENUS	3	20	11th year of Mahadasha	
5.	MERCURY	2	17	5th year of Mahadasha	
6.	SATURN	6	19	6th year of Mahadasha	
7.	MARS-MALEFIC	3	7	4th year of Mahadasha	
8.	MARS-BENEFIC	3			
9.	RAHU	6	18	7th year of Mahadasha	
10.	KETU	3	7	3rd year of Mahadasha	
	TOTAL	35	120 years.		

☞ *Every planet shows its result during the 1/4th or half of its span.*

REMEDIES

REMEDIES FOR DEBILITATING PLANETS

S.NO	PLANET	COLOUR	REMEDIES
1.	JUPITER	YELLOW	GRAM LENTILS (DAL CHANA), GOLD
2.	SUN	COPPER (WHEATISH)	WHEAT, RED COPPER
3.	MOON	MILKY WHITE	RICE, MILK, SILVER
4.	VENUS	WHITE(CURD)	CURD, WHITE PEARL, WHITE BUTTER
5.	MARS	RED	GAYTRI PAATH, RED THINGS, MASUR DAL (RED LENTILS), RED RUBY (NOT VERY BRIGHT) RED CORAL.
6.	MERCURY	GREEN	DURGA PAATH, MOONG (GREEN LENTILS), EMERALD.
7.	SATURN	BLACK	IRON, MAASH (BLACK LENTILS), COAL, LEATHER GOODS
8.	RAHU	BLUE	MUSTARD(SARSON), KANYA WORSHIP (VIRGIN), SAPPHIRE (NEELAM).
9.	KETU	BLACK AND WHITE	SESAME OR TIL (BLACK & WHITE), KAPILA COW, BLACK & WHITE BLANKET

+
REMEDIES   If any of the above planets gives bad results donate the things mentioned against each. Throw them into flowing water or donate them to a poor man or in a religious place e.g. temple or church or mosque or gurudwara. It should be remembered that these articles should be donated for 43 days without break.

FOR INSTANT REMEDIES:

Besides the donation of the articles mentioned in the chart in the foregoing page, do the following for instant relief for 43 days.

1. **MALEFIC MARS:** Throw Rewaries(Sweet made of Jaggery & Sesame) into the flowing water or river or throw crumbs of sweet bread to the birds.
2. **DEBILITATING JUPITER:** Paste saffron on the navel or eat it.
3. **DEBILITATING SUN:** Throw jaggery (Gurh) in the flowing water.
4. **DEBILITATING SATURN:** Mustard (sarson) may be donated.
5. **DEBILITATING MOON:** Place a pot of milk under your pillow and put that milk on the 'KEEKAR' tree in the morning.
6. **DEBILITATING VENUS:** Donate white barley (Jawar).
7. **BENEFIC MARS:** Donate Sweets.
8. **MALEFIC MERCURY:** Put a whole into a copper coin and throw it into flowing water.
9. **MALEFIC KETU:** Throw bread to dogs.
10. **MALEFIC RAHU:** Donate Radish (Mooli) or throw coal into flowing water.

REMEDIES FOR MALEFIC PLANETS (ACCORDING TO RAASHIS IN THE HOROSCOPE) DURING MARRIAGE OR MARRIAGE ANNIVERSARY.

1. **MALEFIC JUPITER :** Take two pieces of gold of equal weight. Throw one into the flowing water after marriage and the other may be kept permanently by the native. It does not matter how small the pieces are. If one cannot afford gold, two pieces of turmeric or Saffron (of equal weight) will give the same results.
2. **MALEFIC SUN :** Adopt the above procedure, but use copper instead of gold.
3. **MALEFIC MOON :** Adopt the above procedure, but use white (milky) pearl or silver.
4. **MALEFIC VENUS :** Adopt the above procedure, but use pearl (curd like colour).
5. **MALEFIC MARS :** Adopt the above procedure, but use red precious stone, which should not be bright.
6. **MALEFIC MERCURY :** Adopt the above procedure, but use diamond or shell.
7. **MALEFIC SATURN :** Adopt the above procedure, but use iron or steel or black salt.
8. **MALEFIC KETU :** Adopt the above procedure, but use a stone with two colours or black & white stone.
9. **MALEFIC RAHU :** The same remedy as for Moon. Remember not to use or wear sapphire (Neelam).

☞ • *Remedies are to be adopted in case of Raashis (signs) only.*
 • *All remedies may be adopted only during the day time as day is ruled by Sun & night by Saturn.*

HOUSES WITH RAASHIS & ASPECTS

TWELVE HOUSES, RAASHIS, AND THEIR DESCRIPTIONS

S.NO.	RAASHI	LORD	EXALTED	DEBILI-TATED	PERMA-NENT HOUSE	BRINGER OF LUCK	RESULT OF PLANET	RAASHI RESULT
1.	ARIES	MARS (BENEFIC)	SUN	SATURN	SUN (BENEFIC)	MARS	MARS	RAHU
2.	TAURUS	VENUS	MOON	NIL	JUPITER	MOON	RAHU KETU	NIL
3.	GEMINI	MERCURY	RAHU	KETU	MARS	MERCURY	SATURN	SATURN
4.	CANCER	MOON	JUPITER	MARS	MOON	MOON	MOON	VENUS MARS KETU
5.	LEO	SUN	NIL	NIL	JUPITER	SUN	SUN JUPITER	NIL
6.	VIRGO	MERCURY KETU	MERCURY RAHU	KETU	KETU	RAHU	MERCURY KETU	SUN MARS JUPITER SATURN
7.	LIBRA	VENUS	SATURN	SUN	VENUS MERCURY	VENUS	VENUS	SUN JUPITER RAHU
8.	SCORPIO	MARS (MALEFIC)	NIL	MOON	MARS (MALEFIC) SATURN	MOON	MARS (MALEFIC)	NIL

9.	SAGITTA-RIUS	JUPITER	KETU	RAHU	JUPITER	JUPITER	JUPITER	SATURN
10.	CAPRI-CORN	SATURN	MARS	JUPITER	SATURN	SATURN	SATURN	MERCURY KETU
11.	AQUARIUS	SATURN	NIL	NIL	JUPITER	JUPITER	JUPITER SATURN	NIL
12.	PISCES	JUPITER RAHU	VENUS KETU	MERCURY RAHU	RAHU	KETU	RAHU	MERCURY

TABLE OF EXALTATIONS AND DEBILITATIONS

	SUN	MOON	MARS	MERCURY	JUPITER	VENUS	SATURN
EXALTATION	ARIES	TAURUS	CAPRICORN	VIRGO	CANCER	PISCES	LIBRA
DEBILITATION	LIBRA	SCORPIO	CANCER	PISCES	CAPRICORN	VIRGO	ARIES

ASPECTS OF PLANETS

	SUN	MOON	VENUS	MERCURY	RAHU	KETU	JUPITER	MARS	SATURN
100% ASPECT	7th	7th	7th	7th	7th	7th	7th,5th,9th	7th,4th,8th	7th,3rd,10th

Ketu is always at the beck and call of Rahu who commands. Ketu has no identity of its own.

☞
- *Partially i.e. 50% — All planets aspect the 5th house and are friends e.g. 2nd aspecting the 6th.*
- *Planets aspect 25% - 8th aspect 6th, 2nd aspects 12th (25%) and vice versa.*
- *8th house aspects the 2nd 100% and not the 2nd aspecting the 8th.*

GRAPH FOR ASPECTS

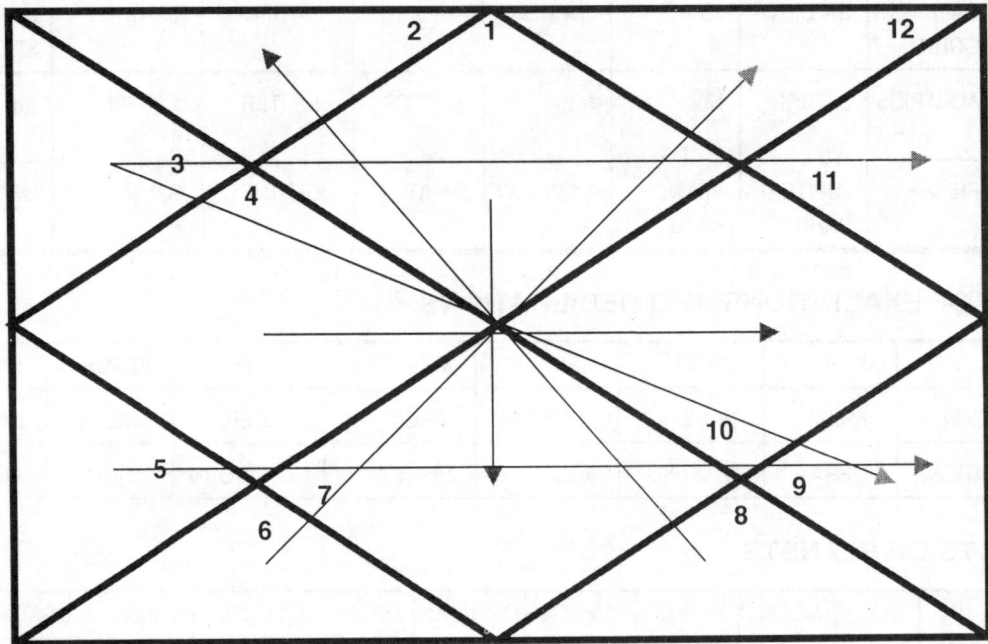

BEGINNING OF ARROW	1ST HOUSE	3RD HOUSE	4TH HOUSE	5TH HOUSE	6TH HOUSE	8TH HOUSE
END OF ARROW	7TH HOUSE	9TH HOUSE 11TH HOUSE	10TH HOUSE	9TH HOUSE	12TH HOUSE	2ND HOUSE

☞
- *5th house does not aspect the 11th house.*
- *2nd house does not aspect the 8th house.*

If the planet so aspected by a friendly planet, the results are good, otherwise bad.

☞
- *Mercury, In the 12th house adversely aspects the 6th and from 9th it adversely aspects the 3rd.*
- *Saturn, In the 6th house is retrograde. It adversely aspects the 2nd house and spells disaster and doom for the planet in that house, even though it may be occupied by his friend, Venus.*

SUDDEN LOSS OR INJURY (LIFE OR PROPERTY OR BOTH)

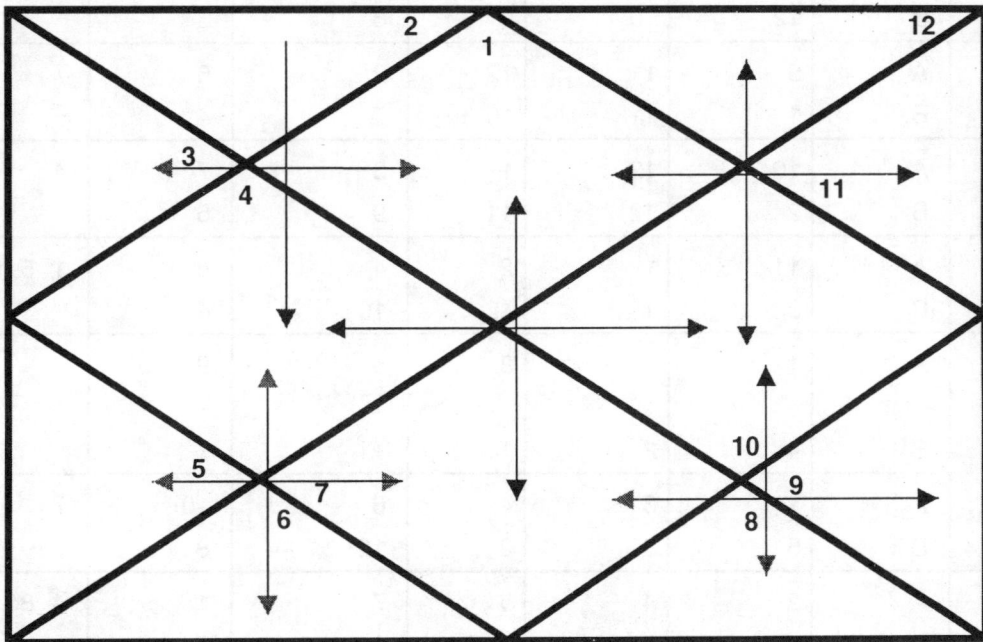

Whether friends or enemies, life or property is endangered. It happens suddenly and without warning e.g. Suppose Venus in the first house moves to the 3rd or vice versa, it may entail loss of property or life. Saving grace is, if it is aspected by Sun or Moon or Jupiter etc.

CHART SHOWING FRIENDS, ENMITY, DECEPTION & SUDDEN DEATH ETC.

HOUSE NO	ASPECT	MUTUAL HELP	BASIC ASPECT	ENMITY	DECEPTION	COMMON TO ALL	SUDDEN LOSS OR INJURY
1	A	5	7	8	10	2	3 7 11
	B	9	7	6	4	12	
2	A	6	–	9	11	11	4
	B	10	–	7	5	1	
3	A	7	9	10	12	4	1
	B	11	9	8	6	2	

39

4	A	8	10	11	1	5	10 6
	B	12	10	9	6	3	
5	A	9	11	12	2	6	7
	B	1	11	10	7	4	
6	A	10	12	1	3	7	4
	B	2	12	11	9	5	
7	A	11	1	2	4	8	1 5 9
	B	3	1	12	10	4	
8	A	12	2	3	5	9	10
	B	4	2	1	11	7	
9	A	1	3	4	6	10	7
	B	5	3	2	12	8	
10	A	2	4	5	7	1	4 8 12
	B	6	4	3	1	7	
11	A	3	5	6	8	12	1
	B	7	5	4	2	10	
12	A	4	6	7	9	1	10
	B	8	6	5	3	11	

☞ A → Can aspect the house.

    B → Can be aspected from the house, e.g, 1st house can aspect the 5th and it can be aspected by the 9th.

- Only friends can see through the common wall and not enemies.

Suppose Rahu in the 1st house in the horoscope, occupies 3rd house in annual chart, it may lead to accident. For this, help will come from 5, 9, 7 & 11 houses occupied by benefic planets. Similarly Mars in the 8th house occupying the 10th house will also lead to an accident; but help will come through benefic planets from 4, 5 & 12.

A planet exalted or debilitating in the main horoscope gives good or bad results only when placed in the house reserved for it in the Annual Chart. For example exalted Jupiter in Cancer gives its exalted effect only when it occupies the 4th and 2nd house in the Annual Chart, so is the case with other planets.

SPECIAL ASPECTS FOR HEALTH, SICKNESS, MARRIAGE, CHILDREN, HOME ETC.

- Third house will be friendly to 5th, whether friends or enemies. 5th will aspect 7th and 7th will aspect 9th - adverse or good effects according to friendly or enemy planets. 6th & 8th and 8th & 10th houses will be opposed to each other except Sun in 9th house which will be like beneficial rain.
- From house no. 10 to house no 5, there are six house i.e., 11th to 4th and from house no. 5 to 10 there are 4 house i.e., 6th to 9th. It means house no. 10 will aspect house no. 5 and not vice versa except Moon in house no.5 which will be like a poison to house no.10.
- As regards aspects of Kendras i.e. 1 to 7 and 4 to 10 and other houses, please refer to prevous pages containing chart of aspects.

PLANET OF DECEPTION OR MISLEADING PLANET

Deception means to mislead. Sometimes a planet deceives or misleads an individual in a good or bad sense. Occasionally a man receives an unexpected windfall or unexpected reverses. Such a planet will be doubly bad or good. Refer to Explanatory Notes under House no.10.

When no.10 occupies the house of deception in a particular year, it will completely and malefically deceive the individual. In other words, he will face unexpected loss or reverses.

Similarly when no.2 (House of personal fate) occupies no.11 (House of income), it will mislead the man in a good sense and he will have better luck that year. (Refer to Column no.6 - deception -in the chart showing friends, enmity, etc as above). Malefic planet will be infact more malefic when it occupies no.8.

Here is the graph of misleading planets :

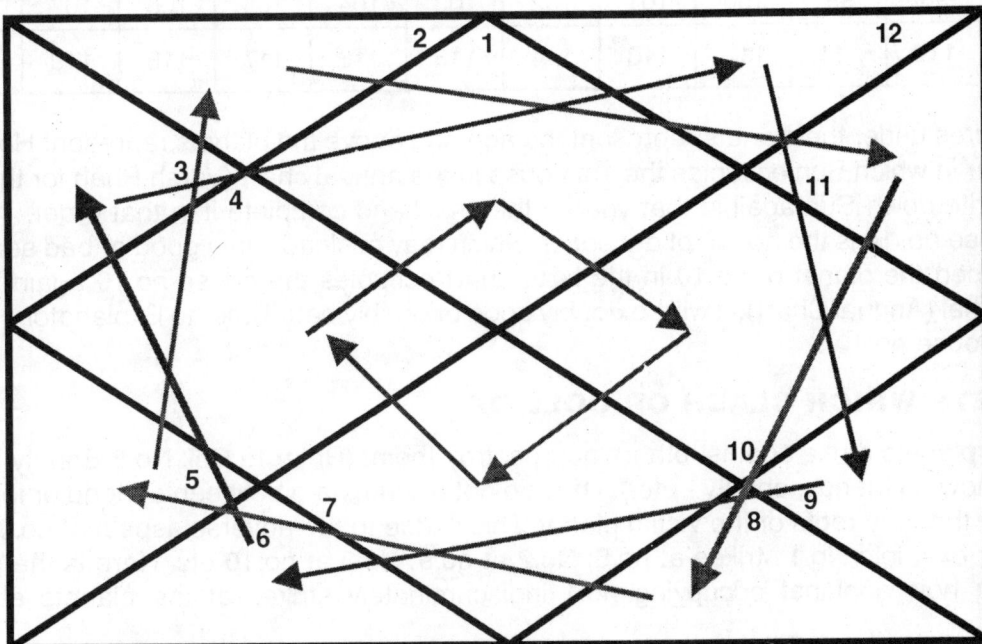

12 YEAR CYCLE OF DECEPTION

Man's total life span is taken as 120 years. Prepare the following chart by multiplying 12 × 10 =120.

Sun House 1	Moon House 2	Ketu House 3	Mars House 4	Mercury House 5	Saturn House 6	Rahu House 7	Planet of House 8 / House 8	Planet of House 9 / House 9	Jupiter House 10	Venus House 11	Planet of House 12 / House 12
1	2	3	4	5	6	7	8	9	10	11	12
13	14	15	16	17	18	19	20	21	22	23	24
25	26	27	28	29	30	31	32	33	34	35	36
37	38	39	40	41	42	43	44	45	46	47	48
49	50	51	52	53	54	55	56	57	58	59	60
61	62	63	64	65	66	67	68	69	70	71	72
73	74	75	76	77	78	79	80	81	82	83	84
85	86	87	88	89	90	91	92	93	94	95	96
97	98	99	100	101	102	103	104	105	106	107	108
109	110	111	112	113	114	115	116	117	118	119	120

Figures under the planets represent the age and above the planets represent Houses. The year in which Sun occupies the 1st house in the annual chart (Varsh Phal) for the first time, write down Sun against that year in the chart and complete it in that order.

House no. 10 is the house of deception which may mislead—in a good or bad sense—Even when the planet of no.10 in the birth chart occupies the house no.10 again in the Varsh Phal (Annual Chart), it will be doubly good or doubly bad (Refer to Explanatory notes under house no.10).

PLANETS WHICH CLASH OR COLLIDE

Certain planets strike against others and destroy them. (Refer to Col. No.5 Enmity in the chart showing friends, enmity - etc.). They do not discriminate between a friend or foe and strike at the very roots of the victim planet. This is due to the adverse aspect at no.8 from self. For example No.1 strikes at no.8; No.2 at no.9; No.3 at no.10 etc. Here is the graph showing how a planet occupying no.1 indiscriminately strikes at the planets at no.8

(whether friend or foe) and so on and so forth.

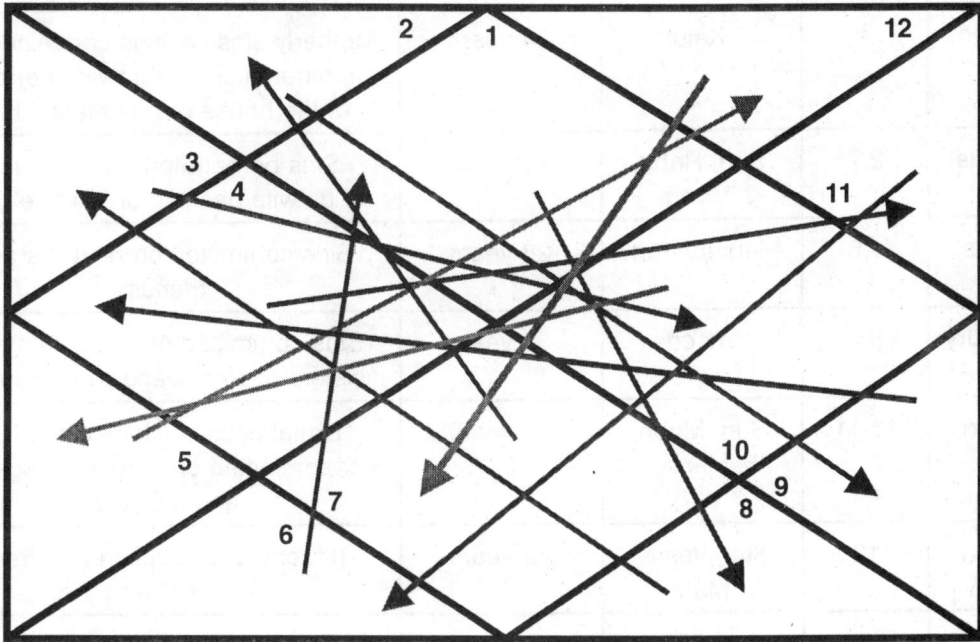

ATONEMENT FOR THE SINS OF ANCESTORS (PITRI RIN)

It is truly said that the sins committed by the ancestors visit upon their children. They become the scapegoats for the sins of their parents. House no.9 is the fundamental one. When Jupiter is destroyed in no.9 or in no. 2, 5 and 12 by the enemy planets, it is a case of 'Pitri Rin' (ancestral sin or debt). In that case remedies for all the planets in no. 2, 5, 9 and 12 are to be adopted. Suppose someone's father or grandfather kills a dog without any provocation, the son or grandson will have to pay for that sin, even though he may have exalted planets in his birth chart. For that he will have to adopt the remedy both for Jupiter (father cr grandfather) and Ketu (dog) as suggested in Ancient texts.

LIST OF VARIOUS TYPES OF DEBTS TO BE PAID BY THE CHILDREN :

Name of Planet	House No.	Enemy Planets	Duration after becoming Major	Types of sins and reasons thereof
Jupiter	2,5,9,12	Venus, Mercury, Rahu	16 years	Ancestral sins i.e., sins committed by ancestors

Sun	5	Venus or wicked planets	22 years	Personal sins
Moon	4	Ketu	24 years	Motherly sins i.e. sins committed on mother such as throwing her out of the house or maltreating her.
Venus	2,7	Sun, Rahu, Moon	25 years	Sins perpetrated on wife such as wife bashing or killing etc.
Mars	1,8	Mercury, Ketu	28 years	Sins committed on relatives and friends.
Mercury	3,6	moon	34 years	Sins committed on daughters and sisters of others and playing fraud
Saturn	10,11	Sun, Moon, Mars	36 years	Brutal actions, Homicide; Sins committed on human beings and animals.
Rahu	12	Sun, Venus, Mars	42 years	Treachery; Deception and fraud on others
Ketu	6	Moon, Mars	48 years	Loose character, Lustful actions; Killing of someone's son or dog or misbehaviour with a Sadhu.

CASTING A HOROSCOPE

HOW TO PREPARE A HOROSCOPE

The following elements are required for preparing a horoscope :
• The date of birth.
• The time of birth.
• The longitude and latitude of the place of birth.
It is very easy to calculate the position of ascendant and planets if the above elements are known.

A. CALCULATION FOR ASCENDANT

STEP 1. CONVERT THE STANDARD TIME INTO LOCAL MEAN TIME.

Standard time is the civil time fixed by the government of the country according to the central meridian of a country. For India, the central meridian is fixed at 82° 30' East longitude.

In India, the standard time has been fixed throughout the country. But the local time would differ depending upon the longitude of the place. Therefore in order to make a horoscope for a place in India, the Indian Standard Time has to be converted first to local mean time.

☞ *As the earth has been demarcated into 360° longitudinally and it takes 24 hours approximately from one sunrise to another, it means that the difference in sunrise would be 15 minutes for a difference of 1° longitude with same latitude.*

The method of conversion can be explained with the following example :-
Suppose we have to calculate the local mean time for Mumbai having a longitude of 72° 50' East, when it is 10.00 A.M. I.S.T.
First calculate the difference between 72° 50' E and 82° 30' E (central meridian for India), which comes out to be 9° 40'.
Then multiply 9°40' by 4 minutes, which is equal to 38 min. and 40 sec.

☞ • *If the longitude of the place is more than the central meridian, add the difference to IST to get local time. If it is less, then subtract.*

So in this case, the local mean time will be (10 - 00 - 00) - (00 - 38 - 40)= (09 - 21 - 20) i.e., 9-21-20 a.m.

STEP 2. CALCULATION OF SIDEREAL TIME.

Another parameter required for finding the position of ascendant is the sidereal time at preceding noon. It is generally given in the Ephemeris for the year, but requires smaller correction.

If we are using Laheri's Ephemeris, the sidereal time given is for 82°30' E longitude and for 1900 A.D. The following steps are required for actual sidereal time : -

a). Note down the side real time for 82°30'E longitude and 1900 AD.

b). Apply correction for different years.

c). Apply correction for the longitude of the locality (for which the birth chart is prepared) to (b). These are at the rate of 0.66 Sec per degree of longitude from central meridian of India (viz. 82°30'E) and positive for west and negative for East. For places in India these corrections are so small as can be safety ignored for ordinary calculations.

The result thus, obtained is the sidereal time for 12h noon local mean time of the place.

d). In order to find the sidereal time at the time of birth, a correction is to be applied. This correction factor can be calculated as under :-

i). Find out time since noon till the local time of birth.

ii). Multiply (i) by 9.8 Sec per hour i.e. acceleration.

Now, add (i) & (ii) to the sidereal time for noon. If the total thus obtained exceeds 24 hours, then 24 hours should be subtracted from it.

Example: Find out the sign, ascending degree and minutes for Bombay at 10 AM on 15 June,1975.

Longitude = 72° 50'E   Latitude = 18 ° 58'N

Local Mean Time at Bombay will be 9 hrs.21 mts.20 Sec. I.e. 9-21-20 AM

		Hours	Minutes	Seconds
(a)	Sidereal time at preceding noon	5	23	24
(b)	Apply correction for different years	-0	0	39
(c)	Apply correction for the longitude of locality	+0	0	6
(d)	Therefore sidereal time for 12h noon local mean time of the place --- (a) + (b) + (c).	5	27	51
(e)	Time since noon till local time of birth	+21	21	20
(f)	Acceleration At 9.8 Sec/hr.	+0	3	31
(g)	Sidereal time for noon - (d) + (e) + (f).	26	52	42

As it exceeds 24 hrs., 24 hrs. should be subtracted from it.

Hours	Minutes	Seconds
26	52	42
-24	00	00
2	52	42

The figure 2 hrs., 52 Mts. & 42 Sec. is called the sidereal time of birth.
From table of Ascendants, with latitude of 18degree 58'N :-

Sidereal Time			Sign Rising		
Hours	Minutes	Seconds	Sign	Date	Month
2	52	0	3	23	12
2	56	0	3	24	6

For 2-52-42 Hrs., the rising sign comes out to be 3-23-21. Therefore, the rising sign or Ascendant is Cancer.

☞ • *The first figure of the longitude indicates the sign completed, the second refers to the degree completed and third to the minutes.*

(B) HOW TO CALCULATE LONGITUDES OF PLANETS

The ascendant is always calculated on the basis of local mean time. But the longitudes of planets are computed on the basis of standard time.

By referring to Lahiri's Ephemeris, the longitudes of various planets can be calculated.

POSITION OF MOON

15th June'1975 ----- 10.00 a.m.	
Time from 5.30 a.m.	4 hrs. and 30 min.
(a) Log of 4 hrs and 30 min.	0.7270
Moon's daily motion on 15/6/1975	14°17'
(b) Log of 14°17'	0.2254
Sum of (a) and (b) ***	0.9524
Log of 0.9524	2°40'
Longitude of Moon = Longitude of Moon at 5.30 a.m. of 15/6/1975 + 2°40'	4S 8° 10' + 2° 40' = 4S 10° 50'

☞ *** Subtract, if the planet is retrograde.

The Moon's longitude 4-10-50 means 4 completed signs and 10°50' in Leo.

In a similar fashion, the position of other planets can be found out. The longitudes of various planets for the above timings are as under :

PLANET	SIGN	DEGREE	MINUTES	RAASHI
Moon	4	10	50	Leo
Sun	2	5	55	Gemini
Mars	11	29	42	Pisces
Mercury	1	26	18	Taurus
Jupiter	11	26	48	Pisces
Venus	3	21	22	Cancer
Saturn	2	26	1	Gemini
Rahu	7	7	5	Scorpio
Ketu	1	7	5	Taurus

The horoscope of the native is as under :-

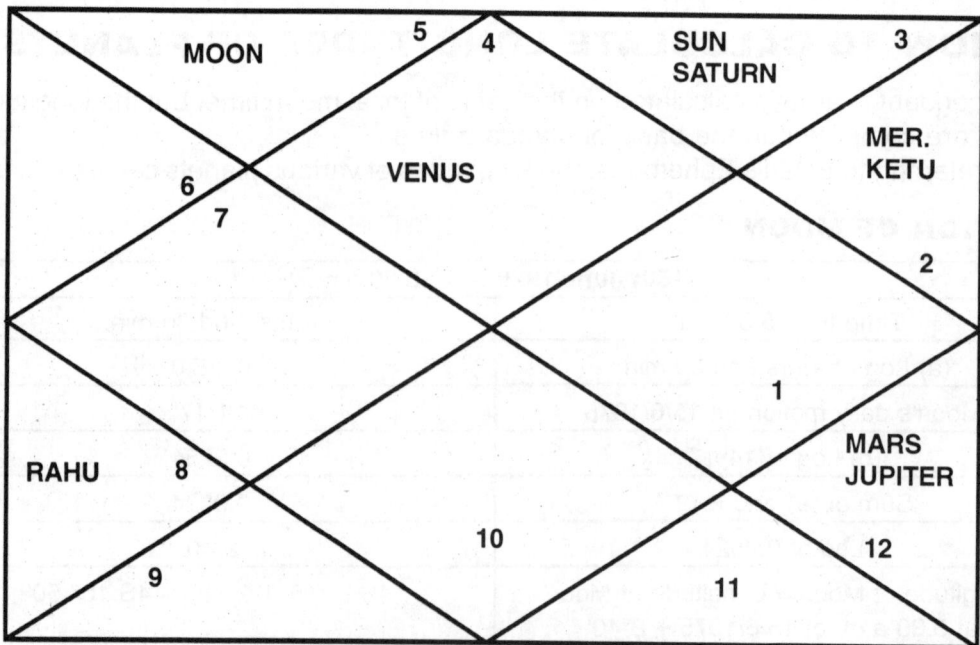

FATE AND PLANETS

If all the four kendras i.e. 1,4,7,& 10 houses are without any planet, search for fate in the 3,5,9 & 11 houses and even if they are vacant then find the planets of fate in the 2,6,8 & 12 houses.

If an exalted planet occupies the first or second house in the Annual Chart it will bring Promotion, power, happiness etc. If these are occupied by debilitating planets misery and misfortune awaits the native.

MAHADASHA (RULING PERIOD) ANTARDASHA (INTERVENING PERIOD) AND PARTANTAR (SUB-PERIODS OF PLANETS)

This method of Calculating the Dasha of planets is peculiar only to Indian Astrology. It means the ruling period of a planet. The wheel of life is fixed at 120 years and every planet has been allotted certain years:

SUN	MOON	MARS	RAHU	JUPITER	SATURN	MERCURY	KETU	VENUS
6 YRS	10 YRS	7 YRS	18 YRS	16 YRS	19 YRS	17 YRS	7 YRS	20 YRS

'Dasha' at the time of the birth is calculated from the position of the Moon at birth. Each lunar mansion extends over 13degree-20' of arc of 800'. The Moon may occupy any degree or minute in a star at epoch.

The order of periods of the nine planets is as under :

Ketu, Venus, Sun, Moon, Mars, Rahu, Jupiter, Saturn, Mercury.

The duration of initial Mahadasha depends upon the distance covered by the Moon in the particular constellation. However, in order to ascertain the balance Mahadasha at birth on the basis of Moon's position, a ready reckoner is given in next page.

Long. of Moon			Moon in Aries, Leo, Sagitt.				Moon in Taurus, Virgo, Capricorn				Moon in Gemini, Libra, Aquarius				Moon in Cancer, Scorpio, Pisces		
			Balance of Mahadasha Y	M	D		Balance of Mahadasha Y	M	D		Balance of Mahadasha Y	M	D		Balance of Mahadasha Y	M	D
0 0		Ketu	7	0	0	Sun	4	6	0	Mars	3	6	0	Jup	4	0	0
0 20			6	9	27		4	4	6		3	3	27		3	7	6
0 40			6	7	24		4	2	12		3	1	24		3	2	12
1 0			6	5	21		4	0	18		2	11	21		2	9	18
1 20			6	3	18		3	10	24		2	9	18		2	4	24
1 40			6	1	15		3	9	0		2	7	15		2	0	0
2 0			5	11	12		3	7	6		2	5	12		1	7	6
2 20			5	9	9		3	5	12		2	3	9		1	2	12
2 40			5	7	6		3	3	18		2	1	6		0	9	18
3 0			5	5	3		3	1	24		1	11	3		0	4	24
3 20			5	3	0		3	0	0		1	9	0	Sat	19	0	0
3 40			5	0	27		2	10	6		1	6	27		18	6	9
4 0			4	10	24		2	8	12		1	4	24		18	0	18
4 20			4	8	21		2	6	18		1	2	21		17	6	27
4 40			4	6	18		2	4	24		1	0	18		17	1	6
5 0			4	4	15		2	3	0		0	10	15		16	7	15
5 20			4	2	12		2	1	6		0	8	12		16	1	24
5 40			4	0	9		1	11	12		0	6	9		15	8	3
6 0			3	10	6		1	9	18		0	4	6		15	2	12
6 20			3	8	3		1	7	24		0	2	3		14	8	21
6 40		Ketu	3	6	0	Sun	1	6	0	Rahu	18	0	0	Sat	14	3	0

7	0		3	3	27		1	4	6		17	6	18		13	9	9
7	20		3	1	24		1	2	12		17	1	6		13	3	18
7	40		2	11	21		1	0	18		16	7	24		12	9	27
8	0		2	9	18		0	10	24		16	2	12		12	4	6
8	20		2	7	15		0	9	0		15	9	0		11	10	15
8	40		2	5	12		0	7	6		15	3	18		11	4	24
9	0		2	3	9		0	5	12		14	10	6		10	11	3
9	20		2	1	6		0	3	18		14	4	24		10	5	12
9	40		1	11	3		0	1	24		13	11	12		9	11	21
10	0		1	9	0	Moon	10	0	0		13	6	0		9	6	0
10	20		1	6	27		9	9	0		13	0	18		9	0	9
10	40		1	4	24		9	6	0		12	7	6		8	6	18
11	0		1	2	21		9	3	0		12	1	24		8	0	27
11	20		1	0	18		9	0	0		11	8	12		7	7	6
11	40		0	10	15		8	9	0		11	3	0		7	1	15
12	0		0	8	12		8	6	0		10	9	18		6	7	24
12	20		0	6	9		8	3	0		10	4	6		6	2	3
12	40		0	4	6		8	0	0		9	10	24		5	8	12
13	0		0	2	3		7	9	0		9	5	12		5	2	21
13	20		20	0	0	Ven	7	6	0		9	0	0		4	9	0
13	40		19	6	0		7	3	0		8	6	18		4	3	9
14	0		19	0	0		7	0	0		8	1	6		3	9	18
14	20		18	6	0		6	9	0		7	7	24		3	3	27
14	40		18	0	0		6	6	0		7	2	12		2	10	6
15	0		17	6	0		6	3	0		6	9	0		2	4	15
15	20	Ven	17	0	0	Moon	6	0	0	Rahu	6	3	18	Sat	1	10	24
15	40		16	6	0		5	9	0		5	10	6		1	5	3

16	0		16	0	0		5	6	0		5	4	24		0	11	12
16	20		15	6	0		5	3	0		4	11	12		0	5	21
16	40		15	0	0		5	0	0		4	6	0	Mer	17	0	0
17	0		14	6	0		4	9	0		4	0	18		16	6	27
17	20		14	0	0		4	6	0		3	7	6		16	1	24
17	40		13	6	0		4	3	0		3	1	24		15	8	21
18	0		13	0	0		4	0	0		2	8	12		15	3	18
18	20		12	6	0		3	9	0		2	3	0		14	10	15
18	40		12	0	0		3	6	0		1	9	18		14	5	12
19	0	Ven	11	6	0	Moon	3	3	0	Rahu	1	4	6	Mer	14	0	9
19	0		11	6	0		3	3	0		1	4	6		14	0	9
19	20		11	0	0		3	0	0		0	10	24		13	7	6
19	40		10	6	0		2	9	0		0	5	12		13	2	3
20	0		10	0	0		2	6	0	Jup	16	0	0		12	9	0
20	20		9	6	0		2	3	0		15	7	6		12	3	27
20	40		9	0	0		2	0	0		15	2	12		11	10	24
21	0		8	6	0		1	9	0		14	9	18		11	5	21
21	20		8	0	0		1	6	0		14	4	24		11	0	18
21	40		7	6	0		1	3	0		14	0	0		10	7	15
22	0		7	0	0		1	0	0		13	7	6		10	2	12
22	20		6	6	0		0	9	0		13	2	12		9	9	9
22	40		6	0	0		0	6	0		12	9	18		9	4	6
23	0		5	6	0		0	3	0		12	4	24		8	11	3
23	20	Ven	5	0	0	Mars	7	0	0	Jup	12	0	0	Mer	8	6	0
23	40		4	6	0		6	9	27		11	7	6		8	0	27
24	0		4	0	0		6	7	24		11	2	12		7	7	24
24	20		3	6	0		6	5	21		10	9	18		7	2	21

24	40		3	0	0		6	3	18		10	4	24		6	9	18
25	0		2	6	0		6	1	15		10	0	0		6	4	15
25	20		2	0	0		5	11	12		9	7	6		5	11	12
25	40		1	6	0		5	9	9		9	2	12		5	6	9
26	0		1	0	0		5	7	6		8	9	18		5	1	6
26	20		0	6	0		5	5	3		8	4	24		4	8	3
26	40	Sun	6	0	0		5	3	0		8	0	0		4	3	0
27	0		5	10	6		5	0	27		7	7	6		3	9	27
27	20		5	8	12		4	10	24		7	2	12		3	4	24
27	40		5	6	18		4	8	21		6	9	18		2	1	21
28	0		5	4	24		4	6	18		6	4	24		2	6	18
28	20		5	3	0		4	4	15		6	0	0		2	1	15
28	40		5	1	6		4	2	12		5	7	6		1	8	12
29	0		4	11	12		4	0	9		5	2	12		1	3	9
29	20		4	9	18		3	10	6		4	9	18		0	10	6
29	40		4	7	24		3	8	3		4	4	24		0	5	3
30	0		4	6	0		3	6	0		4	0	0		0	0	0

HOW TO WORKOUT ANTARDASHAS :

Example I

Suppose we want to calculate the Antardasha of Jupiter in the Mahadasha of Venus, we adopt the following formula :

20 (Mahadasha of Venus) X 16 (Mahadasha of Jupiter) = 320

The first two digits represent the no of Months. The third digit should be multiplied by 3 to get no of days.

Thus 320 means 32 Months and 0 days i.e., 2 years, 8 months & 0 days.

Example II

Calculate Jupiter's Antardasha in Rahu's Mahadasha.

18 (Rahu's Mahadasha) x 16 (Jupiter's Mahadasha) = 288 .

It means 28 months and 24 (8x3) days i.e., 2 yrs, 4 months & 24 days.

HOW TO CALCULATE PARTANTAR

Example :

To calculate Jupiter's Partantar in Jupiter's Antardasha & Venus's Mahadasha.

$$\frac{20 \text{ (Venus Mahadasha)} \times 16 \text{ (Jupiter Mahadasha)} \times 16 \text{ (Jupiter Mahadasha)}}{40}$$

= 128 Days i.e., 4 months and 8 days.

For the convenience of readers, Mahadasha, Antardasha & Partantar charts have been given in the enclosed appendix.

MAHADASHA RESULTS

Mahadasha of an exalted planet confers all happiness but that of a debilitating planet confers misery. But it should be noted that Antardasha of a planet also plays an important role. If the planet is in an exalted Antardasha, it may bring good results.

For example: Jupiter in Venus is bad but Rahu (if exalted) confers power etc.

MAIN LORD & THEIR PERIOD	SUB-LORDS	SUB-PERIOD Y M D			SUN M D		MOON M D		MARS M D		RAHU M D		JUP. M D		SAT. M D		MER. M D		KETU M D		VEN. M D	
SUN'S PERIOD (RAVI MAHADASHA)—6 YEARS	SUN	0	3	18	0	5.4	0	9	0	6.3	0	16.2	0	14.4	0	17.1	0	15.3	0	6.3	0	18
	MOON	0	6	0	0	9	0	15	0	10.5	0	27	0	24	0	28.5	0	25.5	0	10.5	1	0
	MARS	0	4	6	0	6.3	0	10.5	0	7.4	0	18 9	0	16.8	0	20	0	17.9	0	7.4	0	21
	RAHU	0	10	24	0	16.2	0	27	0	18.9	1	18.6	1	13.2	1	21.3	1	15.9	0	18.9	1	24
	JUP.	0	9	18	0	14.4	0	24	0	16.8	1	13.2	1	8.4	1	15.6	1	10.8	0	16.8	1	18
	SAT.	0	11	12	0	17.1	0	28.5	0	20	1	21.3	1	15.6	1	24.2	1	18.5	0	20	1	27
	MER.	0	10	6	0	15.3	0	25.5	0	17.9	1	15.9	1	10.8	1	18.5	1	13.4	0	17.9	1	21
	KETU	0	4	6	0	6.3	0	10.5	0	7.4	0	18.9	0	16.8	0	20	0	17.9	0	7.4	0	21
	VENUS	1	0	0	0	18	1	0	0	21	1	24	1	18	1	27	1	21	0	21	2	0

MAIN LORD & THEIR PERIOD	SUB-LORDS	SUB-PERIOD			SUN		MOON		MARS		RAHU		JUP.		SAT.		MER.		KETU		VEN.	
		Y	M	D	M	D	M	D	M	D	M	D	M	D	M	D	M	D	M	D	M	D
SUN'S PERIOD (RAVI MAHADASHA)—6 YEARS	MOON	0	10	0	0	15	0	25	0	17.5	1	15	1	10	1	17.5	1	12.5	0	17.5	1	20
	MARS	0	7	0	0	10.3	0	17.5	0	12.3	1	1.5	0	28	1	3.3	0	29.8	0	12.3	1	5
	RAHU	1	6	0	0	27	1	15	1	1.5	2	21	2	12	2	25.5	2	16.5	1	1.5	3	0
	JUP.	1	4	0	0	24	1	10	0	28	2	12	2	4	2	16	2	8	0	28	2	20
	SAT.	1	7	0	0	28.5	1	17.5	1	3.3	2	25.5	2	16	3	0.3	2	20.8	1	3.3	3	5
	MER.	1	5	0	0	25.5	1	12.5	0	29.8	2	16.5	2	8	2	20.8	2	12.3	0	29.8	2	25
	KETU	0	7	0	0	10.5	0	17.5	0	12.3	1	1.5	0	28	1	3.3	0	29.8	0	12.3	1	5
	VENUS	1	8	0	1	0	1	20	1	5	3	0	2	20	3	5	2	25	1	5	3	10
	SUN	0	6	0	0	9	0	15	0	10.5	0	27	0	24	0	28.5	0	25.5	0	10.5	1	0
MARS'PERIOD (MARS MAHADASHA)—7 YEARS	MARS	0	4	27	0	7.4	0	12.3	0	8.6	0	22.1	0	19.6	0	23.3	0	20.8	0	8.6	0	24.5
	RAHU	1	0	18	0	18.9	1	1.5	0	22.1	1	26.7	1	20.4	1	29.9	1	23.6	0	22.1	2	3
	JUP.	0	11	6	0	18.6	0	28	0	19.6	1	20.4	1	14.8	1	23.2	1	17.6	0	19.6	1	26
	SAT.	1	1	9	0	20	1	3.3	0	23.3	1	29.9	1	23.2	2	3.2	1	26.5	0	23.3	2	6.5
	MER.	0	11	27	0	17.9	0	29.8	0	20.8	1	23.6	1	17.6	1	26.5	1	20.6	0	20.8	1	29.5
	KETU	0	4	27	0	7.4	0	12.3	0	8.6	0	22.1	0	19.6	0	23.3	0	20.8	0	8.6	0	24.5
	VENUS	1	2	0	0	21	1	5	0	24.5	2	3	1	26	2	6.5	1	29.5	0	24.5	2	10
	SUN	0	4	6	0	6.3	0	10.5	0	7.4	0	18.9	0	16.8	0	20	0	17.9	0	7.4	0	21
	MOON	0	7	0	0	10.5	0	17.5	0	12.3	1	1.5	0	28	1	3.3	0	29.8	0	12.3	1	5

MAIN LORD & THEIR PERIOD	SUB-LORDS	SUB-PERIOD			SUN		MOON		MARS		RAHU		JUP.		SAT.		MER.		KETU		VEN.	
		Y	M	D	M	D	M	D	M	D	M	D	M	D	M	D	M	D	M	D	M	D
RAHU'S PERIOD (RAHU MAHADASHA)—18 YEARS	RAHU	2	8	12	1	18.6	2	21	1	26.7	4	25.8	4	9.6	5	3.9	4	17.7	1	26.7	5	12
	JUP.	2	4	24	1	13.2	2	12	1	20.4	4	9.6	3	25.2	4	16.8	4	2.4	1	20.4	4	24
	SAT.	2	10	6	1	21.3	2	25.5	1	29.9	5	3.9	4	16.8	5	12.5	4	25.4	1	29.9	5	21
	MER.	2	6	18	1	15.9	2	16.6	1	23.6	4	17.7	4	2.4	4	25.4	4	10.1	1	23.6	5	3
	KETU	1	0	18	0	18.9	1	1.5	0	22.1	1	26.7	1	20.4	1	29.9	1	23.6	0	22.1	2	3
	VENUS	3	0	0	1	24	3	0	2	3	5	12	4	24	5	21	5	3	2	3	6	0
	SUN	0	10	24	0	16.2	0	27	0	18.9	1	18.6	1	13.2	1	21.3	1	15.9	0	18.9	1	24
	MOON	1	6	0	0	27	1	15	1	1.5	2	21	2	12	2	25.5	2	16.5	1	1.5	3	0
	MARS	1	0	18	0	18.9	1	1.5	0	22	1	26.7	1	20.4	1	29.9	1	23.6	0	22	2	3
JUPITER'S PERIOD (JUP. MAHADASHA)—16 YRS.	JUP.	2	1	18	1	8.4	2	4	1	14.8	3	15.2	3	12.4	4	1.6	3	18.8	1	14.8	4	8
	SAT.	2	6	12	1	15.6	2	16	1	23.2	4	16.8	4	1.6	4	24.4	4	9.2	1	23.2	5	2
	MER.	2	3	6	1	10.8	2	8	1	17.6	4	2.4	3	18.8	4	9.2	3	25.6	1	17.6	4	16
	KETU	0	11	6	0	16.8	0	28	0	19.6	1	20.4	1	14.8	1	23.2	1	17.6	0	19.6	1	26
	VENUS	2	8	0	1	18	2	20	1	26	4	24	4	8	5	2	4	16	1	26	5	10
	SUN	0	9	18	0	14.4	0	24	0	16:8	1	13.2	1	8.4	1	15.6	1	10.8	0	16.8	1	18
	MOON	1	4	0	0	24	1	10	0	27	2	10	2	4	2	26	2	8	0	28	2	20
	MARS	0	11	6	0	16.8	0	28	0	19.6	1	20.4	1	14.8	1	23.2	1	17.6	0	19.6	1	26
	RAHU	2	4	24	1	13.2	2	12	1	20.4	4	9.6	3	25.2	4	16.6	4	2.4	1	20.4	4	24

MAIN LORD & THEIR PERIOD	SUB-LORDS	SUB-PERIOD			SUN		MOON		MARS		RAHU		JUP.		SAT.		MER.		KETU		VEN.	
		Y	M	D	M	D	M	D	M	D	M	D	M	D	M	D	M	D	M	D	M	D
SATURN'S PERIOD (SAT. MAHADASHA)—19 YRS.	SAT.	3	0	3	1	24.2	3	0.3	2	3.2	5	12.5	4	24.4	5	21.5	5	3.4	2	3.2	6	0.5
	MER.	2	8	9	1	18	2	10	1	26	4	25	4	9	5	3	4	17.3	1	26.5	5	11.5
	KETU	1	1	9	0	20	1	3.3	0	23.3	1	29.9	1	23.2	2	3.2	1	26.5	0	23.3	2	6.5
	VENUS	3	2	0	1	27	3	5	2	6.5	5	21	5	2	6	0.5	5	11.5	2	6.5	6	10
	SUN	0	11	12	0	17.1	0	28.5	0	20	1	21.3	1	15.6	1	24.2	1	18.5	0	20	1	27
	MOON	1	7	0	0	28.5	1	17.5	1	3.3	2	25.5	2	16	3	0.3	2	20.8	1	3.3	3	5
	MARS	1	1	9	0	20	1	3.3	0	23.3	1	29.9	1	23.2	2	3.3	1	26.5	0	23.3	2	6.5
	RAHU	2	10	6	1	21.3	1	25.5	1	29.9	5	3.9	4	16.8	5	12.5	4	25.4	1	29.9	5	21
	JUP.	2	6	12	1	15.6	2	16	1	23.2	4	16.8	4	1.6	4	24.4	4	9.2	1	23.2	5	2
MERCURY'S PERIOD (MER. MAHADASHA)—17 YRS	MER.	2	4	27	1	13.4	2	12.3	1	20.6	4	10.1	3	25.6	4	17.3	4	2.8	1	20.6	4	24.5
	KETU	0	11	27	0	17.9	0	29.8	0	20.8	1	23.6	1	17.6	1	26.6	1	20.6	0	20.8	1	29.5
	VENUS	2	10	0	1	21	2	25	1	29.5	5	3	4	16	5	11.5	4	24.5	1	29.5	5	20
	SUN	0	10	6	0	15.3	0	25.5	0	17.9	1	15.9	1	10.8	1	18.5	1	13.4	0	17.9	1	21
	MOON	1	5	0	0	25.5	1	12.5	0	29.8	2	16.5	2	8	2	20	2	12.3	0	29.8	2	25
	MARS	0	11	27	0	17.9	0	29.8	0	20.8	1	13.6	1	17.6	1	26.5	1	20.6	0	20.8	1	29.5
	RAHU	2	6	18	1	15.9	2	16.5	1	23.6	4	17.8	4	2.4	4	25.4	4	10.1	1	23.6	5	3
	JUP.	2	3	6	1	10.8	2	8	1	17.6	4	2.4	3	18.8	4	9.2	3	25.6	1	17.6	4	16
	SAT.	2	8	9	1	18.5	2	20.8	1	26.5	4	25.4	4	9.2	5	3.4	4	17.3	1	26.5	5	11.5

MAIN LORD & THEIR PERIOD	SUB-LORDS	SUB-PERIOD			SUN		MOON		MARS		RAHU		JUP.		SAT.		MER.		KETU		VEN.	
		Y	M	D	M	D	M	D	M	D	M	D	M	D	M	D	M	D	M	D	M	D
KETU'S PERIOD (KETU MAHADASHA)—7 YRS.	KETU	0	4	27	0	7.4	0	12.3	0	8.6	0	22.1	0	19.6	0	23.3	0	20.8	0	8.6	0	24.5
	VENUS	1	2	0	0	21	1	5	0	24.5	2	3	1	26	2	6.5	1	29.5	0	24.5	2	10
	SUN	0	4	6	0	6.3	0	10.5	0	7.4	0	18.9	0	16.8	0	20	0	17.9	0	7.4	0	21
	MOON	0	7	0	0	10.5	0	17.5	0	12.3	1	1.5	0	28	1	3.3	0	29.8	0	12.3	1	5
	MARS	0	4	27	0	7.4	0	12.3	0	8.6	0	22.1	0	19.6	0	23.3	0	20.8	0	8.6	0	24.5
	RAHU	1	0	18	0	18.9	1	1	0	22.1	1	26.7	1	20.4	1	29.9	1	23.6	0	22.1	2	3
	JUP.	0	11	6	0	16.8	0	28	0	19.6	1	20.4	1	14.8	1	23.2	1	17.6	0	19.6	1	26
	SAT.	1	1	9	0	20	1	3.3	0	23.2	1	29.9	1	23.2	2	3.2	1	26.5	0	23.2	2	6.5
	MER.	0	11	27	0	17.9	0	29.8	0	20.8	1	23.6	1	17.6	1	26.5	1	20.5	0	20.8	1	29.5
VENUS'S PERIOD (VENUS MAHADASHA)—20 YRS.	VENUS	3	4	0	2	0	3	10	2	10	6	0	5	10	6	10	5	20	2	10	6	20
	SUN	1	0	0	0	18	1	0	0	21	1	24	1	18	1	27	1	21	0	21	2	0
	MOON	1	8	0	1	0	1	20	1	5	3	0	2	20	3	5	2	25	1	5	3	10
	MARS	1	2	0	0	21	1	5	0	24.5	2	3	1	26	2	6.5	1	29.5	0	24.5	2	10
	RAHU	3	0	0	1	24	3	0	2	3	5	12	4	24	5	21	5	3	2	3	6	0
	JUP.	2	8	0	1	18	2	20	1	26	4	24	4	8	5	2	4	16	1	26	5	10
	SAT.	3	2	0	1	27	3	5	2	6.5	5	21	5	2	6	0.5	5	11.5	2	6.5	6	10
	MER.	2	10	0	1	21	2	25	1	29.5	5	3	4	16	5	11.5	4	24.5	1	29.5	5	20
	KETU	1	2	0	0	21	1	5	0	24.5	2	3	1	26	2	6.5	1	29.5	0	24.5	2	10

NO. OF YEARS SHOWING BAD (MALEFIC) RESULTS IN A PARTICULAR MAHADASHA

S.NO.	MAHADASHA	YEARS SHOWING BAD RESULTS
1	JUPITER	3 years out of 16 years.
2	SUN	1 year out of 6 years.
3	MOON	1 year out of 10 years.
4	VENUS	8 years out of 20 years.
5	MARS	4 years out of 7 years.
6	MERCURY	7 years out of 17 years.
7	SATURN	4 years out of 19 years.
8	RAHU	11 years out of 18 years.
9	KETU	3 years out of 7 years.
	TOTAL	42 years out of 120 years

EFFECTS OF VARIOUS PLANETS IN A PARTICULAR YEAR, DURING A PARTICULAR MAHADASHA

1	2	3	4	5	6	7	8	9	10	11	12
Venus	Raashi no.12 ends	Sun	Moon	Ketu	Mars	Mercury	Saturn	Rahu	Death Planet in no.8	Ancestral Planet no.9	Jupiter
1	2	3	4	5	6	7	8	9	10	11	12
13	14	15	16	17	18	19	20	21	22	23	24
25	26	27	28	29	30	31	32	33	34	35	36
37	38	39	40								

From the above chart it is clear that no. 1 indicates 1st year of Mahadasha, No.2

indicates 2nd year of Mahadasha etc. though Mahadasha of a planet may commence from any year of life.

Example : Suppose Mahadasha of Venus of an individual starts from 23rd year, substitute no.1 with 23, No. 2 with 24 and so on and so forth. Another point to be noted is that Mahadasha of Venus ends at the 20th year and the planet occupying no. 20 in the above chart is Saturn; hence in the 20th year of Mahadasha of Venus, we will have mixed results of both the planets i.e., Venus and Saturn.

ANNUAL CHART (VARSH PHAL)

Whether you prepare the Annual Chart on the basis of ancient astrological calculations or other systems, conclusions are almost the same.

EXAMPLE: A gentleman was born on 17.03.1930 at 11.55 P.M., his horoscope as prepared by the Astrologers is as under :

BIRTH CHART ON 17.03.1930

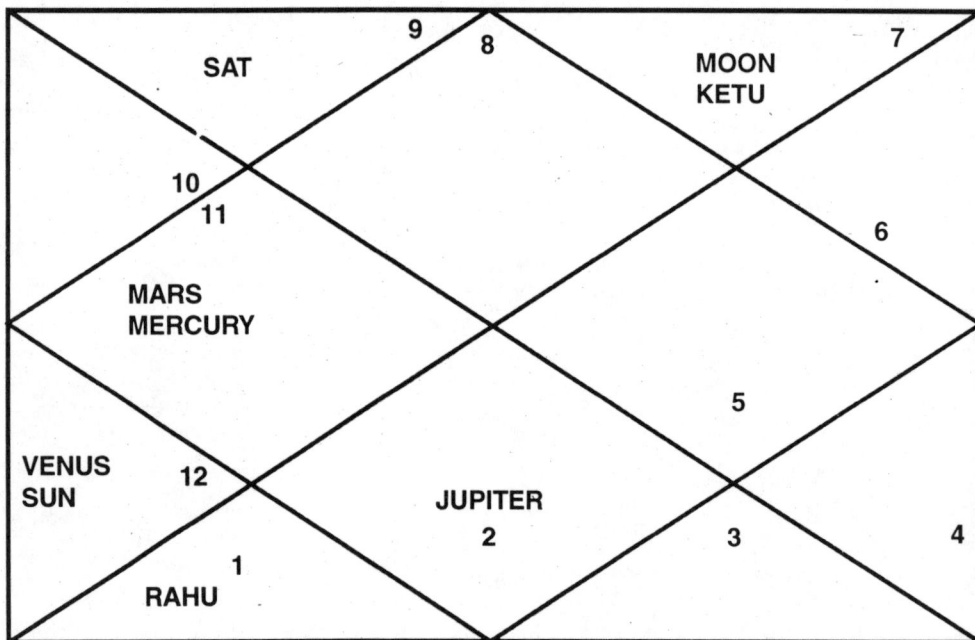

9 SAT	8
10 11	7 MOON KETU
MARS MERCURY	6
VENUS SUN	5
12	JUPITER 2
1 RAHU	3 4

BIRTH CHART (ACCORDING TO ANCIENT TEXTS AND RESEARCH)

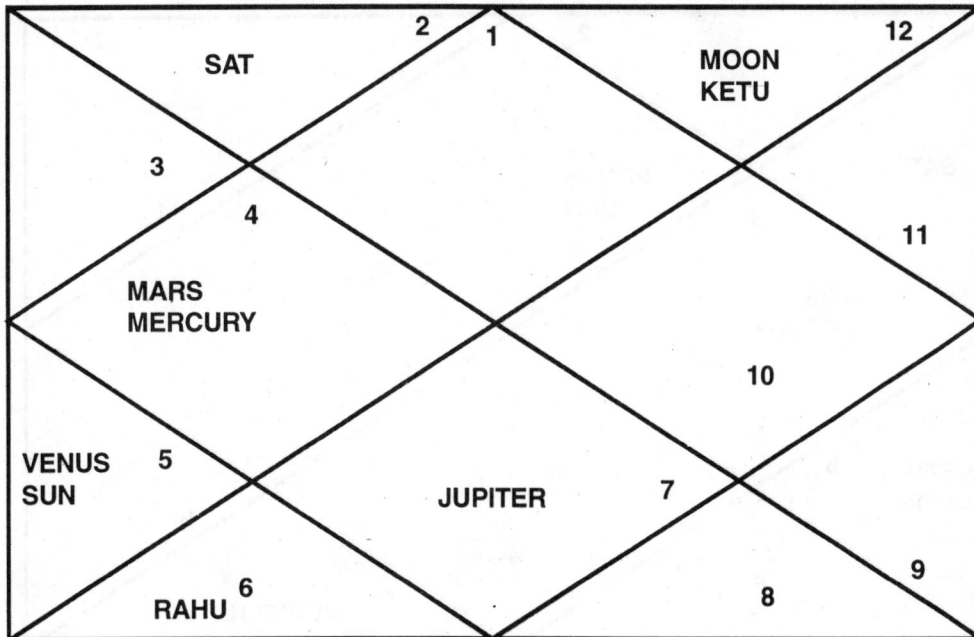

The horoscope indicates that the native is very intelligent must have the gift of gab (a fine orator) - because of Venus in 12th sign and sun in 5th house, He is fond of music, poetry and astrology. His children must be well educated. Saturn in II house in Sagittarius is exalted, hence he earns a lot during Saturn's Mahadasha and enjoys complete domestic happiness and personal fate, Jupiter in 7th house indicates he must suffer from asthma or bronchitis and must be helpful to his parents and relatives; must live away from relatives. Moon and Ketu suggest that he suffers from some allergy on his feet and he must always be tense. Rahu indicates his dominance and victory over others. But as it aspects the 12th house, he must be a spend thrift.

Here is an example of his 29th year :

ANNUAL CHART FROM 17.03.1958 TO 17.03.1959 (AGE 29TH YEAR)

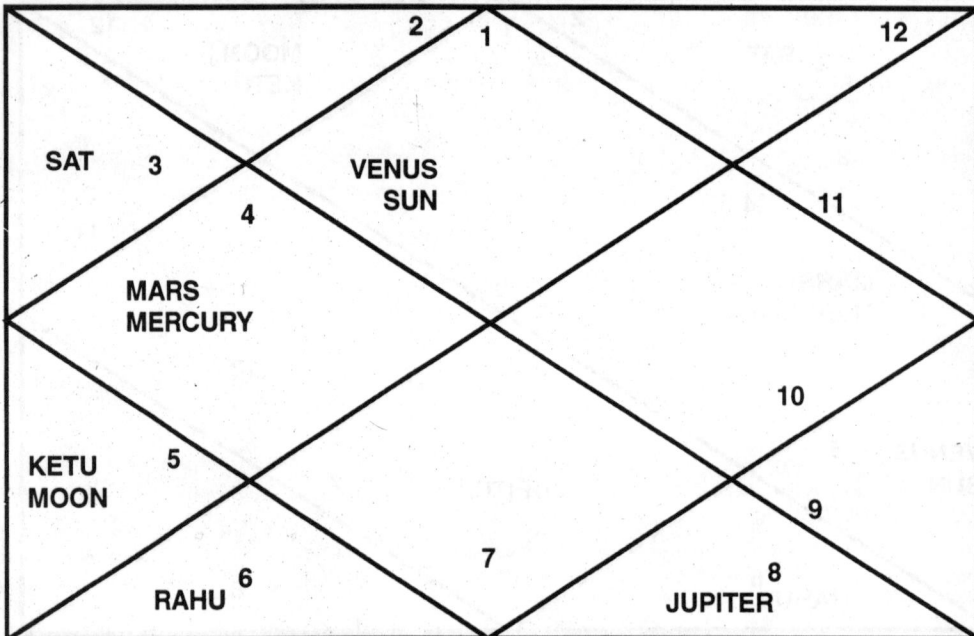

```
                          2  | 1                    12
         SAT    3                VENUS
                      4          SUN                    11
              MARS
              MERCURY

                                                   10

              KETU    5
              MOON
                                                   9
                6                       8
           RAHU              7      JUPITER
```

In order to prepare the monthly chart, position of sun may be moved as under. As he was born in March (i.e. 3rd Month), sun will occupy the 3rd house in the Monthly Chart i.e., on 17.05.1958, 3rd month will start.

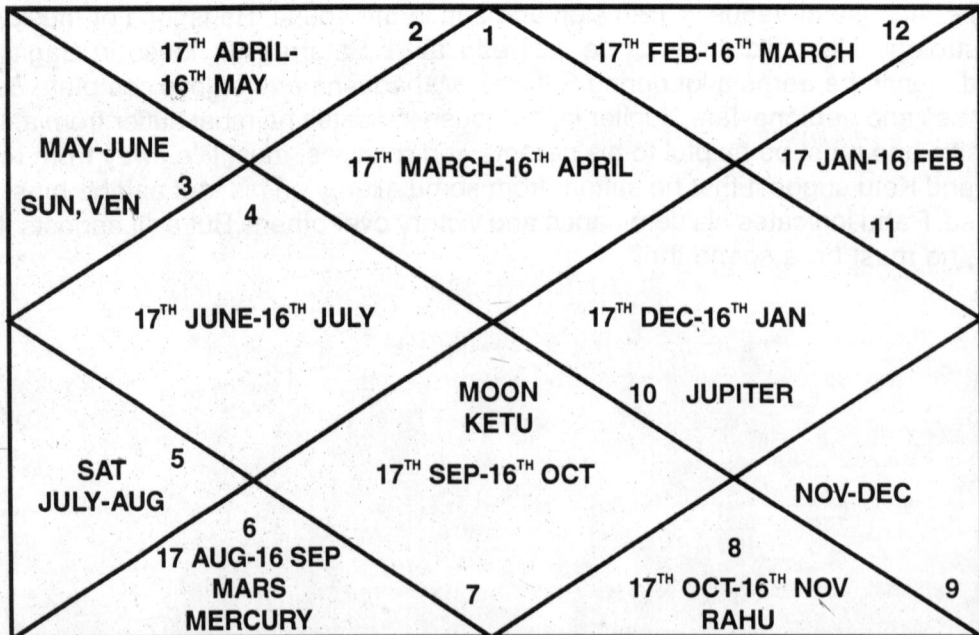

```
                       2  | 1
    17TH APRIL-                   17TH FEB-16TH MARCH      12
    16TH MAY
   MAY-JUNE                                        17 JAN-16 FEB
                          17TH MARCH-16TH APRIL
   SUN, VEN    3
               4                                          11

   17TH JUNE-16TH JULY         17TH DEC-16TH JAN

                            MOON
                            KETU       10   JUPITER
   SAT     5
   JULY-AUG               17TH SEP-16TH OCT
                                               NOV-DEC
           6
   17 AUG-16 SEP                           8
   MARS                  7       17TH OCT-16TH NOV        9
   MERCURY                       RAHU
```

64

Venus and Sun in the 1st house in the Annual Chart are exalted and therefore the native must have got a good job between 17.05.1958 to 16.6.1958. This month must have been the best for him. Exalted Saturn in the 3rd house; Moon-Ketu in the 5th and Rahu in the 6th house in the annual chart must have conferred very good results in the months indicated against each in the monthly chart.

DAILY KUNDALI

Just as Sun is shifted in the Monthly Chart so in order to determine the daily chart, move Mars. 15th day (12+3) of the 3rd month may be assigned to Mars. Mars will move to no. 8.

DAILY CHART

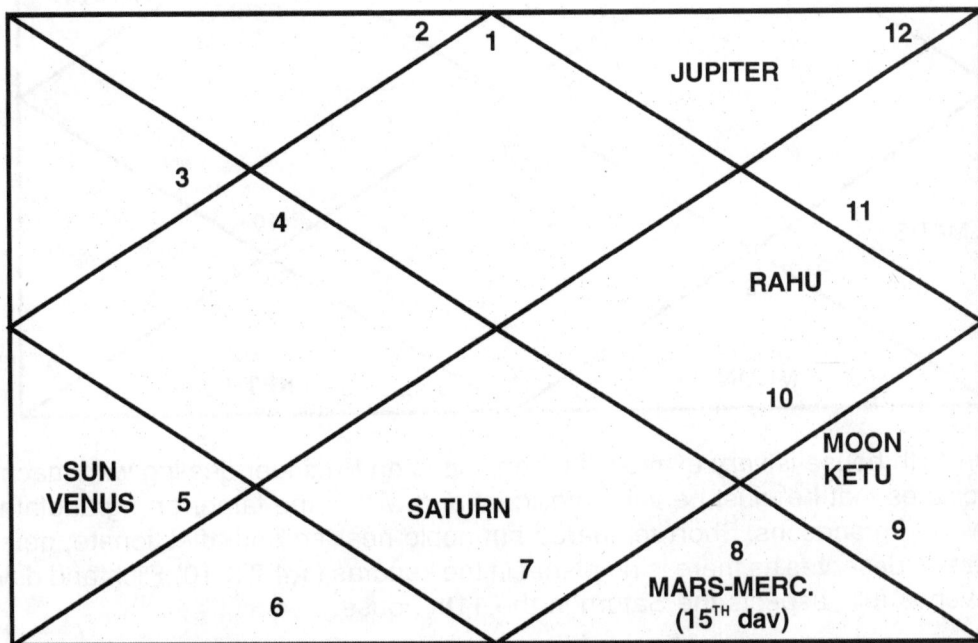

Similarly for a person born in May (5th month) - 17th day may be assigned to Mars i.e., 12 + 5 = 17th in the daily chart.

EXAMPLE NO.2

The native was born on 07.06.1965 at 03.14 A.M. His horoscope is as under :

BIRTH CHART ON 7/8.06.1965

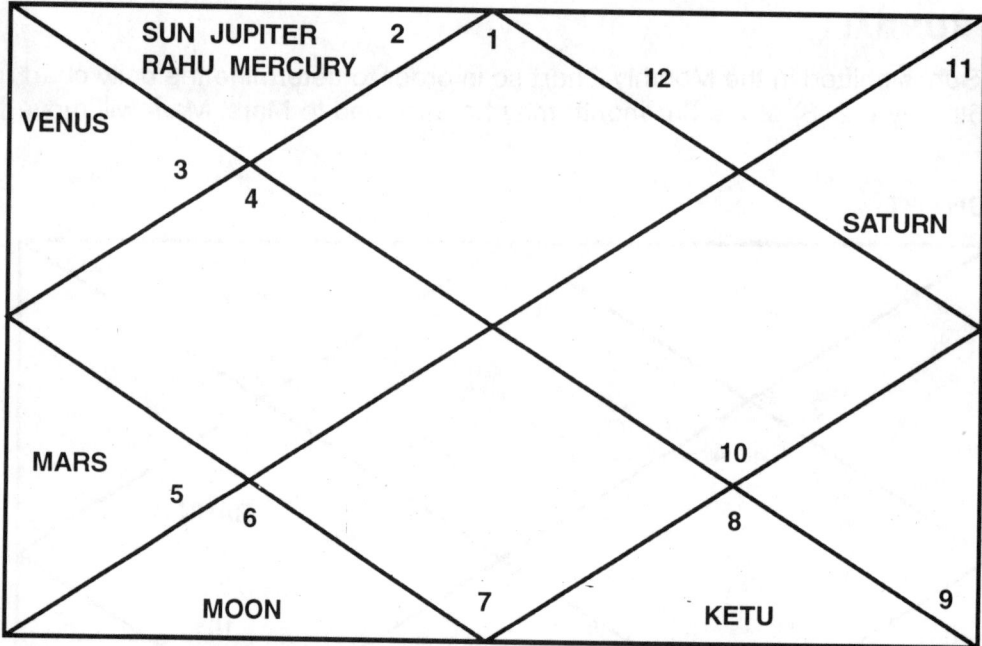

```
                    SUN JUPITER      2   1
                    RAHU MERCURY              12              11
      VENUS
               3
                 4
                                                       SATURN


      MARS                                       10
           5                                           8
             6                                                    9
                MOON               7        KETU
```

Saturn in 11th house is very exalted; it means he is an Engineer dealing with machines. Mars indicates that he must be very intelligent and will be the father and grandfather of rich sons and grandsons. Short tempered but noble hearted and affectionate; gets less than what he deserves as there is no planet in the kendras (1,4,7 & 10);Rich and devoted wife as Venus fully aspects the Saturn in the 11th house.

ANNUAL CHART FROM 07.06.1981 TO 07.06.1982 (AGE 17TH YEAR)

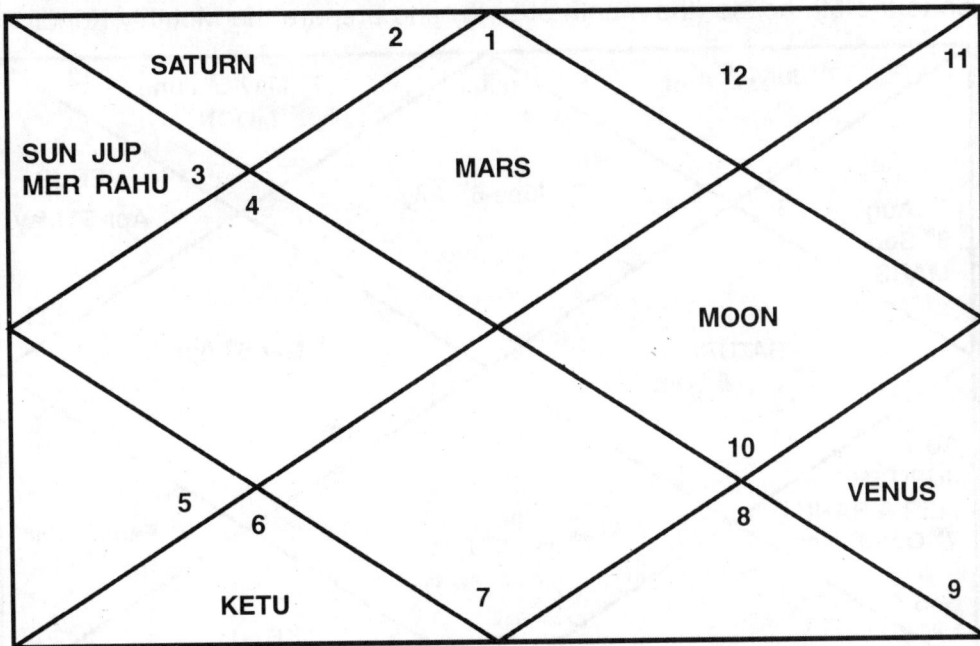

```
┌─────────────────────────────────────────────────────────┐
│            2  ╲  ╱ 1                              11       │
│     SATURN     ╲╱              12                          │
│              ╱╲  ╱╲                          ╱╲           │
│  SUN JUP    ╱  ╲╱  ╲        MARS            ╱  ╲          │
│  MER RAHU 3╱   ╱╲   ╲                      ╱    ╲         │
│          ╱ 4 ╱    ╲   ╲                  ╱      ╲        │
│         ╱    ╱      ╲   ╲              ╱        ╲        │
│        ╱    ╱        ╲   ╲          ╱   MOON    ╲       │
│       ╱    ╱          ╲   ╲      ╱              ╲      │
│      ╱    ╱   5        ╲   ╲  ╱        10        ╲     │
│     ╱    ╱    ╱╲        ╲  ╱╲        ╱╲    VENUS  ╲    │
│    ╱    ╱ 6 ╱  ╲        ╱╲  ╲      ╱ 8  ╲         ╲   │
│   ╱        ╱    ╲      ╱  ╲  ╲    ╱      ╲      9   │
│   KETU    ╱  7   ╲    ╱    ╲  ╲  ╱        ╲         │
└─────────────────────────────────────────────────────────┘
```

Mars in the fist house in the Annual Chart and Saturn in 2nd house (both exalted) confer eminence on him. He must have obtained some position in the University and Saturn in 2nd house must have brought personal happiness to him. He must have joined a good Engineering College based on his merits. Similarly, Annual Charts for various years may be prepared according to the Catalogue .

MONTHLY KUNDLI

Shift Sun to the 5th house (the month of birth) and prepare the Monthly Kundli.

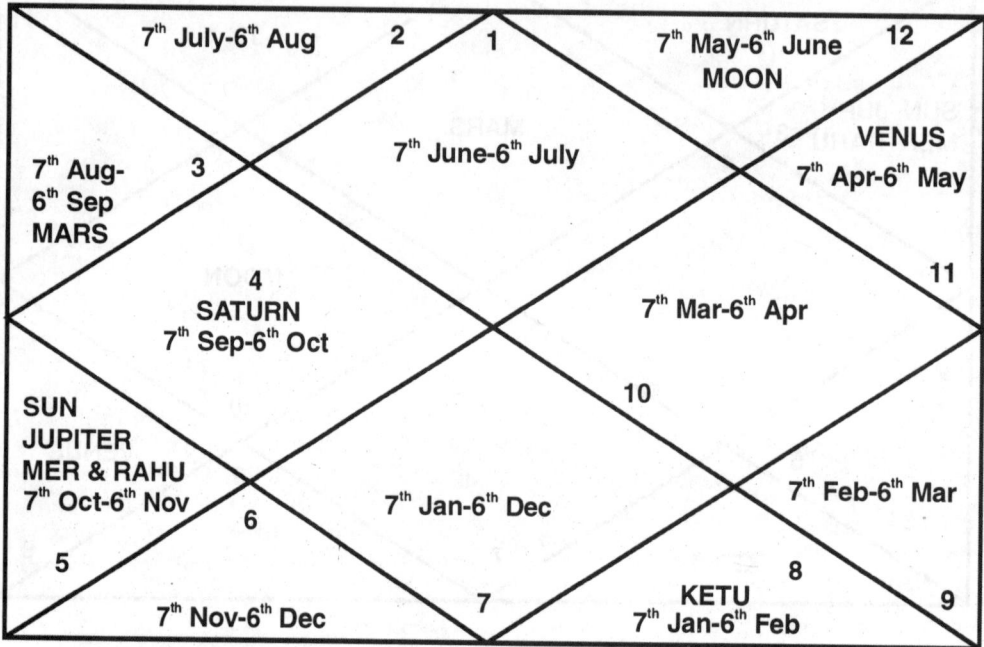

7th July-6th Aug **2** / **1**	7th May-6th June **MOON** **12**	
3 7th June-6th July	**VENUS** 7th Apr-6th May	
7th Aug-6th Sep **MARS**		**11**
4 **SATURN** 7th Sep-6th Oct	7th Mar-6th Apr	
	10	
SUN JUPITER MER & RAHU 7th Oct-6th Nov **6**	7th Jan-6th Dec	7th Feb-6th Mar
5		**8**
7th Nov-6th Dec	**7**	**KETU** 7th Jan-6th Feb **9**

Assign 17th day to Mars i.e., 12+5=17th day in the Daily Chart. Mars will move to no. 7.Daily chart is as under :

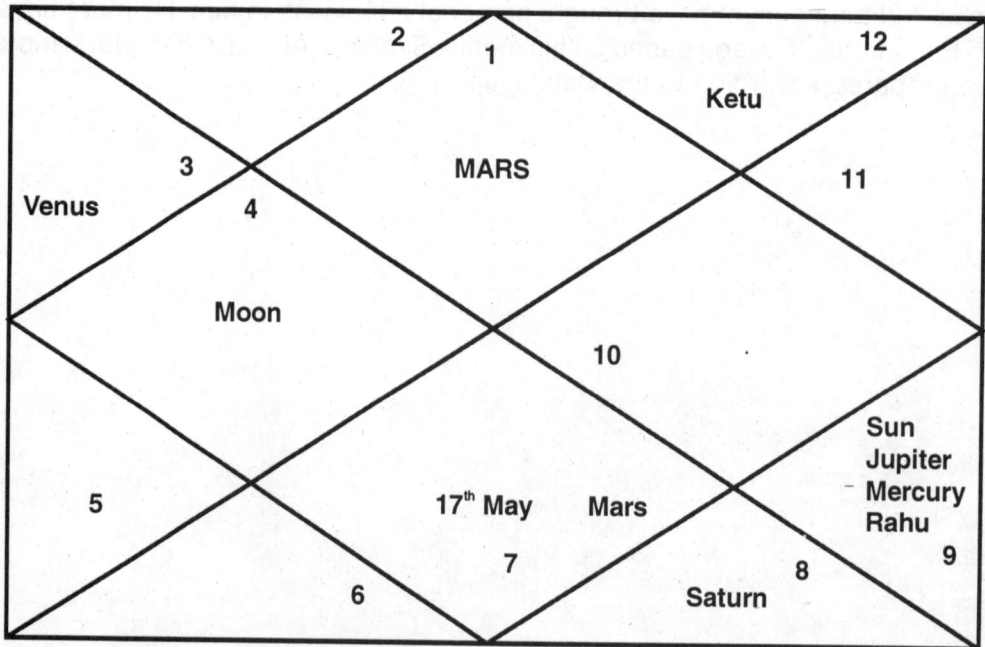

2 / **1**	**MARS**	**Ketu** **12**
3		**11**
Venus **4**		
Moon		**10**
		Sun Jupiter Mercury Rahu
5	17th May **Mars**	**8** **9**
	7	**Saturn**
	6	

68

While determining the effect of a planet in a particular House and in a particular year, divide the year of age of the native with the number of the house in which a particular planet is placed in the birth chart. The remainder will give the result in that particular year concerning that house. In case of House no.1, divide the age by 12; in case of House no.2, divide it by 11 and for House no.3, divide the age by 10. For all other houses, divide the age of the person by that particular house no.

Example : Suppose a person is interested in knowing about the children (Progeny). For children, house no.5 is reserved. If house no.5 is vacant in the birth chart, refer to the position of Ketu in the annual chart. Suppose a person desires to know about the children during the 25th year, divide it by 5 (house for children) . The remainder is zero; hence study the result of house no.5 in the horoscope. If there is no planet in the house no.5 in the horoscope, refer to Ketu's position in the birth chart. If a person wants to have information regarding children in his 26th year, divide it by 5, remainder will be 1. Now study house no.1 for results in the birth chart. If no.1 is vacant, then refer to house no.5 in the horoscope for results.

I have worked out the annual/monthly results in the annual chart according to English (Gregorian) Calendar for the sake of easy comprehension. But sometimes it is also advisable to work out the monthly results in terms of Hindu Astrological Calendar. In Astrology Sun's position is the most significant as it starts from 1st of Baisakhi in Aries, which approximately falls on 13th April. Of course, there will be a minor variation of a few days, while computing the monthly results in terms of English Calendar.

Beginning of a month is to be taken from the date and time of birth. Suppose a person is born on 31st of a particular month, he will complete the month on the 30th of next month (e.g., from 31st July to 30th August, etc.)

Annual Chart's results - favourable and unfavourable - will be visible from the position of the Sun. It will give bad results if it is placed in the 7th house (during 7th month from birth) and other planets will give results according to their positions in the Annual Chart.

It may be remembered that Sun's position in the annual Chart is the fundamental one. The house in which Sun is placed in the Annual Chart may be given the month of birth and then the monthly chart be prepared. A person born in May, his Sun will be allotted 5th, month from birth i.e., Sept. - in the monthly chart and Sun's results will be available in Sept.- Oct.. and so on and so forth (as per examples given in the preceding pages).

CATALOGUE OF ANNUAL CHART

Figures 1 - 12 written against Age indicate the house nos. of the birth chart and the figures under Age indicate the year.

Example: If Jupiter is in the 5th house in the Birth Chart it will be in the 12th house in the 16th year.

AGE	1	2	3	4	5	6	7	8	9	10	11	12
1	1	9	10	3	5	2	11	7	6	12	4	8
2	4	1	12	9	3	7	5	6	2	8	10	11
3	9	4	1	2	8	3	10	5	7	11	12	6
4	3	8	4	1	10	9	6	11	5	7	2	12
5	11	3	8	4	1	5	9	2	12	6	7	10
6	5	12	3	8	4	11	2	9	1	10	6	7
7	7	6	9	5	12	4	1	10	11	2	8	3
8	2	7	6	12	9	10	3	1	8	5	11	4
9	12	2	7	6	11	1	8	4	10	3	5	9
10	10	11	2	7	6	12	4	8	3	1	9	5
11	8	5	11	10	7	6	12	3	9	4	1	2
12	6	10	5	11	2	8	7	12	4	9	3	1
13	1	5	10	8	11	6	7	2	12	3	9	4
14	4	1	3	2	5	7	8	11	6	12	10	9
15	9	4	1	6	8	5	2	7	11	10	12	3
16	3	9	4	1	12	8	6	5	2	7	11	10
17	11	3	9	4	1	10	5	6	7	8	2	12
18	5	11	6	9	4	1	12	8	10	2	3	7
19	7	10	11	3	9	4	1	12	8	5	6	2
20	2	7	5	12	3	9	10	1	4	6	8	11

AGE	1	2	3	4	5	6	7	8	9	10	11	12
21	12	2	8	5	10	3	9	4	1	11	7	6
22	10	12	2	7	6	11	3	9	5	1	4	8
23	8	6	12	10	7	2	11	3	9	4	1	5
24	6	8	7	11	2	12	4	10	3	9	5	1
25	1	6	10	3	2	8	7	4	11	5	12	9
26	4	1	3	8	6	7	2	11	12	9	5	10
27	9	4	1	5	10	11	12	7	6	8	2	3
28	3	9	4	1	11	5	6	8	7	2	10	12
29	11	3	9	4	1	6	8	2	10	12	7	5
30	5	11	8	9	4	1	3	12	2	10	6	7
31	7	5	11	12	9	4	1	10	8	6	3	2
32	2	7	5	11	3	12	10	6	4	1	9	8
33	12	2	6	10	8	3	9	1	5	7	4	11
34	10	12	2	7	5	9	11	3	1	4	8	6
35	8	10	12	6	7	2	4	5	9	3	11	1
36	6	8	7	2	12	10	5	9	3	11	1	4
37	1	3	10	6	9	12	7	5	11	2	4	8
38	4	1	3	8	6	5	2	7	12	10	11	9
39	9	4	1	12	8	2	10	11	6	3	5	7
40	3	9	4	1	11	8	6	12	2	5	7	10

AGE	1	2	3	4	5	6	7	8	9	10	11	12
41	11	7	9	4	1	6	8	2	10	12	3	5
42	5	11	8	9	12	1	3	4	7	6	10	2
43	7	5	11	2	3	4	1	10	8	9	12	6
44	2	10	5	3	4	9	12	8	1	7	6	11
45	12	2	6	5	10	7	9	1	3	11	8	4
46	10	12	2	7	5	3	11	6	4	8	9	1
47	8	6	12	10	7	11	4	9	5	1	2	3
48	6	8	7	11	2	10	5	3	9	4	1	12
49	1	7	10	6	12	2	8	4	11	9	3	5
50	4	1	8	3	6	12	5	11	2	7	10	9
51	9	4	1	2	8	3	12	6	7	10	5	11
52	3	9	4	1	11	7	2	12	5	8	6	10
53	11	10	7	4	1	6	3	9	12	5	8	2
54	5	11	3	9	4	1	6	2	10	12	7	8
55	7	5	11	8	3	9	1	10	6	4	2	12
56	2	3	5	11	9	4	10	1	8	6	12	7
57	12	2	6	5	10	8	9	7	4	11	1	3
58	10	12	2	7	5	11	4	8	3	1	9	6
59	8	6	12	10	7	5	11	3	9	2	4	1
60	6	8	9	12	2	10	7	5	1	3	11	4

AGE	1	2	3	4	5	6	7	8	9	10	11	12
61	1	11	10	6	12	2	4	7	8	9	5	3
62	4	1	6	8	3	12	2	10	9	5	7	11
63	9	4	1	2	8	6	12	11	7	3	10	5
64	3	9	4	1	6	8	7	12	5	2	11	10
65	11	2	9	4	1	5	8	3	10	12	6	7
66	5	10	3	9	2	1	6	8	11	7	12	4
67	7	5	11	3	10	4	1	9	12	6	8	2
68	2	3	5	11	9	7	10	1	6	8	4	12
69	12	8	7	5	11	3	9	4	1	10	2	6
70	10	12	2	7	5	11	3	6	4	1	9	8
71	8	6	12	10	7	9	11	5	2	4	3	1
72	6	7	8	12	4	10	5	2	3	11	1	9
73	1	4	10	6	12	11	7	8	2	5	9	3
74	4	2	3	8	6	12	1	11	7	10	5	9
75	9	10	1	3	8	6	2	7	5	4	12	11
76	3	9	6	1	2	8	5	12	11	7	10	4
77	11	3	9	4	1	2	8	10	12	6	7	5
78	5	11	4	9	7	1	6	2	10	12	3	8
79	7	5	11	2	9	4	12	6	3	1	8	10
80	2	8	5	11	4	7	10	3	1	9	6	12

AGE	1	2	3	4	5	6	7	8	9	10	11	12
81	12	1	7	5	11	10	9	4	8	3	2	6
82	10	12	2	7	5	3	4	9	6	8	11	1
83	8	6	12	10	3	5	11	1	9	2	4	7
84	6	7	8	12	10	9	3	5	4	11	1	2
85	1	3	10	6	12	2	8	6	5	4	9	7
86	4	1	8	3	6	12	11	2	7	9	10	5
87	9	4	1	7	3	8	12	5	2	6	11	10
88	3	9	4	1	8	10	2	7	12	5	6	11
89	11	10	9	4	1	6	7	12	3	8	5	2
90	5	11	6	9	4	1	3	8	10	2	7	12
91	7	5	11	2	10	4	6	9	8	3	12	1
92	2	7	5	11	9	3	10	4	1	12	8	6
93	12	8	7	5	2	11	9	1	6	10	3	4
94	10	12	2	8	11	5	4	6	9	7	1	3
95	8	6	12	10	5	7	1	3	4	11	2	9
96	6	2	3	12	7	9	5	10	11	1	4	8
97	1	9	10	6	12	2	7	5	3	4	8	11
98	4	1	6	8	10	12	11	2	9	7	3	5
99	9	4	1	2	6	8	12	11	5	3	10	7
100	3	10	8	1	5	7	6	12	2	9	11	4

AGE	1	2	3	4	5	6	7	8	9	10	11	12
101	11	3	9	4	1	6	8	10	7	5	12	2
102	5	11	3	9	4	1	2	6	8	12	7	10
103	7	5	11	3	9	4	1	8	12	10	2	6

☞ *Please remember that if the exalted planet occupies its own house or house No. 1 or 2 it brings promotion and happiness, and a debilitating planet in its own house or house No. 1 or in enemies house brings misery.*

Example: *Jupiter in Cancer is exalted. If it occupies 1,2,4,9 houses, it brings happiness. It is debilitating in 10th house & brings misery. Similarly, Sun may bring happiness in 1,2 & 5th houses, but will be bad in 7th house. There is a provision that all, these planets must not be adversely aspected by enemies.*

JUPITER

THE GREAT GURU, LORD BRAHMA—THE CREATOR

Jupiter during the first 8 years of its Mahadasha does not give bad results, even if it is debilitated or surrounded by enemies. It reserves the 1st, 2nd, 8th & 10th and 14th years as 'Guru Dakshina' and hence these are very beneficial. Of course the remaining years 9th, 11th, 12th, 13th, 15th and 16th give bad or good results according to the Antardasha of planets - friends or enemies.

Jupiter in 1st to 5th and 12th houses helps Saturn and Sun both. In 6th to 11th, it helps Saturn only.

JUPITER IN HOUSE NO.1

Chemist researcher, saffron colour, Bold like Tiger, Sadhu.
The native rises after marriage. Even Sun helps and brightens his life. Enemies though in larger number will be defeated. Everything is exalted such as service, wealth, prosperity, victory in litigation and property; Will have children for eight years; thereafter there will be no children. Sun's chariot is driven by Lion and Saturn will protect it; Age not less than 75 years. Scholar, intelligent and highly learned, but short tempered; Can see through the wicked designs of others; Good eye sight and health; a loving person. Happiness from children. Jupiter gives the best results; At 16th year, good luck to his parents. In old age he receives fame and name, Mother's blessings. Mother lives at least till the native is 51 years old or more.

Example: Jupiter in 1st or helped by friendly planets in 1 or 2 or 4 -- His copper coin is like a gold coin in terms of wealth, service & fame.

If Jupiter is malefic and the native is not educated, he leads the life of a Sadhu or a beggar with a begging bowl. In a nutshell, if the native is educated he is like a King and if uneducated he is just a beggar or Faqir.

WITH JUPITER IN 1ST HOUSE IN COMBINATION WITH OTHER PLANETS

PLANET	HOUSE NO	EFFECT
Sun, Mars or Moon	1,2,4	His copper coin is like a gold coin in terms of wealth, service & fame.
Mars	7	Rich ancestors.
Sun	9	Long life.

WITH MALEFIC JUPITER IN 1ST HOUSE IN COMBINATION WITH OTHER PLANETS

PLANET	HOUSE NO	EFFECT
Venus or Mercury	2,5,9,12 or with malefic Jupiter in no 1.	Loss of wealth.
Saturn	Same as above	Bad health; urinary troubles etc.
Saturn-Malefic or in malefic house	Any	Bad for children & parents.
Rahu	8 or 11	Father may die of asthma or heart failure.

JUPITER HOUSE NO.2 (PERMANENT HOUSE)

Hospitality, worship, wealth, gram Dal

This is the real house of Jupiter. Moon in 2nd sign is very exalted as she is Jupiter's friend. No planet can harm it as it is Guru's dwelling. Native will have exalted position in Government for 27 years and results will be sweet and milky. The native receives wealth, esteem, property, promotions etc. effortlessly; Will inherit property from father as well as father-in-law; comfortable life; Pious, teetotaller, noble, honest and man of resolutions.

CERTAIN EXAMPLES:

JUPITER IN 2ND HOUSE IN COMBINATION WITH & IN RELATION TO OTHER PLANETS

PLANET	HOUSE NO	EFFECT
Mars	8 or 9	Honest and a powerful officer
Rahu	8 or 9	Bold and thoughtful
Ketu	8 or 9	Honest, intelligent, sharp brain, noble & powerful officer, will have premonition of death
Sun	10 or 12	Famous
Benefic	2,8 or 6	Lottery and property from others
Any planet	8,9,10 or 12	Happy life and good children
Saturn	12	Brave like Napoleon
Saturn exalted or in combination with	Any	Intellectual and knowledgeable

☞ • *If Jupiter is debilitated and malefic, the native brings disaster and misfortune on the family.*

MALEFIC JUPITER IN 2ND HOUSE IN COMBINATION WITH & IN RELATION TO OTHER PLANETS

PLANET	HOUSE NO	EFFECT
Saturn	2 in annual chart	Bad health & loss of wealth in the father-in-law's house.
Bad planet	8 or 2	A wet blanket; full of ill omen.

REMEDY : As per chart at pages 15 & 16 for Jupiter.

JUPITER HOUSE NO.3 (DURGA WORSHIP; EDUCATION)

A sincere friend, but a cruel enemy; sycophancy and flattery will bring his downfall. If Mars is benefic both Jupiter and Mars confer happiness and knowledge; A Justice loving; happiness from In-laws and children, but not towards maternal uncles; Intelligent wise, loving nature, comfortable life, good job.

If Mars is malefic in the horoscope reverse will be the case. He will be a terror for others; will loot other's property; unlucky, quarrelsome, Bully; Ill health for 20 years.

JUPITER IN 3RD HOUSE IN COMBINATION WITH & IN RELATION TO OTHER PLANETS

PLANET	HOUSE NO	EFFECT
Saturn	4	Will become rich after looting & cheating others.
Saturn	9	Very rich man, lot of property etc.

JUPITER HOUSE NO.4 (GOLD, GRAND HOUSE, GODDESS OF WEALTH)

Jupiter is very exalted, ocean, over-brimming with milk. Even Moon becomes exalted. His seat is like Vikramaditya's throne; Winner of lottery, wealthy; takes after parents in eminence; Full of fortitude, courage of conviction in difficulties; Tranquility of mind;. Imposing house, smiling face. Laxmi touches his feet; maintains best of relations with all irrespective of creed and colour; Beautiful wife; obedient children; bringer of good luck for parents; Education for 24 years; In fact, the best planet.

JUPITER IN 4TH HOUSE IN COMBINATION WITH & IN RELATION TO OTHER PLANETS

PLANET	HOUSE NO	EFFECT
Mercury	10	Bad,responsible for his own misfortune after 34 years of age.
Saturn	2	Freedom loving, leader, best luck till death.
Sun	1	Best results of both.
Saturn	9	Best fortune and lucky for all.
Saturn	10	Will have cars etc.
Moon	1	
Moon	2	Will rise very high, better than parents.
Sun	10	Travel will bring good results like a pearl in a shell.
Moon--benefic	Any	

MALEFIC JUPITER : Will be poor when Rahu and Ketu are malefic,debilitating and are aspected by Venus, Saturn & Mercury from 10th house.

JUPITER IN HOUSE NO 5 (PERMANENT HOUSE)

Nose, Saffron, Milk of human kindness, respected by all, short tempered
Good and eminent children, property & wealth. Jupiter in 5th and 9th is exalted, provided 2,9&11 are not occupied by wicked planets; Short tempered but a noble soul.

JUPITER IN 5TH HOUSE IN COMBINATION WITH & IN RELATION TO OTHER PLANETS

PLANET	HOUSE NO	EFFECT
Sun, Mars, Moon	9	Best luck; his small boat will be like a big ship.
Saturn	9	Very lucky, sweet breeze.
Mercury, Venus, Rahu or Saturn (not as malefic planets)	2,5,9,11,12	Wealthy father, self and children.

JUPITER HOUSE NO 6 (SIGN RESULT)

Eagle (a bird of Prey), enjoys life at others expenses, Ketu's remedy for bad days, Parasite
Father dies early, if alive he will be a rich man; prosperous; will be a parasite enjoying lavishly at others' expense; will not have to work hard for living, but will get everything effortlessly; Hedonistic approach to life (eat,drink and make merry).
Jupiter 6 - Mars 12 - Bad for fathers' life.

JUPITER HOUSE NO 7 (SIGN RESULT)

Books, Asthma, frog, a vagrant Sadhu - Remedy of Moon for bad days.
A Sadhu in previous life; unhappy with Brothers and Sisters; Rise after marriage; will help relatives but unlucky to have their gratitude;Will be blessed with a son at a late stage, may be near about 39 years; Beautiful children, who will get every thing from him but will not be helpful to him; may live away from brothers; An eminent astrologer; luxurious life for 40 years; bad investments; Must seek Moon's assistance (i.e. Remedy for Moon).

JUPITER IN 7TH HOUSE IN COMBINATION WITH & IN RELATION TO OTHER PLANETS

PLANET	HOUSE NO	EFFECT
Saturn	9	Thief, dacoit, will loot others.
Mercury	9 or 7	Unhappy married life.

JUPITER HOUSE NO.8

Rumour, Blessings of an ancestor, voice of people, Sadhu

If Mercury is not in the 9th house, long life of ancestors; Rising fortune, full of courage, may extract gold and wealth, even when in distress; Long life, Rich; If Mars is malefic, ill health, otherwise good health; Grandfather may have died before his birth or within 8 years of his birth. Now, this house will not be a house of death, rather it will be the house of life. It will confer gold, promotion and rise in family fortune.

Jupiter No.8 - Mars No.4 - Coward, indolent and lazy.

JUPITER HOUSE NO 9 (PERMANENT HOUSE)

Planet of rising fortune, Exalted, Ancestral property, Blessings of ancestors, eminent family.

Noble soul, man of word, an expert Jeweller. If Jupiter is malefic, the native is atheist. Age 75 years; If aspected by both Venus and Moon - life is like a pendulum - sometimes rich and sometime poor. Noble, helpful attitude; Travel; fathers' blessings, leadership of family members (but spoilt by Venus and Mercury). An exalted Sun further brightness Jupiter. Indeed a very exalted planet for fate and best fortune.

JUPITER IN 9TH HOUSE IN COMBINATION WITH & IN RELATION TO OTHER PLANETS

PLANET	HOUSE NO	EFFECT
Saturn	5	Exalted fate, wealthy but bad for son.
Sun-exalted	Any	Raj yoga.
Mercury	4	
Moon	5	Bad results.
Mercury	3	
Moon	3	Best results.
Mercury	5	
Mars	3	Wealthy in-laws & will give monetary help.
Mars	3	Best results for all these houses.
Sun	5	

JUPITER HOUSE NO. 10

Most debilitating; Dry Peepal Tree; Loss of money; Disruption of studies; throw copper coin in river during bad days.

Very bad from 27 to 36, but good later on; Very bad investments, loss of money and disruption in studies; does not get anything from parents in life and even after their death. Donate gram (chana) Dal, and throw copper coins for 43 days into flowing water .During bad days keep a yellow handkerchief and saffron in your pocket.

JUPITER IN 10TH HOUSE IN COMBINATION WITH & IN RELATION TO OTHER PLANETS

PLANET	HOUSE NO	EFFECT
Moon	4	Will earn bad name if helps some one out of the way.
Sun	5	More than one marriage.
Mercury	4	Worst condition.
Saturn Aspected by sun	9	Incidence of fire, profit from gold, silver & cloth; but loss from iron & machinery.
Moon-benefic	Any	Advantage from travel on government duty.
Sun with benefic moon	4	
Saturn	9	Power to loot others, however lowly placed.

JUPITER IN HOUSE 11

Bringer of Good Luck, lonely like Palm tree, Reign of Saturn, Gilt.
During fathers' life, happiness and wealth; after his death, he again becomes Zero; Father will not leave him any thing after death. Only Good and Noble life is the redeeming feature; will fill his coffers with money. Malefic Mercury renders both Jupiter and Saturn ineffective. Benefic Saturn makes Mars benefic also.

JUPITER IN 11TH HOUSE IN COMBINATION WITH & IN RELATION TO OTHER PLANETS

PLANET	HOUSE NO	EFFECT
Friendly planets	3	Will gain wealth for 12 years. Thereafter ill health.
Mercury	3	Will get nothing from father.
Mars	3	Auspicious for in-laws, but sad on account of deaths in his own family.
Saturn-exalted	Any	Although no help from father, yet will have a good life and money. Mars will not be malefic.

JUPITER HOUSE NO 12

Green Peepal tree, life, copper, Yogi, humane

Lot of money, but lot of expenditure. A good adviser; lot of wealth during 25 years of Venus period . Rahu will entail unnecessary expenditure, which will be used for household goods. No savings; Yogi; full of milk of human kindness; will not care for money.

JUPITER IN 12TH HOUSE IN COMBINATION WITH & IN RELATION TO OTHER PLANETS

PLANET	HOUSE NO	EFFECT
Saturn	9	Lot of wealth, but will not care; philanthropic; gain from machines.
Venus	Any condition	Will be auspicious.
Mercury & Ketu- may be malefic	Any	There will be no scarcity of wealth.

CHAPTER 10

SUN

LORD VISHNU; SUPPORTS AND SUSTAINS LIFE

SUN HOUSE NO 1 (PERMANENT HOUSE)

Exalted, Day time, Honest Administrator

Very wealthy, Self-made rich but will not hanker after wealth; Handsome in body and soul, humane, helpful, purity of soul; man of honesty and integrity; Philanthropist; intellectual; happiness from wife and children, Father will have a long life; Himself will live long(100 years); Vehicles;Esteem and respect everywhere. First child will be Son - born during day time or after midnight to morning - full of milk of human kindness; short tempered like a snake.

SUN IN 1ST HOUSE IN COMBINATION WITH & IN RELATION TO OTHER PLANETS

PLANET	HOUSE NO	EFFECT
Vacant	7	Early marriage is beneficial.
Friends like Mars, Jupiter & moon	Any	Self made, rich, successful, eminent.
Venus	7	Parents die in childhood.
Mercury	7	A good man, away from lust & greed.
Moon	2	Eminent position, prosperous and man of property.
Saturn	11	
Mars	5	Death of son.
Saturn	8	Death of wife.

SUN HOUSE NO2

Wheat, Barley, Philanthropist, faith in own powers

Comforts of conveyances. All amenities of life; wealthy; upholder of traditions; Army Officer; Good reputation; Bringer of good fortune for In-laws, children, relatives; In Short will lead a bright and glorious life and will bring happiness to others.

SUN IN 2ND HOUSE IN COMBINATION WITH & IN RELATION TO OTHER PLANETS

PLANET	HOUSE NO	EFFECT
Mars	1	Indolent, lazy & poor.
Moon	12	
Moon	6	Moon will confer best results.
Mercury	8	Brave.
Ketu	8	Honest, truthful.
Rahu	8	Technical mind.
Mars	9	Fashionable.
Vacant	8	Sun will give exalted results.
Saturn	10	People will respect him.
Mars	8	Greedy.
Moon	8	Should not accept donations & bribes.

☞ • *If Sun is alone in this house, the no. of women will become fewer. Remedy lies in donating coconut or almonds.*

SUN HOUSE NO 3

Day time children, nephews, wealthy, self-made man

Now Moon will not be malefic; mother will have long life, provided Moon is not debilitating. Ancestors may be poor, (not necessarily) but he will be rich at the fag end of life. If Mars is benefic in the birth chart, Sun and Mars will have good effects, but if Mars is malefic, it will show bad results, but Sun will give good results. Rahu and Ketu, if malefic and debilitating, will adversely affect the maternal uncles. The native will be an expert mathematician and Astrologer.

SUN IN 3RD HOUSE IN COMBINATION WITH & IN RELATION TO OTHER PLANETS

PLANET	HOUSE NO	EFFECT
Moon-malefic	Any	He will be robbed & looted in broad day light.
Debilitating	9	Poor parents.

SUN HOUSE NO 4

Will accumulate wealth for others and children

Inventor; will produce pearls out of shell i.e. Very rich man; Exalted Sun, and therefore, exalted Moon; Exalted Position; Beneficial travels in and outside country in connection with the state matters; Multi Millionaire; Himself may lead a frugal life, but will leave millions for children; good health; wealth will flow like a fountain.

SUN IN 4TH HOUSE IN COMBINATION WITH & IN RELATION TO OTHER PLANETS

PLANET	HOUSE NO	EFFECT
Mars-benefic	Any	Man of perseverance, good intentions.
Mars	10	One eyed man, but lucky.
Moon	1	Impotent.
Sat & Venus	7	
Saturn	7	Night blindness.
Jupiter	10	Jupiter will not be debilitating. Benefits from travel on state matters. A pearl in the shell.
Moon-benefic	Any	
Jupiter	10	Incidence of fire & theft of gold - when aspecting each other in annual chart. Benefits from gold, silver & cloth business; loss in machine & hardware business.

SUN HOUSE NO 5 (RESULTS OF PLANET AND HOUSE)

Mascot (Bringer of good fortune), Only Son, Red faced monkey, Grand son, Promotion of family

Sun's personal result will never be bad. Tiger's vehicle being driven by Lion i.e., Jupiter and Sun - Both will be exalted; Excellent Government Job; if good hearted, excellent old age and children. Sun is the lord of soul, body and health; If benefic, best health; if malefic bad results.

SUN IN 5TH HOUSE IN COMBINATION WITH & IN RELATION TO OTHER PLANETS

PLANET	HOUSE NO	EFFECT
Saturn	9, 11	Humane, sympathetic, blessings of parents. No scuffle between sun & Saturn.
Moon	4	King like; eminent position.
Moon-benefic	4	Eminent personality & position.
Jupiter-benefic	9	
Jupiter-benefic	9	Rajyoga; excellent position.
Mercury-benefic	4	
Mars- benefic	3	Jupiter's results will be excellent
Jupiter-benefic	9, 12	
Jupiter	10	More than one marriage
Saturn	3	Bad for children, even their death; full of grief & sorrow.
Enemies	1, 5	Sun will help the enemies even at no 1, 5.

SUN HOUSE NO 6 (SIGN RESULTS)

Wheatish colour, problem with Feet, carefree, Remedy lies in Mercury: For the help of Maternal uncles give Jaggery/Gur to monkeys.

Mars even in Cancer will not be malefic; no worries about job, but short tempered; good job; will leave jobs many times, but after the birth of son he will stick to the job; Birth probably in Maternal uncles' house or at place away from house.

SUN IN 6TH HOUSE IN COMBINATION WITH & IN RELATION TO OTHER PLANETS

PLANET	HOUSE NO	EFFECT
Ketu	1,7 Either in birth or annual chart	Son must be born.
Mercury	12	Besides income from job, there will be problem in service also.
Saturn	12	Death of wife.

Mars	1,6	After 24, father & son will serve at different places. Will leave jobs many a time; father will have bad health during his 5, 11 & 23 years.
Rahu or Saturn	1	Solar eclipse, when Rahu & Saturn occupy 1st house in annual chart it will bring disaster.
Rahu	2	Bad results.
Saturn	8	
Moon	12	Either the native or his wife will be one eyed.

SUN HOUSE NO 7 (DEBILITATING SIGN RESULTS)

Red Cow (copper colour), Defect in soul, white cow inauspicious, but Black Cow auspicious. Fewer family members).

The most debilitating planet; Even Gold turns into dust. If Mercury is not in 7th house or if it is debilitating man is unlucky. He can become prosperous only with the help of Mercury which should be benefic. If Sun is in the 7th house and is already aspected by Saturn, the remedy lies in throwing a drop of milk in fire.

MALEFIC SUN: Ill fated; Ill tempered; Peevish; irritable; rude; selfish; prone to flattering and self-praise; life of darkness; such a person is his own enemy, but eminent for self; Bad domestic life. If he is polite and soft spoken officer or short-tempered businessman, he will be destroyed. Moon and Mercury lend their strengths to it; if Mercury is exalted, such a man is rich but not wise; Wife from a rich family; if Mercury is debilitating or bad, unhappy married life; will die at home and not while travelling. If the woman is just like 'Touch me not' i.e. honest to husband, domestic life will be comfortable, otherwise not. If sun is malefic, son may be dumb or mentally retarded.

SUN IN 7TH HOUSE IN COMBINATION WITH & IN RELATION TO OTHER PLANETS

PLANET	HOUSE NO	EFFECT
Mercury	7	Courageous.
Venus	1	Wife's ill health; madness, mentally retarded.
Wicked planets & Venus	1	Bundle of misfortunes; very unfortunate.
Jupiter or Mars or Moon	2	Eminent position
Mercury-exalted & Helped by Mars	Or 7 Any	Rich but not wise

All planets Bad or malefic	Any Any	Suicidal tendency but courageous; remedy lies in placating Jupiter; unhappy married life
Jupiter or Venus or wicked planet Malefic Mercury	1 Other house	Death in family; unhappy service, unhappy marriage. Asthma, suicide, madness, irritable, selfish, will destroy everything.
Mars or Saturn	3, 12	Leucoderma
Moon	1	

Sun is dim in 7th house; it will regain its brightness when planet in No.8 occupies house No.2 in the Annual Chart i.e. at age 13, 29, 41, 54, 64, 72, 78, 86, 98 & 119.

✚
REMEDIES • Bury 7 copper square pieces in the earth (for wealth, domestic life and male child)
   • Take some sweet, while doing auspicious work.
   • Sprinkle a drop of milk on fire in the hearth.
   • Throw morsel of food on fire before taking meals (for domestic happiness).

SUN HOUSE NO 8

CHARIOT, TRUE FIRE, KING DOING PENANCE

• Conqueror of death . Death fears Sun in 8th house; Will not see any death in family in presence; Will be away at the time of death in the family.
• From 23rd year onwards (for 22 years) i.e., upto 45th year of age, Rich; promotion in service.
• Even Mars in 8th house will not be malefic (Manglik) as Sun combusts it.
• He should not behave like the three proverbial dogs i.e., must not be subservient to In-laws, sisters & maternal uncles.
• If sun is alone in the house no 8, he should not be lustful, must be affectionate towards his elder brothers; otherwise unlucky.

SUN IN 8TH HOUSE IN COMBINATION WITH & IN RELATION TO OTHER PLANETS

PLANET	HOUSE NO	EFFECT
Friendly planets Or benefic Mars	1 or together Exalted	Malefic Saturn will give good results instead of bad. Sun will confer best results.

Saturn	3	Short lived, if there is not elder brother or if he is inimical to his elder brother, then mars will be malefic.
Bad Jupiter Or Mars-malefic	1, 5	
Venus	1, 5, 10	Bad results
Jupiter-bad	Any	Good for others, but bad for self.

SUN HOUSE NO 9

BROWN BEAR, SUN AFTER THE ECLIPSE, LONG LIFE, SUPPORTER OF FAMILY.
The native will shed his all for his family members; Will not demand anything in return; Long life of ancestors; self & children; Should donate silver for prosperity, but should not accept gifts of silver; Long life upto 100 years, provided Mercury is not in the 9 th house; Parents good officials; humane; Sun's period after 22 - Best results for service; auspicious for parents. Sun in 9th brightens the 5 th house also. Family life a little disturbing; but mother's blessings are plenty. In short, sun in 9th gives best results.

SUN IN 9TH HOUSE IN COMBINATION WITH & IN RELATION TO OTHER PLANETS

PLANET	HOUSE NO	EFFECT
Mercury	5	Rise in life after 34
Mercury	3	Bad results and unlucky life. Mercury will befool both the Sun & Saturn.
Saturn	11	
Rahu	1, 3, 5	Should not be over-polite or over-rude; irreligious & luxurious life; parasite.

SUN HOUSE NO 10

BROWN MANGOOSE, BROWN BUFFALO, HONOUR, HEALTH, WEALTHY BUT SUPERSTITIOUS.
Man of honour; healthy & wealthy, but superstitious; White cap is auspicious. If all alone in 10th, it brings bad results for parents inherited property and service matters. River water and underground water will be beneficial.

SUN IN 10TH HOUSE IN COMBINATION WITH & IN RELATION TO OTHER PLANETS

PLANET	HOUSE NO	EFFECT
Malefic Moon	5, 6	Short lived & unfortunate.
Unhelpful Mars and Jupiter	Any	
Moon	5	Short lived if not helped by masculine planet.
Moon	4	Best service.
Venus	4	Father dies in his childhood.
Saturn-malefic	Any	
Moon-exalted	Or in 2	Bad for mother in his 24th year, she may die even.
Wicked planets	6 & 7	Worst till 34.
Vacant	4	May be talented but is ignored by superiors.

+
REMEDIES   Throw copper coins for 43 days continuously in a flowing water, stream or river.

SUN HOUSE NO 11

RED COPPER; RELIGIOUS MINDED, BUT SELFISH; LUXURIOUS LIFE.
If Vegetarian & religious minded, long & happy life. Must not touch wine & should not be lustful- it will bring disaster; Will earn wealth but will adopt fraudulent ways & means because of effect of Saturn.

SUN IN 11TH HOUSE IN COMBINATION WITH & IN RELATION TO OTHER PLANETS

PLANET	HOUSE NO	EFFECT
Moon	5	Age 12 years only, when not helped by male planets.
Moon	8	Though long lived yet a cheat & liar.
Saturn-malefic	Any	
Mercury	3	

91

✚
REMEDIES • Radish, carrot, turnip etc and almonds may be kept under pillow at night and then donated in the morning for 43 days.

SUN HOUSE NO 12

BROWN ANT; MENTALLY UPSET; ARTIFICIAL SUN (VENUS & MERCURY); VICARIOUS PLEASURES; HAPPY & COMFORTABLE SLEEP BUT WORRIED ABOUT OTHERS.
Comfortable sleep, but worried for the others; No clash between Sun & Saturn i.e., father & son; even Venus & mercury will not be bad. Happy couple; property; free life; noble soul; lively & knowledgeable. Machinery business will not be beneficial, but trade will bring good results.

SUN IN 12TH HOUSE IN COMBINATION WITH & IN RELATION TO OTHER PLANETS

PLANET	HOUSE NO	EFFECT
Venus & Mercury together	Any	Will never lose his job. If govt. Service is not profitable, business will make him rich.
Saturn	6	Even if Venus is debilitating, Saturn will give good results regarding domestic happiness.
Ketu	2	Self made rich after 24.
Wicked planet	1	Sleepless nights; hand to mouth living. Remedy lies in forgiving enemies.
Moon	6	One eyed man or wife.

MOON

LORD SHIVA & MOTHER EARTH

WHITE COLOUR (MILK); OCEANIC & AIR BORNE HORSE (PEGASUS); SIGN RESULTS IN 8TH - SAVES FROM DEATH; IN 7TH MAKES A MAN WEALTHY & IN 3RD PROTECTS IN BATTLEFIELD.

MOON'S WATER AND EDUCATION OF THE NATIVE

MOON'S HOUSE	WATER'S CAPACITY	EDUCATIONAL EFFECT
1	Pure water in a pitcher	Money spent on education will never go waste.
2	Fountain of water gushing out of mountain	Most exalted; mother and education; ancestral property; wealth, moon's blessings; business of horses or silverware beneficial;will not be a teacher.
3	Jungle or desert full of water.	The more the education the worse will be the father's monetary condition; education will not stop, if Ketu is good; mother will act as father.
4	Sweet fountain of water	Complete education and beneficial. mother's blessings
5	River or canal water irrigating the establishment	Money spent on education will not yield full results; however talented & may get technical education etc.
6	Ground water, hand pump etc.	Education will be beneficial, but will face great difficulty in getting it.
7	River or canal irrigating the land	Will complete education before marriage; either bad investments or very rich.
8	Divine 'amrita' or poison	Such a person will either be highly educated or will prevent his children from studying.

9	Ocean	Will educate all like lord Indira; full of comforts; may not be highly educated himself but will not be illiterate.
10	Water blocked by hills	Impediments in education; but will have knowledge of medicines. If 8th is malefic, bad results, but when no.2 is exalted results will be beneficial.
11	Torrential rains	If educated, complete education.
12	Rains, hailstones, snow or stinking drain water	If malefic, it will be like a dirty drain. if Sun & Jupiter are benefic, results will be good i.e., water without any impurity.

MOON HOUSE NO 1

HEART, GARDEN, LEFT SIDE, LEFT CORNEA OF EYE, WEALTH & PURE MILK TILL MOTHER'S LIFE.

Marriage before 28 years destroys mother's life and is bad for children; Marriage at 24 will harm mother. Take milk in a cup of silver for the benefit of children. Fix 4 copper coins on four legs of cot. Or else place a few drops of water on Banyan tree. Sun's result is exalted; Honour & success in service matters; Happiness for 27 years & happiness from children. Age 90 years. If moon is benefic the native will have landed property; Must receive mothers' blessings for long life, good job and wealth.

MOON IN 1ST HOUSE IN COMBINATION WITH & IN RELATION TO OTHER PLANETS

PLANET	HOUSE NO	EFFECT
Jupiter	4	Comfortable life, conveyance at command.
Saturn	10	
Venus	7	Daughter-in-law & mother-in-law will have cordial relationship like daughter & mother; but problem during marriage and for children.
Sun	4,10	Advantage from travels in connection with govt. Affairs.***
Jupiter	10,4	
Mercury	7,11	Not wise; but wealthy & may travel abroad on govt. affairs to his advantage. ****
Sun	6	Bad; poverty. If son has bad health & bad eye-sight, he will bring back wealth at 19. ***
Saturn	6	

Good	7,8	His mud will be converted into gold.
Mars-malefic or Mercury-malefic or	Any	Grief stricken & unhappy.
Malefic	8	

☞   *** *Moon in 1st house is benefic.*
           **** *The same results will be obtained if moon is in the 5th house.*

MOON HOUSE NO 2

(EXALTED, BRINGER OF GOOD LUCK, MOTHER, MILK, RICE, SPIRITUAL WHITE HORSE, GODDESS OF SELF-MADE WEALTH)

Handsome, must have brothers and parents(if not his own, may be his wife's). Such a person usually does not have sisters, but must have brothers. Like a white horse; comforts from parents; rich; must have conveyance; Age 85 to 96; A person with Moon in Taurus (2nd) must have a son even though other planets may be hard for children. Even Jupiter confers best results. Exalted Moon in 2nd gives the exalted result of Jupiter in 2nd . When Moon occupies the first house in Annual Chart(Age 2,14,26,38,50,62,81,98 etc), the best results are available regarding Wealth, Mother, Children and Father. It will be like a cool refreshing breeze, as long as there is old rice in the house; wealth for 27 years; complete happiness; Must bury milk and sugar in the foundations of his own built houses. He himself becomes rich and marries in a rich family, if Moon is exalted.

MOON IN 2ND HOUSE IN COMBINATION WITH & IN RELATION TO OTHER PLANETS

PLANET	HOUSE NO	EFFECT
Rahu, Ketu & Saturn	4,6,8,9,10	His mother lives upto 48 years of age or even more.
Venus-exalted	Any	Moon's results excellent; successful lover.
Jupiter	4	Exalted results of both the planets. Wealthy, flag on his car.
Saturn	4	Ancestral property.
Mercury	6	Mother's blessings, but weak eyesight.
Sun	1	Eminent position; Wealthy & lot of property.
Saturn	11	

Malefic planet	1,2,7,10,11	Bad results.
Saturn	10	Old age is bad.
Jupiter	11	Old age is bad.
Wicked planets	9,10,12	Mother may die in 9,18 or 36 years.
Mercury, Venus & Ketu	1	All these planets will give bad results.

MOON HOUSE NO 3

(HORSE, LORD SHIVA, THE SAVIOUR, PROTECTS FROM THEFT AND DEATH)

Best results regarding wealth, life, mutual love and affection of the couple. If Venus 3 is good for household. Moon 3 is good for meditation and devotion to Lord Shiva who is the great Saviour. Moon in 3 must protect both life and property. Even Mars no longer remains malefic (even Mars in Cancer); Victory in all battles. If Mars is malefic enmity with mother, but good for self. In short every third day, month or year will bring luxury and comfort; Age 80 years . Mother is bold like father, when Moon is in 3.

MOON IN 3RD HOUSE IN COMBINATION WITH & IN RELATION TO OTHER PLANETS

PLANET	HOUSE NO	EFFECT
Vacant	9,11	Mars will not be malefic, rather benefic.
Mercury	11	Good for family; age 80 years.
Mercury-malefic	Any	Women will be worshipped & honoured in this house.
Moon in annual chart	1	
Sun	1	Rajyoga; parents long-lived; have their blessings; fountain of peace & wealth.
Saturn	11	
Mercury	5	
Jupiter-benefic	Or 9,4	
Malefic	8	Loss of wealth but not theft.
Mars	4	Mars becomes benefic, courageous self-respecting; victory over enemies.
Mars	10	Best results; help from others.

MOON HOUSE NO 4

Exalted planet; bringer of luck; Water tank; well; fountain; peace of mind; cloth merchant; The more the spending, the more the income.

When Moon is all alone in 4th house, the more the native spends the more he will earn; will have mother's blessings, whether real or stepmother; Will succeed as cloth merchant, if mother is with him; failing which he will incur losses; Successful in ancestral business. If Mars is benefic his elder brother, uncles will be successful in life; Will bring good luck to parents. Moon in 4th house is like milk; person should place pot full of milk in the temple before doing auspicious work. It will auger well. Moon's enemies (Venus and Mercury) will not harm it. Even Rahu and Ketu swear not to remain wicked. Even Malefic Saturn and Mars will not be poisonous. No.8 - 2 will no longer be malefic, rather planets in No.1,7,4,10 will be benefic; long life; good old age.

MOON IN 4TH HOUSE IN COMBINATION WITH & IN RELATION TO OTHER PLANETS

PLANET	HOUSE NO	EFFECT
Jupiter	6	Successful in ancestral business.
3 other planets	4	Wealth four times; sons, daughters & daughters-in-laws will be helpful.
Saturn	9,11	Good man; purity of blood; help from parents.
Sun	5	Exalted status; good luck after birth of son.
Jupiter	5	
Sun	5	Exalted status; king like.
Jupiter	2,9	
Mercury	10	May visit abroad for business & service matters-beneficial.
Venus	7	
Rahu	10	Breaking of head.
Mars	10	Dominating; government job; wealthy
Jupiter	10	Bad; do not help people out of the way. It may bring bad name.
Venus	10	Best relations between mother & wife.

MOON HOUSE NO 5

Mothers' milk; godly canal; bird of good omen; partridge (beautiful bird).
Man of God; Honour in service; Though a traveller of jungles and hill yet not successful. A great fighter, full of courage in distress; good for mother and sons, even though wicked planets may be together or aspecting. Rahu will lose its sting. Sun brightens Moon in this house; Soft spoken, polite, but wealthy and may travel abroad for 9 years; Age 100 years; Average height; intelligent; truthful; just and fair; compassionate, but bad for business.

MOON IN 5TH HOUSE IN COMBINATION WITH & IN RELATION TO OTHER PLANETS

PLANET	HOUSE NO	EFFECT
Friendly	2-3	Good results.
Enemy	9-11	
Mercury	7,11	Moon is like a pearl & best;may travel abroad even though 3,8 may be malefic.
Vacant	9	Moon is asleep. Take sweets before leaving home.
Good planets	10,12	Moon's result is bad.
Jupiter	9	Bad results
Mercury	3	
Sun	10	Short lived; 10 days only.
Sun	11	Short lived; 11 years only
Moon--malefic	5	Like the knight (horse) of chess, moving 2½ houses & destroying them (3,8,10,12).
Enemies	2,3	Worst like lightning.
Friends	9,11	

MOON HOUSE NO 6

Female rabbit; travel; full lunar eclipse because of Ketu; bitter water.
'As you sow, so shall you reap'.
Resourceful; wise. Good to those who are good to him and vice versa; Tit for tat; more daughters; Bad health for 6 years after birth; Moon, if alone confers all comforts during youth.

MOON IN 6TH HOUSE IN COMBINATION WITH & IN RELATION TO OTHER PLANETS

PLANET	HOUSE NO	EFFECT
Good	2	Honour & respect.
Good	4	Wealthy.
Good	8	Long life.
Jupiter	2	Good results; donate milk.
Venus, Ketu-bad	Any	Bad for maternal & paternal side for 34 years.
Mercury	12, 2	Very bad; may commit suicide, when mercury occupies 1st house in annual chart.
Sun	12	One eyed either self or wife.
Mars or	4,8	Mother may die in his childhood.
Mercury	6	
Mars or	6, 12	Short lived.
Mercury	8	
Venus-malefic	Any	In-laws will be financially destroyed.
Ketu-malefic	Any	Parental side ruined.
Mercury-malefic	Any	Maternal side ruined.

✛
REMEDIES • Donate wheat, gram, Dal and rice. Do not take milk at night ; may take cheese.

MOON HOUSE NO 7 (SIGN RESULT)

LANDED PROPERTY(SELF ACQUIRED OR INHERITED BUT NOT URBAN); INCARNATION OF LAXMI.

Saturn may be in 3rd or Jupiter may be in 7th (howsoever poor), Moon in 7th (sign) makes the native very rich. In short, he is the incarnation of goddess Laxmi (wealth), provided Rahu and Ketu do not adversely affect or aspect it; will die at his ancestral place. Pure hearted like milk; enjoys respect and esteem; Can be a great poet and astrologer; very intelligent; can read future and is master of the occult; should not marry at 24 or 25, Otherwise clash between mother and wife, A clash with old mother will destroy him. Moon may destroy Mercury but Moon will be exalted. Will be respected by colleagues and officers; noble children and mother; comforts of conveyance etc., If Moon is destroyed by wicked planets the native will be critically ill for 15 years; 85 years age. The native will enjoy all pleasures and will have a noble wife.

MOON IN 7TH HOUSE IN COMBINATION WITH & IN RELATION TO OTHER PLANETS

PLANET	HOUSE NO	EFFECT
Mercury-benefic	Any	Very intelligent; can see through the veil of mystery; spiritual powers; master of occult.
Vacant	8	
Mercury-benefic	Any	Very rich even though Saturn no. 3 (shortage of wealth) & Jupiter no. 7 (lack of son) may be there.
Venus-benefic	Any	Peaceful & happy domestic life and job or business.
Jupiter	7	Unhappy childhood. Mars will be malefic; bad results in business.
Malefic Mercury	2,8	
Venus-malefic	Any	Venus (domestic happiness) will be destroyed, but will be wealthy & very lucky.
Venus with bad planet	Any	May lose children early.
Jupiter	7	Bad childhood.
Saturn	7	Death with a weapon.
Venus	1	Clash between mother & wife.
Mercury	1	Addiction to drugs & wine.

MOON HOUSE NO 8

MOST DEBILITATING: BRINGER OF GOOD LUCK, LONG LIFE LIKE THE VAST OCEAN, HIMSELF OCEAN LIKE, EPILEPSY; FITS; HEART AILMENT; BURNT MILK, DEAD MOTHER.

Moon may be debilitating, but such a person must have a son. If combined with Saturn moon may show off, but will be like a dirty drain of water. His ancestral property will be of no use to him. If there is a well or tank near his ancestral house he will have still worse luck. In short when Moon is in No,8 even Rahu loses its wicked ways. But if Mars is debilitating it may lead to mothers' death; enmity with people; ailments of the heart; epileptic fits etc. Should not deal in jewellery.

MALEFIC MOON: Unlucky; trouble after trouble; bad in all worldly matters; opposing colleagues; ill health for 6 years. In short this house belongs to Mars (malefic) and Saturn and both of them create problems. Nevertheless, long life (90 years); Must keep silver, rice in his house. Loss of sensation will be a bad omen. In-laws may gain through him.

MOON IN 8TH HOUSE IN COMBINATION WITH & IN RELATION TO OTHER PLANETS

PLANET	HOUSE NO	EFFECT
Jupiter, Saturn	2	Rahu will not be malefic. Moon will not be debilitating.
Any three malefic planets	3, 4	Loss of ancestral property; bad for children.
Venus or Mercury with malefic Saturn	Any	Bad for health, children & wealth.
Jupiter & Sun-malefic	Any	Physically handicapped.
Malefic	1	Hand to mouth living till 34th year.

+
REMEDIES • Keep rice, silver in your house; Donate rice for 43 days. Keep water from a hand-pump or tap in the cremation ground in your house.

MOON HOUSE NO 9

ANCESTRAL PROPERTY, BIG PEARL, HUMANE, PROTECTOR OF THE DOWN TRODDEN, OCEAN; PARTIAL LUNAR ECLIPSE.

If Moon is benefic such a person is exceptionally polite, humane, compassionate and like a pearl which is nine times beautiful. He is infact Moon incarnate. It gives the same exalted effect after 24 as is the case with Moon - Jupiter. Moon-Sun-Moon, Jupiter- Venus or Moon-Sun- Venus combination. When Moon is exalted in No.9, even the 5th house helps and brightens it as regards children; Noble, religious minded; visits abroad; good man and protector of the down trodden and poor; Must travel abroad for 20 years; Age 75 years, specialist in Mathematics.

MOON IN 9TH HOUSE IN COMBINATION WITH & IN RELATION TO OTHER PLANETS

PLANET	HOUSE NO	EFFECT
Jupiter	5	Very lucky; his small boat will be like a big ship. Moon will be like a big ocean full of milk.
Friendly planet	3	Wealthy.
Any planet	4	Very lucky.
Friendly planet	5	Best for children.
Venus	3	Mother may lose eye-sight.
Ketu	2	Financial condition will considerably improve after 34 / 48 years, but will not be bad before that.
Mercury	5	

MOON HOUSE NO 10

NIGHT, UNDERGROUND WATER BUT POISONOUS AND SOUR; MILK OF AAK (MADAR) LEAVES.

Remedy from planets in No.2 and if that is vacant help from the house occupied by Jupiter. Moon in 10th is like Snake's mother who will eat up her own children. Such a person will be a meaningless physician although he may be a learned physician; may of course be a very competent surgeon. If Mars is malefic such a person is a cheat and insincere. When Moon and Saturn occupy the first house, it will spell disaster- such as illness, trouble, enmity with mother and bad name. Nevertheless, may earn for 42 years; Age 90 years.

MOON IN 10TH HOUSE IN COMBINATION WITH & IN RELATION TO OTHER PLANETS

PLANET	HOUSE NO	EFFECT
Saturn or Venus	4,1	Blessings of parents. Lustful conduct may spell doom.
Sun or Jupiter	4	Best like the rain of white pearls.
Saturn	1, 4	Cheat, fraudulent behaviour & ill-gotten money.
Saturn	3	Thief; dacoit.
Sun	7	Death by drowning.
Venus &	7	Death of children, even mother.
Wicked planet	4	

To lessen the intensity of malefic effects, do not take milk at night.

MOON HOUSE NO 11

SILVER, WHITE PEARL, BLOODY WELL, MOVING CLOUDS
Moon in No.11 is Zero (cipher) and malefic; is like fake butter(without ghee) . When it (benefic moon) occupies No.1 in Annual Chart, it is exalted; One conquers enemies; good for service matters; Increase in wealth for 12 years; 90 years of age.

MOON IN 11TH HOUSE IN COMBINATION WITH & IN RELATION TO OTHER PLANETS

PLANET	HOUSE NO	EFFECT
Mercury	3	Bad for brothers & ancestral property.
Mercury	5	Good results of both the houses.
Jupiter	5	Wealthy.
Sun & Mercury	4	Good income.
Ketu	3	Bad for mother's life, loss of wealth.

✚

REMEDIES • Donate sweets made of milk (Khoya) for 43 days. Heat a gold wire and then put it into the milk eleven times & then take that milk for 43 days, if Moon in No.11 is malefic.

MOON HOUSE NO 12

FLATTERY, WHITE CAT, FLOODED RIVER WHICH DESTROYS CITIES, BATHE WITH RAIN WATER
Dreamer; one fondly remembers ones' ancestral glory i.e. good old days, but himself is nothing; just a dream.

PIDRAM SULTAN BOOD - TURACHEY ?

"My father was a King - but what are you?" Now all bad results for his and in-laws property; rather unfortunate; in distress; happiness from wife; wise and intelligent. Fear of water for 45 years, Age 90 years.

MOON IN 12TH HOUSE IN COMBINATION WITH & IN RELATION TO OTHER PLANETS

PLANET	HOUSE NO	EFFECT
Sun & Mercury	3	Good for family.
Exalted Jupiter & sun	Any	Wealthy moon will confer happiness & wealth.
Moon	1st house in annual chart	Very bad; will be like flooded river destroying land & property. This will happen at the age of 12, 24, 35, 46, 59, 75, 82, 97 or 106.
Moon	12th house in annual chart	Very bad; will be reduced to zero; full of tears, destruction of property & land. This will happen at the age of 4, 17, 28, 48, 55, 68, 80, 90, 101.
Mercury & Venus or wicked planet	2,6,12	Ancestral wealth will be destroyed.

VENUS

GODDESS LAXMI

BENIGN COW; WHITE COLOUR OF CURD; WOMAN LIKED AND LOVED BY MAN.

Goddess of wealth; woman loved and adored by man. One-eyed Venus (Libra Sign) is exalted by Saturn, but debilitated by Sun. If it is exalted it brings domestic happiness, comfort of the world, peace of mind etc., but if it is malefic it causes endless pain, grief and domestic sorrow. Saturn sees all round and Venus borrows one eye from Saturn. Whenever Saturn is in trouble, Venus is the martyr. Venus, if alone, does not give bad results, in whatever house it may be placed. When it occupies its own house i.e. 7th, it confers its strength on the other planet in the 7th house. In 3rd house, Venus behaves like man; in 9th, it is like malefic Mars and in 6th,its results are debilitating. It is the most exalted in 2nd and 12th house and in 10th, it does the role of Saturn i.e. it becomes Saturn itself. In the first it is "KAAG REKHA", whereas, in 4th troubled by Moon i.e. (Mother-in-law). In 5th it is tough Mud and in 11th it spins like a top. In 8th, all planets are debilitating and so is Venus. It confers all blessings and comforts, if it is the celestial Cow (Kam Dhenu) i.e., exalted.

VENUS HOUSE NO.1

RISE AND FALL ASSOCIATED WITH KAAG REKHA AND MACHH REKHA; LOVE OF ANOTHER WOMAN; VENUS' KITE)

May be irreligious; may not even differentiate between various religions in matters of love. But he will excel in service, business etc. Venus, if benefic will bring lot of wealth and if malefic, may spell monetary disaster. If benefic, it will be "Machh rekha" - best for wealth and children and family and if malefic it will be "Kaag Rekha" - when one-eyed Venus will create problems.

> **KAAG REKHA (CROW LINE)**—If Saturn is malefic or No.7 & 10 are not vacant and they are not occupied by wicked planets and Mercury - that constitutes "Kaag Rekha" (Crow Line). If Saturn and Venus are in 1st house - It is also called Kaag Rekha.
>
> **MACHH REKHA (FISH'S LINE)**—If Saturn is benefic or No.7 & 10 are vacant or they are occupied by Rahu, Ketu, Saturn and Mercury - they constitute"Machh Rekha. (Fish's Line).

Nevertheless one will have comforts, conveyance. Man will be lover of woman or like a moth hovering around candle. He will be like a broken melon, i.e. whole family even wife's parents etc. will get advantage from him and himself will have nothing before marriage. Wife's health bad, but not his own; will be leader in the family and among compatriots. If married on 25th year, especially when 7 & 10 are not vacant, it will mean destruction of wealth and death of woman. If wife's health is impaired, donate (seven cereals e.g. Rice, Wheat, Barley, Gram Dal, Mustard, Moong, linseed, Masoor Dal, Urd etc.) If 7th is occupied by enemies of Venus, man suffers from T.B. or Cough. In this house Venus may give bad results but Sun is benefic and good.

VENUS IN 1ST HOUSE IN COMBINATION WITH & IN RELATION TO OTHER PLANETS

PLANET	HOUSE NO	EFFECT
Sat-benefic	In its own house	Marriage before personal employment or job. She will be the lord of the house.
Mercury	3,6	Very good results. Moon's effect will be good; victorious in litigation.
Venus-malefic	1	Moon's effect will be bad on mother's life.
Rahu	7	Wife's health bad; mental illness & madness.
Moon	7	Clash between mother & wife.
Mars	7	Very good for children; wealth & comfortable life.
Sun Sun with wicked & enemy planet Venus aspecting sun	7 7	III health of wife; mentally retarded; henpecked; philanderer(runs after women); ill-mannered; lustful-bad for health; but Venus will not have bad effect on sun.
Saturn-malefic	In any house	Relatives will not be helpful. Venus will give the results of no. 10 i.e., Exalted. But his wife will be like a perennial flower, radiating beauty and fragrance of love; the man will lead a luxurious life.

VENUS HOUSE NO.2 (PERMANENT HOUSE & PLANET RESULT)

POTATO; COW SHED FOR COW; GHEE; WHITE MICA; CAMPHOR; LUXURIES, HAPPY DOMESTIC LIFE FULL OF COMFORTS AND WEALTH)

One earns for 60 years; may not be hardworking, but will have God's grace, In this house, i.e. No.2, Venus is very exalted. Incarnation of goddess Laxmi; Jupiter sheds its enmity with Venus in House No.2. Victory over enemies; Really very exalted regarding wealth, domestic happiness, children, exalted status etc.

VENUS IN 2ND HOUSE IN COMBINATION WITH & IN RELATION TO OTHER PLANETS

PLANET	HOUSE NO	EFFECT
Saturn	9 or any house	Both will give exalted results.
Venus	2 or any house	Both are exalted.
Saturn	9	
Jupiter	2	Most exalted regarding love & wealth.
Saturn	2,9	Exalted.
Jupiter	6,12	Help from relatives, who will be in good position.
Not aspected by any planet	From no 8	Laxmi yoga; rich, beautiful but infertile wife.

It Venus is malefic in No.2, in a man's horoscope, his wife will be barren and infertile and vice versa. When Venus is associated with wicked planets in No.2, man may adopt some one.

VENUS HOUSE NO.3

MARRIAGE, SACRIFICING WIFE, LEGEND OF SAVITRI - SATYAWAN.

Now Venus will not have an adverse effect on the 9th house. When Mercury is benefic, Venus will confer good results. Travel for 20 years; When Ketu is exalted the woman behaves like a man. She is bold and devoted to her husband. She will inspire her husband. If Mars is benefic, Venus will confer best results; and bad results, if Mars is malefic. If a person is true to his wife, she will serve him; if he is faithless, she will dominate him.

VENUS IN 3RD HOUSE IN COMBINATION WITH & IN RELATION TO OTHER PLANETS

PLANET	HOUSE NO	EFFECT
Saturn	9	Best results; Now no 9 will not be destroyed.
Ketu-exalted	Any	Women will be respected in his house; wife will be devoted & there will never be a theft.
Jupiter	9	Bad health; unhappy; illness.
Mercury	11	Venus will be destroyed; bad till 34 years, thereafter revival of earlier fortune.

> Satyawan died young; his dead body was being carried by lord Yama to the nether world. Savitri, his wife brought him back to life by means of sheer devotion, tenacity of purpose and boldness. Such a man's wife is bold and inspires her husband in times of distress.

VENUS HOUSE NO.4 (SIGN RESULT)

FOUR FOOTED ANIMAL, BIRD, CURD, REMEDY FOR JUPITER.

Travel on land will be beneficial; Moon is always on the move. It is the Moon who is the enemy of Venus; Whereas, Venus is not inimical to Moon. Till four years after marriage, life will be full of comforts, luxuries and peace; but later clash between mother-in-law (Moon) and Venus (daughter-in-law), it is the mother who is responsible for the clash. Bad for maternal uncles (remedy lies in appeasing moon) or else throw gram dal in flowing water.

Only two woman will be alive at a time; one old and the other young and fashionable. Even then lack of children; may be issue-less. It happens only when No. 2 & 7 are vacant and Venus is not associated with any other planet.

When Venus is associated with any other planet, bury a kernel of peach (round) stuffed with "Surma" in grass at a deserted place or jungle; it will benefit the wife and children. Marriage at 22,24,29,32,39,47,51, 60 will be inauspicious.

As regards benefits of children, it will be good only in the second round of Saturn, Ketu or Mars i.e. when they occupy house No.1 in the Annual Chart or are helpful to Venus.

- Venus in house no. 4 with malefic Saturn will result in lack of children; Lustful conduct spells disaster.

VENUS HOUSE NO.5

REWARD, BRICK KLIN, FAMILY FULL WITH CHILDREN.

Family full of children; attached with family and tribe; If noble, good results; if lecherous or lustful, worst results; but it will not have adverse effect on wife and children; may earn a lot for 5 years after marriage

VENUS IN 5TH HOUSE IN COMBINATION WITH & IN RELATION TO OTHER PLANETS

PLANET	HOUSE NO	EFFECT
Mer., Ketu & Saturn--benefic	Any	Noble; wife like 'Laxmi'; bringer of luck & fortune.
Male planet-benefic or in association with	5th	Very good results; lover of family & tribe; wealthy.
Sun Moon	1 10	Best results.
Venus-malefic	5	Lustful conduct, but will not have adverse effect on children i.e., He will be blessed with children.
Sun, moon & Rahu	1	Lustful; lecherous; but no bad effect on children.
Moon-malefic	Any	Moon's bad results will be observed on Venus i.e., Badly effected domestic happiness; donate rice or silver etc.

+
REMEDIES • Regarding health (whether man or woman), wash your private parts with milk instead of water.

VENUS HOUSE NO.6

DEBILITATING; SPARROW; GIRL; EUNUCH; WHITE COW INAUSPICIOUS; UNRELIABLE WOMAN.

Insulting attitude towards relatives; raises accusing finger at all friends and relatives; wants to be leader among compatriots; irreligious; indulges in flattering and praising women; a carpet knight; good health; good eye-sight and power of speech; good results from wife's relatives. It is certain that he insults and humiliates his friends often. Problems in domestic life as Sun and Venus are enemies. Such a person's wife must not walk bare footed; She should wear socks; The skin of her feet must not touch the earth, it may otherwise result in loss or theft. The native with Venus No.6 may do foolish acts but his fate helps him. When Ketu is malefic or bad, wife may either be barren or may produce daughters only.

MALEFIC VENUS IN NO.6: Such a man does many foolish acts; may even distribute his wealth among the poor; will not enjoy staying in a house built by him. Old age will be comfortable; Donate Rice or Silver or Milk. If Venus is in 6th, Jupiter, Sun and Moon will not confer good results. If aspected by or associated with a helpful male planet, he will be wealthy; Venus will be like a precious diamond (if sun or Jupiter or both are in No.2, 6). Venus in 6th will never be bad, if Moon is benefic. The native must be affectionate and indulgent towards his wife for exalted results, otherwise she will destroy his happiness and peace.

VENUS IN 6TH HOUSE IN COMBINATION WITH & IN RELATION TO OTHER PLANETS

PLANET	HOUSE NO	EFFECT
Ketu	6	Bad results, though sun, moon & Jupiter may be helpful.
Jupiter	12	
Rahu	12	Death of first wife.

VENUS HOUSE NO.7 (PERMANENT HOUSE AND EXALTED PLANET)

BRINGER OF GOOD LUCK; BARLEY; WHITE COW; UTENSILS OF BRASS; LOVE OF THE SPOUSE.

If alone, Venus is exalted; otherwise gives the effect of associated planet. Venus is one eyed; even then it brings wealth. Whenever, Venus occupies No.1(31ST Year) in the Annual Chart or if any other planet is benefic in the horoscope, Venus will have exalted results. Domestic happiness, wealth etc will last at least for 25 years, if Venus is in 7th house. Wife will be noble and good looking provided she should not be black or exceptionally beautiful. When Venus in 7th is exalted, it will be a happy couple; parents of both the spouses will be wealthy; life 80 or 90 years.

It is said "the woman may be one eyed but she should be harbinger of fortune, domestic happiness and all pleasures and comforts" so is the case with Venus No.7 (exalted). Such a person does return from foreign lands; will never die in a foreign country. If Venus in 7th is malefic, the person must not do business in partnership with the relatives of his wife; That will lead to losses.

VENUS IN 7TH HOUSE IN COMBINATION WITH & IN RELATION TO OTHER PLANETS

PLANET	HOUSE NO	EFFECT
Sun, Moon, Rahu (enemies)	1,7,9,11	Increase in wealth; Venus will give exalted results.
Sat, Mercury, Ketu (friends)	1,7,9,11	Venus will give same results as one of these four.
or Saturn	9,11	
Mer-benefic	4,6,2	Best results after marriage - for 37 years.
Venus-exalted	7	Best results regarding marriage, domestic happiness, age, etc.
Venus	7	For children-see Ketu's position.
		For domestic happiness—see Saturn's position.
		For wealth—see Rahu's position.
Moon	4	Will keep away from lustful conduct.
Venus & Jupiter Together	Malefic Venus in no.7	Bad for business & problems in the birth of children.
Jupiter-malefic		
Sun, Moon, Rahu (enemies)	1	Theft; loss of wealth (4,16,28,40,52,64,76,88,100 years of age)
& malefic in annual chart	3	
Venus-malefic	7	
Moon	1	Harmonious relations between mother & wife; but problems in marriage & children.
Moon	1	Incapacitated; castrated; eunuch; impotent man & barren woman or else coward.
Sun	4	
Saturn	7	
Sun or Mercury	8	Death of wife.
Rahu	8	Bad for wife; she should not wear black & blue clothes.

Vacant	1	Good results of Venus.
Jupiter	2	Deprived of son or unhappy with the son.
Mars (combust or malefic)	Any	
Saturn & moon	6	Wife may suffer from heart disease.

VENUS HOUSE NO.8

CARROT; GRAVEYARD; WHITE COW WITHOUT HORNS - BAD.

Naughty, imperious, foul mouthed and dominating woman. But this planet is not always bad; gives bad results for the first 25 years and good results during the next 25 years. Must not marry till 25th year of age. If the moon is benefic, Venus will not be bad. If Moon is malefic, Mercury may help; if Mercury is debilitating then Mars will be helpful . If Mars is malefic, have Rahu's assistance i.e., throw Copper coin or flower into a dirty drain. In order to ward off the adverse effect of Venus No.8, one must donate and pray in religious place of his faith.

VENUS IN 8TH HOUSE IN COMBINATION WITH & IN RELATION TO OTHER PLANETS

PLANET	HOUSE NO	EFFECT
Vacant	2	Late marriage; woman's death; may suffer from venereal disease.
Enemy planet	8	Should not stand surety for others; if lustful, may suffer from venereal disease.

VENUS HOUSE NO.9

WHITE COLOURED COW INAUSPICIOUS; BURY A SQUARE PIECE OF SILVER IN A NEEM TREE; CRUEL; UNSYMPATHETIC; MALEFIC MARS; THUNDERSTORM OF BLACK DUST.

Though ancestors may be rich, yet bad for children, specially sons; good for travel; wise, resourceful, administrator; may be very rich but will have to earn his livelihood. For good results, regarding monetary conditions, bury a square piece of silver in a NEEM tree.

In order to ward off the evil effect of Venus on children especially sons, put a piece of silver besmeared in honey in the foundation of the house. Hardworking; Bad for children; Will spend on wife's health.

VENUS IN 9TH HOUSE IN COMBINATION WITH & IN RELATION TO OTHER PLANETS

PLANET	HOUSE NO	EFFECT
Planets in no 4— Malefic or Sun, Moon, Rahu	4	Loss of wealth & reputation, when they are in no 1 in annual chart (4,16,28,40,52,64,76,88,100th year)
Moon-malefic	Or in no.7	Bad for sons & wealth.
Jupiter-malefic	Any	Bad for children.

VENUS HOUSE NO.10

MUD; COTTON; HEIR TO SATURN; IF SATURN EXALTED, EVERYTHING EXALTED.
This planet will give all comforts during old age,. During youth one may indulge in love making with another woman which may lead to bad results for Son; Brother may repent and Mother may be unhappy. One must have good character. If a philanderer, may be deprived of son for 12 years; ill health of wife; Venus will be as powerful as Saturn; In youth lover of other woman, but pious during old age. Good health; lot of wealth for 12 years after marriage.

VENUS IN 10TH HOUSE IN COMBINATION WITH & IN RELATION TO OTHER PLANETS

PLANET	HOUSE NO	EFFECT
No aspect; vacant	4	Good health; husband lean & wife fat.
Saturn-exalted	Or in 9	Mercury will be benefic; will not meet any accident; good house; landed property; orchards.
Any planet	1,5	Comfortable life; luxurious life during youth.
Moon alone	7,4,2	Even mud will turn into sweet sugar; car etc.

For the good of children, one must remain away from lustful conduct; must not cohabit with other woman; Must wash his/her private parts with curd. Venus at No.1 (10,22,32,47,58,70,79,97 years of age) in the Annual Chart or Venus at No.7 (4,16,33,44,50,66,76,.94 years of age) in the Annual Chart or Saturn in the same house in the Annual Chart, as it occupies in the main horoscope - results will be beneficial provided he does not drink.

Venus in 10th house with malefic Saturn --- Venus will give bad results; wife will become blind & unhappy.

VENUS HOUSE NO.11

COTTON; PEARL; WHITE CURD LIKE - BEAUTIFUL WOMAN/MAN; SPINNING TOP REGARDING WEALTH.

Woman may appear to be the bringer of good luck, but she will herself be responsible for the disaster. During the period of wicked planets, donate oil. At the time of marriage, donate white cow. Beautiful wife; rich man; wealth for 12 years; otherwise impotent and prone to skin diseases.

VENUS IN 11TH HOUSE IN COMBINATION WITH OTHER PLANETS

PLANET	HOUSE NO	EFFECT
Mercury or moon-benefic		Secretive; changes like a chameleon, but rich; will be beheaded; wealth for 12 years, otherwise impotent.
Rahu	12	The more the girls, the more the wealth.

Such a man appears to be a simpleton, outwardly; but is very clever & shrewd.

Venus in 11th house with Mercury in 3rd—Woman will destroy her husband's wealth, outwardly she may appear to be bringer of good luck; She will not give wealth to her daughters, but will give it to her husband's relatives.

VENUS HOUSE NO.12

EXALTED; PROVIDER OF EVERYTHING (KAM DHENU COW); FOUR FOOTED ANIMAL; WIFE PROVIDES ALL HAPPINESS AND PLEASURES (FOR 27 YEARS)

Wife incarnation of goddess of help & strength for husband.

Conjugal pleasures; wife is like the proverbial 'Kam Dhenu' Cow; respect for wife will provide all pleasures and comfort; Good luck after marriage; Even Moon and other male planets will be three times benefic and even No.2, will be benefic. It will be just like exalted Venus in No.2; Exalted status in service matters; Domestic happiness for 27 years or more even.

VENUS IN 12TH HOUSE IN COMBINATION WITH & IN RELATION TO OTHER PLANETS

PLANET	HOUSE NO	EFFECT
Jupiter & Saturn	12	Children will be happy; wife will be happy.
Mercury-benefic	2,6	Musician; poet; long life (96 yrs); exalted results, very happy family.

Venus in 12th house confers all domestic pleasures. The native's wife inspires him at the time of distress and difficulties. If wife does not keep good health, she should bury blue flower in a deserted place during evening. During bad days or when in distress, the native's wife or husband should bury rice, wheat or mustard in a deserted place. The native with an exalted Venus in No.12 is the supporter of the family; domestic happiness; loves his wife, who serves him well; full of zeal; poet; and fond of music. Wife will provide all pleasures but not vice versa, victorious over enemies.

MARS

MARS (BENEFIC)—"HANUMAN"; RELIEVER OF ALL DISTRESS.

MARS (MALEFIC)—LORD SHIVA, THE LORD OF DEATH.

MARS IN VARIOUS HOUSES

HOUSE NO 1	SWORD OF JUSTICE; ARMY OR POLICE.
HOUSE NO 2	SUPPORTER AND HELPER OF OTHERS.
HOUSE NO 3	TIGER CHAINED IN A ZOO.
HOUSE NO 4	OCEAN ON FIRE; DEATH & DESTRUCTION ON ALL.
HOUSE NO 5	ANCESTOR OF RICH SONS & GRAND SONS, IF BENEFIC; BAD FOR ALL, IF MALEFIC.
HOUSE NO 6	SADHU & SAGE; RELIGIOUS MINDED.
HOUSE NO 7	'VISHNU LIKE '; SUPPORTER OF OTHERS.
HOUSE NO 8	DEATH TRAP FOR BROTHERS.
HOUSE NO 9	EXALTED; THRONE OF KING.
HOUSE NO 10	EXALTED; KING; EMINENT STATUS.
HOUSE NO 11	GUISE OF A SADHU; BEE-HIVE FULL OF HONEY.
HOUSE NO 12	FOLLOWER OF TRADITIONS & FAITH; RAHU BECOMES INEFFECTIVE.

CERTAIN IMPORTANT POINTS

• Mars in 10 is Royal and King-like; whereas Saturn in 3rd is malefic and leads to loss of wealth.

- If Mars aspects Saturn, bad for children; bad results if man joins the army or police, but very good results if he is a Mechanical Engineer or a Mechanic.
- If Saturn aspects Mars - both dacoits helping each other - both show very good results.
- If Mars aspects Rahu, Rahu will be ineffective.
- If Rahu aspects Mars, diseases of stomach, arms, a lot of pain in the Right side of the body. Remedy lies in appeasing Moon i.e. Donation of rice, milk or silver.
- If Sun and Mercury are together in the horoscope, Mars will be benefic.
- If Sun and Saturn are together in the horoscope Mars will be malefic.
- Malefic Mars (1;4,7,8) believes in Tit for Tat; but if Sun and Moon help it, it will not be malefic. If Mercury is malefic Mars becomes most malefic and debilitating. Mars is no longer malefic if it is associated with Sun which combusts it.
- If Mars is alone in Aries or Scorpio (1 or 8 sign) and without Sun, it is malefic.
- If Mars (Malefic) is helped or aspected favourably by Sun or Moon, it is no longer malefic.
- If two wicked planets (Saturn-Rahu; Saturn-Ketu) or two enemies (Mercury-Ketu; Sun-Venus) are in combination with Mars, it will not be malefic.
- If Mars and Saturn are together, results will be very bad. Their effect will be that of Mars in Cancer and Saturn in Aries. Remedy is for Mars in no. 4 and Saturn in no. 1.
- When Mars and Ketu aspect or face each other, results will be bad regarding fate. It will be a fight between a tiger and a ferocious dog. For remedy, refer to Mars-Ketu.

MARS (BENEFIC)

MARS IN HOUSE NO 1

PERMANENT HOUSE; RESULT OF THE PLANET.

32 teeth; Bringer of good luck; Remedy for Sun & Moon - whereby results will be good; Sword of Justice - Army or Police. He should be an elder brother; or else will become the eldest. In short, his elder brother will die before his death. If Sun & Moon are on the left & right side of the Mars, such a person will be like the sword in the sheath. His parents may die when Mars period (14-28 or 13-15) starts; but he will be a master swordsman i.e., a brilliant Army or Police officer. 32 or even 31 teeth indicate benefic Mars; Probably no sister; but if there is one, she will be queen like. Brother sick & unhappy; Resourceful, Beaurocrat; enemies though many will be vanquished. Profit in timber business; Sun & Mars will confer good results; Advantage from Govt.; Service for 28 years, if Mars is benefic. If it is malefic, illness & body troubles.

MARS IN 1ST HOUSE IN COMBINATION WITH & IN RELATION TO OTHER PLANETS

PLANET	HOUSE NO	EFFECT
Together with sun & no aspect	1	Brave; courageous; 32 teeth.
Mercury	3	Two brothers; will see rise & fall; sometimes poor & sometimes rich, but sisters will be wealthy.
Sun	2	Indolent & poor.
Moon	12	

MARS (BENEFIC) IN HOUSE NO 2

Leopard; deer; supporter of brothers.

If he is not the eldest brother, he will die before his elder brothers; Will get property from in-laws, who will be like a bee-hive brimming with honey; all comforts; wealthy; leader of the family; Mars & Jupiter together will confer best results, and he will be a self-made rich man. If Mars is malefic, ill-fated and may remain sick for 9 years and may die in a battle field. Rich In-laws; may inherit property from them. If he helps others, he may earn more.

MARS IN HOUSE NO 3 (PERMANENT HOUSE)

Stomach; Lips; Chest; Ivory - auspicious.

If malefic, it will be like a man - eater; otherwise meek like a deer. It will be like honey with a sprinkling of poison; Unreliable Mars; Self respecting; helps the poor & down-trodden. If Mars is benefic, happiness from friends, relatives, brothers & children; courageous; good eye-sight; justice loving; expert in martial arts; Rich in-laws & happiness from them.

MARS IN 3RD HOUSE IN COMBINATION WITH & IN RELATION TO OTHER PLANETS

PLANET	HOUSE NO	EFFECT
Jupiter & sun or	9,11	Bad results, if he pokes his nose into other's affairs; good for family.
Moon & Mercury Or	9	
Saturn Or both	11	
Mercury	9,11	Bad results, if he pokes his nose into other's affairs, but good for in-laws.
Jupiter	11	Good for self; but unhappy on account of deaths of relatives.

Jupiter, Sun or Moon	7	
Mercury or Saturn or both	3,7	Bad results for poking nose into other's affairs; but will be helpful to in-laws.
Jupiter	9,11	Rich in-laws & will help him monetarily.
Saturn	9,11	No death or mishap or bad event in the family.

MARS IN HOUSE NO 4 (SIGN RESULT)

Most debilitating & malefic; Remedy of Moon; Sword; Diseases between the navel & the throat; Ocean on fire & death.

Mars in the 4th house (Cancer) is the most malefic. It is full of fire which can burn even the ocean. It may cool down only if Moon is in the 3rd, or 8th houses. If its enemies occupy 4th,8th or 3rd houses, Mars becomes the most malefic & spread fire & death all around. If Sun or Jupiter are in the 3rd, 8th or 9th houses, malefic Mars spreads milk instead of poison. Malefic Mars turns everything (even sugar & honey) into coal. Such a person is born in a family where about one or two generations ago his ancestor, must have been like a king, a great land lord & very rich. Such a person is haughty & insolent; believes in the maxim of ' Physician heal thyself first.'

Wet blanket; Ring leader of evil-doers; has the evil capacity of burning ocean with fire; God Shiva, the lord of death & destruction. Mars is malefic, when Sun & Moon are not in 8th, 4th or 3rd houses or it may not get help from Sun, Moon or Jupiter. Mars becomes all the more malefic, if it is associated with debilitating Saturn or Ketu (even though it may be helped by Sun, Moon or Jupiter).

Mars is also malefic, if it is alone in any of the 8th, 4th or 3rd house; the other two remaining houses are occupied by Mercury & Ketu -- the family will have widows who will destroy the family.

MARS IN 4TH HOUSE IS NOT MALEFIC UNDER FOLLOWING SITUATIONS :

- If any two wicked planets (e.g., Saturn, Rahu or Saturn, Ketu) or two mutual enemies (e.g., Mercury & Ketu) are together.
- Moon or Venus alone or associated with Mars in no. 3,4 or 8 will not allow Mars to be malefic.
- Friendly planets (Sun, Moon, Jupiter) are in no. 3,4,8 or 9 i.e., they are helping Mars. In that case, Mars will not be malefic.

MARS IN 4TH HOUSE IN COMBINATION WITH & IN RELATION TO OTHER PLANETS

PLANET	HOUSE NO	EFFECT
Moon	6	Mother dies in one's childhood.
Mercury	6	Mother dies in one's childhood; otherwise both unhappy.
Wicked planet	9	Problems in children; will destroy in-laws & maternal uncles.
Moon	3	Courageous & honourable.
Mercury	12	Worst results; ill-fated; poor; foolish Sadhu.

♦ If Mars is alone in 4th house, it will be malefic Mars and will destroy both life & property. If it is alone in 8th house, it will destroy only wealth.

MARS IN HOUSE NO 5

Brother; Neem tree; Father of rich children & grand children.
Happiness from wife and children. If Mars is good, cool-minded & peace-loving; otherwise just the reverse i.e., Short-tempered. Now Mars will be indulgent & kind towards its enemies occupying 9th house. Planets in no.3 will also help & benefit Mars like the tail of Hanuman. Very wealthy; like god of wealth; Father of very rich children & grand children : like a Neem tree; the older he grows, the richer he will be; but will have sleepless nights-should keep a glass of water under his head (below the pillow) at night. Intellectual; Man of education; scholarship & learning; best children.

MARS IN HOUSE NO 6 (SIGN RESULT)

Navel; Remedy for Saturn; A contented Sadhu.
All pleasures from wife & friends; Brothers may earn less; but they will also grow, as he rises in life; Sweet tongued; will rise high in life; a Sadhu, who is full of contentment; noble, pious; Sun's effect will be good; a successful writer; even Rahu in 12th house will be ineffective and will lose its sting.

MARS IN 6TH HOUSE IN COMBINATION WITH & IN RELATION TO OTHER PLANETS

PLANET	HOUSE NO	EFFECT
Benefic Venus or Benefic planet or Saturn, Mercury or Ketu	Any 7 7	Long life; may see prosperous grand children.
Jupiter, Sun & Mercury- Benefic (even though Ketu no 8 & Saturn no 5)	Any	Noble & auspicious children.
Mercury (no help from Sun or Moon)	8,12	Death in childhood.
Mercury	12	Brothers may create problems; Mar's results will be bad.

MARS IN HOUSE NO 7

Cereals; Dal Masur; First son; Sweet pudding.
Mars & Venus will show good results, provided they are not associated with Mercury or Mercury is malefic; happy family life; noble; adviser; jolly & jovial; honourable; expert in Maths; If malefic, keep a silver piece or donate rice, milk or silver.

MARS IN 7TH HOUSE IN COMBINATION WITH & IN RELATION TO OTHER PLANETS

PLANET	HOUSE NO	EFFECT
Venus or Jupiter	1	Very rich; landed property; all comforts - family happiness; will get his wish fulfilled once.
Jupiter Or Sun or Moon Or Mercury Or Sun & Mercury	1,7 1 **** 7	Will create problems for himself by meddling in the affairs of others; but will be helped by family members.

**** The same results will apply for Mars in 1st house also.

MARS IN HOUSE NO 8 (PERMANENT HOUSE; PLANET'S OWN RESULT)

Death trap; if malefic mars - body without arms - Remedies as suggested for Mars no 4.

If Mars is benefic, man is happy & victorious; happy family life; The more exalted the Mercury, the worst results are conferred by Mars i.e., Mars is bad when Mercury is good. Hard working; bold; can face enemies boldly; Justice loving.

MARS IN 8TH HOUSE IN COMBINATION WITH & IN RELATION TO OTHER PLANETS

PLANET	HOUSE NO	EFFECT
Moon, Sun, Jupiter	2	Mars confers good results.
Or vacant	2	
Moon	1,3,4,8 or 9	Mars will not be malefic:
Mercury	8	Both give good results.
Mercury	6	Death of mother in his childhood.

BENEFIC MARS IN HOUSE NO 9

Red colour; Ancestral greatness; If malefic - atheist & notorious.
All the planets become exalted . At the age of 13 or 14, parents will have eminent position and at the age of 28, himself will become great & eminent; Must keep red coloured things with him. Sun will confer best results;since his very birth, he is bringer of good fortune for parents & self; Royal up-bringing; Royal way of living & royal employment; will be very wealthy . In short, an incarnation of god of wealth, power & eminence; though may be born in a poor family, will achieve exalted status during the period of Mars i.e., after 28 years of age.
* Mars in 9th house with Mercury in 12th results in unhappy parents, who live from hand to mouth.

MARS IN HOUSE NO 10

Very exalted; Honey; Sweet food; God visiting a poor man's house.
Mars in 10th or 11th house (Saturn's house) is like a tiger, who will not be a man-eater; but bold, courageous & brave like a tiger; his ordinary chair will be like a throne. If associated with Venus or any other planet or if Sun is in the 6th house, may be blessed with a son in old age (upto 45 years). To be exalted, Mars should be alone in no. 10,11; Very rich; employment for 28 years. If associated with Saturn or is helped by Saturn, such a person is very naughty & notorious; wealthy; lot of property; good health; all comforts; comfortable family life; man of resolution & determination; In no. 10, Mars, if alone & not aspected by any other planet, is like a king; Parents will also be noble & eminent; provided Mars is alone & no. 2 is not occupied by a female planet.

MARS IN 10TH HOUSE IN COMBINATION WITH & IN RELATION TO OTHER PLANETS

PLANET	HOUSE NO	EFFECT
Sun	4	One-eyed.
Sun	6	May lose son.
Moon	5	One-eyed.
Moon	4	Short-tempered; haughty; dominating; good govt. Job.
Saturn	3	Lack of cash, but lot of landed property; will have sons & grandsons.
Saturn	3	Long life; sons & grandsons; may not utilise landed property, but may have cash.
Moon	4	
Saturn	4	May go to jail for theft.

BENEFIC MARS IN HOUSE NO 11

Vermilion (Used by Hindu married woman); Red Ruby; Beehive brimming with honey.
If benefic, person is like a beehive full of honey; If Mercury is good, noble, rich; will collect wealth for 24 years. Mars is like a tiger, but commanded by its trainer i.e., Jupiter. If Jupiter is exalted, Mars is doubly exalted. No benefits from brothers & relatives. If alone and without aspect, Mars makes the man King-like.

MARS IN HOUSE NO 12

Loud voice; Mahout of an elephant.
If benefic, wealthy; good wife; even Rahu will be ineffective & will give up its evil ways. Mars is the Mahout, who will ride over the elephant, which can not go amuck. Even Mercury or Ketu cannot have adverse effect, on no. 1 or 8. Good results, when blessed with a son or younger brother. If Sun is no. 3,11, one will be saved from death & disease.

MARS IN 12TH HOUSE IN COMBINATION WITH OTHER PLANETS

PLANET	HOUSE NO	EFFECT
Ketu	3	Even a poor man becomes rich & will become eminent.
Jupiter, Venus & Ketu	1,3,8,11	Enemies will go in hiding.

MARS (MALEFIC)

Lord Shiva - the Lord of death, fire & destruction.

Mars if alone in Aries, Cancer & Scorpio (1,4,8) and not helped by Sun or Moon is malefic, base & debilitating. It is like fire, red flag, cruel butcher, haughty, domineering, rich, lack of children; Such a woman may lose her child at 8 or 18; good height; ferocious; roaring voice; fiery eyes like those of a tiger. Unhappy wife or husband; its main job is to create diseases; litigation, fight and to act against religion; Malefic Mars is enemy of everyone. Without Sun, malefic Mars is most debilitating. It will spell doom, death & destruction. Only Moon and Sun can stop it from its evil actions. If Mercury is benefic, Mars will not be malefic.

- If Sun is not in Aries or Scorpio (1,8) or if it is in 6,7,10 or 12 or if Moon is not helping Mars, such a Mars will be most debilitating.
- Without Sun, Mars in Aries, Cancer and Scorpio i.e., 1,4,8 is malefic.
- Mars in 1,4,8 is also malefic, if it is not favourably aspected or associated with Sun, Moon or Jupiter.
- Mars in no.1 or 8 is also malefic, if Sun is in no.6,7,10 or 12.
- Mars in no.1 or 8 is also malefic, if Sun is in combination with Venus in no.7 or with Rahu in no.5 or 9 or with Ketu in no.3 or 6.
- Even if Mars receives help from Sun or Moon or Jupiter, but if it is associated with Saturn or Mercury or Ketu, everything will be nullified and Mars will be malefic.
- When Mars & Ketu aspect each other, both will be malefic and bad.
- Malefic Mars will have its adverse effect on relatives, but not on self.
- Malefic Mars facing Mercury or Saturn or both, may adversely affect honour, health and wealth.
- Malefic Mars facing female planets i.e., Venus or Moon, may adversely affect women of the family.

+ Must use 'White Surma'.

MALEFIC MARS IN HOUSE NO 1

Wet blanket; ill-fated; evil-minded; ungrateful; Wretch; Bad from 28 to 34 years. Fire of malefic Mars will engulf the family after his birth. If black in complexion, good results.

MALEFIC MARS IN HOUSE NO 2

May ward off enemy's attack; but will destroy his own family; ill-fated; quarrelsome; If Mars & Ketu are together in this house, exalted results (one is prosperous & rich).

MALEFIC MARS IN HOUSE NO 3

Bad for enemies, cousins, other brothers, uncles regarding death & disease; Fighter, notorious, but coward; Bad for business; may die fighting others.

MALEFIC MARS IN HOUSE NO 4 (RED PEPPER)

Naughty, picks up quarrels; diseased, coward; cruel; bad for life & wealth; Malefic Mars (Manglik) is when it is in Cancer or Scorpio (4,8); woman may die; no happiness from children; If man is 'Manglik', wife will die & if woman is 'Manglik', husband will die.

Mars in 4th house with Jupiter in 8th house will make the man lazy & indolent.

REMEDY FOR MANGLIK

✛
REMEDIES ❖ Donate rice, milk, silver, wheat & copper.
❖ Put some milk in the mud taken from the roots of a 'Banyan' (Burr) tree and put a dot of this mud on the fore-head and navel for diseases of stomach.
❖ Fill an earthen pot with honey & bury it in a deserted place.
❖ Throw crumbs of sweet bread to sparrows & birds.

Otherwise it will spell disaster, death & loss of life and property.

MALEFIC MARS IN HOUSE NO 5

Naughty; enmity with the world; fear of fire; bad eye-sight; unhappy regarding children; always travelling; children may die at 8 days, 8 months or 18 years. Deaths of men in the family; If Mercury & Ketu (its enemies) are in 9,10, may have restless nights; keep a glass of water under your bed at night.

MALEFIC MARS IN HOUSE NO 6

Bad results; loss and clash in every matter; Mars & Ketu will have adverse effect.

MALEFIC MARS IN HOUSE NO 7

Unfaithful wife; fear of fire for 17 years; wife & intelligence will not help; lustful; bad character; unlucky; will have illicit relation with other women; beloved may die.

MALEFIC MARS IN HOUSE NO 8

Own house of malefic Mars; 'Manglik'; fear of death & adverse results till 28 years; expert in military affairs & intelligent; If Manglik, wife may die; but if Sun, Moon or Jupiter are in no. 4, house no. 8 will not be the house of death . The native will have a long life. Sun in 4th house will shatter and disperse the smoke created by Mars; Difference of age between the native & younger brothers will be about 8 years; Wound & burn marks on the body.

Remedy : The same as suggested for Mars no. 4.

MALEFIC MARS IN HOUSE NO 9

Irreligious; notorious; atheist; secret in his birth; monetary condition of parents will be bad after his birth, till Mar's period is over; parents unhappy, if Mercury is debilitating.

MALEFIC MARS IN HOUSE NO 10

Trouble for 15 years; interested in magic, occult & tantra.

MALEFIC MARS IN HOUSE NO 11

Unhappy regarding children; Uncomfortable life; monetary condition of parents bad.

MALEFIC MARS IN HOUSE NO 12

May spend money foolishly; loss for 5 years; unhappy regarding wife; bad eye-sight & loss of wealth.

Mars in 12th house with Mercury in 8th house will cause early death of mother, if not aspected by Sun & Moon.

MERCURY

ALL POWERFUL GODDESS DURGA

Green colour; Parrot (male and female); lord of speech; Round and green diamond, which may kill, if tasted on tongue; but so delicate as may be cut with a blunt instrument even.

Mercury, if alone, is unattached and impartial. In houses No.2,4,or 6, it is Royal and King like. In seventh it is like philosopher's stone, which changes baser metals into gold i.e. it helps the associated planet. In 9.8.12 & 3, it is like a leper to be avoided. In these houses, Mercury is bad and malefic. If Mercury is in No.1 & 2, it helps Saturn; in No.3 to 8, it helps Sun and in 9 to 12, it helps Saturn.

MERCURY HOUSE NO.1

KING; ADMINISTRATOR; BUT SELFISH AND NOTORIOUS; LOUD VOICE; BOLD; EXALTED POSITION.

In woman's horoscope, It is indeed very exalted. Sun's result will indeed be good; Profit from govt. job; all wicked planets including Saturn will be at Mercury's command. Such a person is selfish and ungrateful; if Mercury is alone it will confer honour and fame for 11 years. Mars' results may be bad but Sun will confer good results. When Mars is in No.12, Mercury will never be malefic in No.1. If Mercury is malefic in No.1, such a person lives abroad and is selfish and greedy, but leads a luxurious life in youth; but bad for business and should avoid green colour.,

MERCURY IN 1ST HOUSE IN COMBINATION WITH & IN RELATION TO OTHER PLANETS

PLANET	HOUSE NO	EFFECT
Vacant	7	A throne without broken props (legs); mercury's own result bad, but Rajyoga - good for others.
Venus or Saturn	7	Courageous & bold, provided black complexioned.
Moon	7	Drug addict.

MERCURY HOUSE NO.2

YOGI RAJA; STANDING EGG; EFFIMINATE; MOONG; NIB OF A PEN; BEAK, SISTER-IN-LAW

Yogi Raja but selfish; Royal and exalted position; intelligent and fortunate; victorious over enemies; good for in-laws; witty; good speaker and writer; full of determination; Wavering nature; comfortable life; will earn wealth for 36 years. If Mercury is alone in No.2, such a person will be helpful to all like a Yogi Raja; Self-made rich; long life, mother may live upto 80 years; self confidence; in short, a comfortable life.

MERCURY IN 2ND HOUSE IN COMBINATION WITH & IN RELATION TO OTHER PLANETS

PLANET	HOUSE NO	EFFECT
Moon's help	From 12 & 8.	Will not be bad for father's life & business.
Jupiter	6,7	Bad for father's life & business.
Jupiter	9,12	Will earn name & fame; long life of mother.
Mars or Jupiter & Mars	6	Will not adversely effect father's life & age.
Saturn	6	Sharp & smart (in good sense) like a flying snake.

If Mercury in no.2 is malefic(bad), it will create problems in the birth of a male child, but such a person will definitely have a male child after all.

MERCURY HOUSE NO.3 (RESULT OF PLANET)

VERY BAD;LEPER; NIECE; LIKE A BAT; SHADOW LESS GHOST; GOOD FOR SELF; WHITE ANT; REMEDY FOR MOON.

It is malefic; destroys not only the 9th, but also 11th, 4th and 5th houses. It may be three times malefic in 3rd house, but is afraid of Sun when it is in the 11th house. If the 7th house is occupied by wicked planets it may bring death and disaster on father and maternal uncles. Age not less than 80; for others bad but may be good for self, regarding money, if Mercury is benefic.

MERCURY IN 3RD HOUSE IN COMBINATION WITH & IN RELATION TO OTHER PLANETS

PLANET	HOUSE NO	EFFECT
Mars	1	Good results.
Sun	11	Long life; good for children; a doctor specializing in asthma & respiratory diseases.
Mercury-asleep	3	Its results will be good.
Vacant	9,11	
Venus	4	Late birth of son.
Moon No.6 not occupied by friendly planets.	8	Bad for domestic happiness & wealth.
Moon	5	Bad results.
Jupiter	9	
Mars-malefic	5,11	Bad results of both the houses.
Moon	11	Very bad results regarding brothers & ancestral house.
Good Venus & no aspect.	Any	Now Moon's effect will not be bad.
Bad Venus & no aspect	Any	Moon's effect will be bad, step mother.
Sun	9	Worst life.
Saturn	11	
Saturn	7	Bad for father's life & business.

✚

REMEDIES • **REMEDY:** If a person stammers , then Mercury is not bad. Use alum for cleaning teeth ; wash "MOONG" at night and then throw them to the sparrows and birds. Take three big leaves of "Palah" or Dhak ; Wash them with milk and bury them in a pit in a lonely deserted place and put a black stone over it. Don't bring back home the shovel or spade with which the pit has been dug & the pot of milk with which the leaves have been washed. Also burn yellow coloured cowries, and throw the ash into the stream.

MERCURY HOUSE NO.4

RAJ YOGA; SKILLFUL; MENTALLY AGILE; PRECIOUS DIAMOND; PARROT; GILT; STANDING EGG; PATERNAL AND MATERNAL AUNT - MULTI-MILLIONAIRE, UNUSED PITCHER (GOOD OMEN)

If alone, Mercury in Cancer (No.4) is the most exalted; confers royal status on the native; Like a philosopher's stone for the family. If associated with Rahu and Ketu, he will be weak hearted, who is like an unused pitcher which breaks if hit even gently. Remedy lies in appeasing Sun i.e. donation of wheat and jaggery. For wealth, take the help of Jupiter (donate Yellow things). Many a time useless and meaningless travel, if associated with Rahu and Ketu.

Very wealthy; but bad for mother's health. If Jupiter is exalted, increase in wealth for 22 years.

MERCURY IN 4TH HOUSE IN COMBINATION WITH & IN RELATION TO OTHER PLANETS

PLANET	HOUSE NO	EFFECT
Moon	2	Rajyoga; exalted status; Mercury & Moon will give good results; if 32 teeth, malefic Mars will no longer be malefic. Best for family; even Mercury & Venus will confer good results.
Sun, Moon, Jupiter	3,5,11 or 9	Best results for family, wealth & life.
Moon or	6,3	Long & comfortable life of parents.
Vacant	2	
Jupiter-exalted	Any	Rajyoga; exalted status; long & best life.
Rahu	Bad	Bad for male members.
Ketu	Bad	Meaningless travel.
Moon-malefic	Or in 6	May commit suicide.

MERCURY HOUSE NO.5

BAMBOO; VOICE OF A SADHU OR GOD; BLESSINGS; GRAND-DAUGHTER; PROSPEROUS.

Man of knowledge; will utter truth i.e. word of God; very good for self and wife, but bad for father. As the Jupiter is helped by Sun, so is the case with the son who is helped by sun. When Mercury is in No.5, everything becomes good and beautiful & showers wealth. In short, Sun, Jupiter, Moon & Saturn will always be good & beneficial.

MERCURY IN 5TH HOUSE IN COMBINATION WITH & IN RELATION TO OTHER PLANETS

PLANET	HOUSE NO	EFFECT
No aspect		Good results; kind-hearted.
Sun, Jupiter, Moon	3,9	Best luck after 24th year.
Moon	3	Good results.
Jupiter	9	

✛   If Mercury in 5th house is malefic, keep a copper coin.

MERCURY HOUSE NO.6

EXALTED; LARGE HEARTED; FLOWER; DAUGHTER; STANDING EGG; DOMESTIC HAPPINESS FOR 37 YEARS; SUCCESSFUL BUSINESS.

Mercury in 6th house will act as a faithful dog or a servant to the native. Self made, rich and life 'beautiful like a flower'; Large hearted; Mercury will enhance the good result of other benefic planets in the horoscope. If Venus is exalted, Mercury is equally exalted; good results of sea travel. Successful businessman; learned; a successful writer and a speaker. Honesty will pay; must worship virgins, while doing auspicious work; if a greedy doctor he will be a loser and the first issue will be a daughter; must shun ill gotten wealth.

MERCURY IN 6TH HOUSE IN COMBINATION WITH & IN RELATION TO OTHER PLANETS

PLANET	HOUSE NO	EFFECT
Alone; not aspected by any planet		Good results of Moon; will gain from paper business & printing press.
Saturn	9,11	Wife from a rich family.
Jupiter, Sun or Saturn	1	Rajyoga; exalted status; wealthy.
Jupiter-good	Any	Rajyoga; paper business; printing press will be beneficial if he is honest.
Venus-malefic	Any	Bury a pot of milk in a deserted place.
Mars	4,8	Mother may die early; bad for house-hold.

Venus	4	Son after 34th year; woman may wear silver bangle or ring in the right arm.
Ketu-bad	Any	
Jupiter & Moon	2	Bad eye sight; bad old age.
Or Moon	2	
& Jupiter	11	

MERCURY HOUSE NO.7 (PERMANENT HOUSE)

Green grass; goat; philosopher's stone for others.

Such a person is like the philosopher's stone for others i.e. he will help others to the maximum; will have a comfortable old age; a successful businessman; good writer; always victorious; like a diamond, which enriches the family. If Mercury in this house is debilitating, it destroys the effect of Mars and Venus also. If Mars is in No.7, it will be malefic Mars; age 80 years; good speaker; If associated with Venus in 7th house, both will confer best results; will love his wife and will provide all comforts to her.

MERCURY IN 7TH HOUSE IN COMBINATION WITH & IN RELATION TO OTHER PLANETS

PLANET	HOUSE NO	EFFECT
Any planet	1	Like a precious diamond for the family.
Moon	1	May travel abroad & get benefit.
Saturn	3	Rich & lucky wife.
Ketu	1,8	Bad results for domestic comforts.
Jupiter	9	Problems in marriage & domestic life.
No aspect		Like a deserted jungle; bad for domestic life.

MERCURY HOUSE NO.8

RECLINING EGG; FADING OR DYING FLOWER; WHITE ANT; HOUSE OF DISEASES AND DOOM; TRAP OF DESTRUCTION; MONETARY LOSS; LEPER; POISONOUS.

Malefic results, if alone; may be good for health but will be like a poison for teeth and stomach i.e., will create dental and intestinal problems; it is like a leper to be shunned or is like the trap of destruction and gallows, may create financial problems; will work on the sly; loss in status. Its bad results will be evident when the stairs are broken; will spell financial doom.

MERCURY IN 8TH HOUSE IN COMBINATION WITH & IN RELATION TO OTHER PLANETS

PLANET	HOUSE NO	EFFECT
Alone		Very bad
Vacant (in the horoscope or in annual chart)	2	Worst for fate & life.
Jupiter	2	Father's life & fortunes in danger from 16 - 21 years of age.
Moon	2	Donate rice or milk.
Malefic	6	Bad for all planets except Jupiter.
Male planet	6	Mother may die early, otherwise both.
Mercury	8,12	Mother and Son will be unhappy.
Vacant	12	Diseases of thighs etc.
Moon, Sun or benefic planet	4	Good results after 34 years of age.
Mars	12	Mercury will not be bad.
Male planet	8	Good results; same as those of associated planets.
Mars	8	Good results though individually both give bad results.

☞ • *It may be noted that Mercury in No.8 is not bad when associated with male planet in No.8 .*

REMEDIES FOR MALEFIC MERCURY IN NO.8

✚
REMEDIES • Whenever Mercury occupies the 8th house in the Annual chart, bury a small earthen pot filled with honey - one 34th day before the birthday and one 34th day after the birth day - in a deserted place away from the city.
• Keep rain water or milk over the roof for 43 days.
• The Girl child should wear a silver nose ring.
• Avoid Red coloured clothes.
• Mercury in No.8 alone, adversely aspects the planets in house No.2. Remedy may be adopted for the planet in No.2, either in the horoscope or annual chart.

MERCURY HOUSE NO.9

LEPEROUS KING; UNFORTUNATE; MAGICAL GHOST; WITHOUT A SHADOW; BAT; AVOID GREEN COLOUR; STAMMERING; GREEN JUNGLE OF VEGETATION AND TREES.

Mercury in 9th sign will be unreliable, malefic and bad. There is some secret in his birth and such a person stammered in his childhood. If associated with Sun or Mars or both, his fate will be totally unreliable and will play 'Hide and Seek' with him. His fate and position is like that of a bat hanging by a rock (bad fate indeed) especially during 1,4,13,15,17,28 & 34th years.

MERCURY IN 9TH HOUSE IN COMBINATION WITH & IN RELATION TO OTHER PLANETS

PLANET	HOUSE NO	EFFECT
Jupiter alone	8,6,10,11	Short lived; life span either 8 months or 8,16,32,40,48 or 64 years.
Moon or Jupiter or both	3,6,7	Long life; but problems in marriage & children.
Vacant	1	Notorious; creates problems for others.
Moon, Ketu & Jupiter	1,3,6,7,9,11	Mercury will not be bad; wealthy & comfortable life.
Moon, Ketu	11	Good; but if these planets are not in no.11, very bad results in 7,15,25,37,49,66 & 76 years of age.
Moon	1	Mercury may dominate others, but is afraid of Moon; best results.

REMEDIES FOR MERCURY IN NO.9

+

REMEDIES
- For a girl child, pierce the nose and wear nose ring made of silver and gold.
- Always avoid green colour.
- Wear new clothes after washing them.
- Bury a piece of silver in the foundation of the house.
- Keep a piece of silver with you.
- For good results in service matters, donate Mushrooms in an earthen pot in a temple.
- Paint red a small ball of iron and keep it.

134

MERCURY IN HOUSE NO 10 (SIGN RESULTS)

TEETH; DRY GRASS; WINE ADDICTION; ATHEIST; RECLINING EGG; REMEDY FOR SATURN; COMFORTABLE LIFE; SYCOPHANT AND FLATTERER .

Such a man is selfish, problem creator, schemer, sycophant & cunning; his victim falls an easy prey to his manipulations. If addicted to wine and other vices, Saturn will have bad effects; house of lac (which can be easily destroyed); blast of explosives; poisonous fang of a snake; tail of a mad dog. Mercury will act according to the dictates of Saturn; if Saturn is good, Mercury's result will naturally be benefic and if Saturn is bad or made through wine and vices, Mercury will also give worst results. Father may or may not be helpful according to the positioning of Saturn.

MERCURY IN 10TH HOUSE IN COMBINATION WITH & IN RELATION TO OTHER PLANETS

PLANET	HOUSE NO	EFFECT
Moon	4	Beneficial sea travels on business etc.
Saturn-benefic	Any	Best results of both Saturn & Mercury.
Benefic	2	Mercury will be doubly lucky; will fill coffers with wealth.
Malefic	8	Bad results of Mercury.

MERCURY HOUSE NO.11

UNUSED PITCHER; PARROT WHO PREACHES; SHELL; DIAMOND; ALUM; TOPSY TURVY PITCHER; WEALTHY; AFTER 34 YEARS WILL BE LIKE A DIAMOND.

Mercury's bad or good effect will depend upon the position of Jupiter. Mercury will be like a diamond, making the man rich after 34th year. It will help even those whose Saturn, Jupiter and Moon are malefic. The year in which Mercury in No.11, occupies the first house in the Annual Chart (viz. 11,23,36,48,57,72,84,94th year) will give best results regarding money, even though No.3 is bad.

✚ Keep a copper coin with you to ward off the evil effects of Mercury, if malefic.

Debilitating; Remedy for Ketu; Bad egg; mad dog; comfortable life, but sleepless nights and victim of vagaries of fate,

If Jupiter and Saturn are together in the horoscope, Mercury in 12th house will lose its sting and will not be bad. Further, if Saturn is also in No.12 Mercury will never be bad. Except Saturn in No.12, Mercury in No.12 poisons all the planets in No.12 or No.6; but Sun (Monkey) saves himself from its poisonous bite. Mercury in No.12 is like a rabid dog; unreliable person of wavering nature; Bad for speculations and all activities concerning Mercury.

MERCURY IN 12TH HOUSE IN COMBINATION WITH & IN RELATION TO OTHER PLANETS

PLANET	HOUSE NO	EFFECT
Jupiter & Saturn	2,12,3	Mercury will confer monetary benefits & will give best results regarding wealth & family.
Jupiter	2,12	Man will earn name, fame & power, but may lose money through lavish living or theft etc.
Sat & Jupiter	7	Mercury will give exalted results for self, if Jupiter & Saturn are together in some other house different from the one occupied by Mercury.

Mercury in Pisces (Sign No.12), if alone, is indeed very malefic. Such a person blows hot and cold in the same breath; one moment he may encourage others with inspiring words, but immediately thereafter may back out; foul mouthed; poisonous tongue; liar . In man's horoscope, it is the worst, but its effect is not so bad in a woman's horoscope. If Rahu is malefic, the man with Mercury in No.12 may face bad name, humiliation, loss of wealth on account of embezzlements, dishonesty, fraud etc.(whether actually committed of fabricated).

MERCURY IN 12TH HOUSE IN COMBINATION WITH & IN RELATION TO OTHER PLANETS

PLANET	HOUSE NO	EFFECT
Saturn	6	Unreliable; addiction to vices; may squander wealth.
Sun	6	Bad for career & money.
Malefic Mars	4	Mother may die in his childhood; both unhappy.
Jupiter	6	Bad for father's life & wealth
Moon	6	Bad for mother's life; may commit suicide.
Mars	6	Brothers will create problems, but will themselves be losers.
Rahu or Ketu	6	Bad for in-laws (Rahu) & for son (Ketu); unhappy.
Venus	6	Bad for domestic happiness & wealth.
Moon	5	If one travels in a green colour car, one meets with an accident.

Saturn	9	
Rahu	12	

+

REMEDIES
- For a woman, she must pierce her nose and wear a nose ring made of silver and gold.
- Wear yellow thread, around the neck.
- Wear an iron ring (it should be pure iron without any joint of other elements).
- Gently throw an unused pitcher in the flowing water.
- Always keep your cool ; fulfill your promises and don't lose temper.
- Avoid green colour.

SATURN (BLACK SNAKE)

IF BENEFIC, HELPFUL; IF MALEFIC, STINGS LIKE A COBRA, SPELLS DEATH AND DESTRUCTION.

Saturn in No.1 is three times malefic and in No.3 it is twice malefic; In No.6 it is retrograde and destroys the domestic happiness, as it hits House No.2; but it is always not bad. In No.4, it is like a water snake and in No.5 it feeds on its own children. In No.2, it is subservient to Jupiter and imbibes the qualities of the great guru. Its headquarter is No.8; It is the most exalted in No.9, 7 &12 - the bringer of good fortune and wealth; In the 10th house, it is like a blank paper and in No.6, it is all ink. In 11th, it is exalted in fate and washes all blackness. In 11, it confers great wealth and income. If may be noted that Saturn has offered its own house at No.10th to Mars, where the latter is like a king; Instead Saturn in 3rd house, whose lord is Mars, is only the caretaker who watches wealth, but does not spend it. In No.2,9,.12 (the Permanent Houses of Jupiter), Saturn is very exalted and gives best results; whereas, Jupiter in No.10 (Saturn's House) becomes debilitating and gives worst results. An exalted Saturn is as powerful as Jupiter. Saturn and Ketu together and aspected by Rahu, give good results; but if any third planet joins Saturn and Ketu (combined), result of both of them will be bad . Saturn combined with any male planet will never give bad results. If there are two male planets combined with Saturn or are in its direct aspect, the result will not be bad. But when two planets (male and female) or more combine with Saturn, the result will be bad. If Saturn is alone with Sun or in house No.1 (whose lord is Sun), final result will be that of mercury i.e., combination of brightness and darkness. It may be remembered, that Saturn in association with Jupiter or in No.2, 9,12 (Jupiter's houses) will always give exalted results. Malefic Saturn, stings like a poisonous cobra, when it occupies the bad houses reserved for it. Remedy lies in donating almonds or things made of iron.

SATURN HOUSE NO.1

DEBILITATING; KAAG REKHA i.e. WORST FATE; DIRTY INSECT; IF MALEFIC, THREE TIMES BAD; IF BENEFIC, GOOD RESULTS.

If Saturn and Venus are in No.1, it will mean the worst fate; may be born in a rich family, but will be reduced to utter poverty; But confers long life; Saturn and Venus in No.1 dominate all the planets, and person is like a dry wood eaten up by white ants. If Rahu and

Ketu are malefic, Saturn in No.1 spells destruction and loss of wealth; If mercury is bad, there will be disruption in studies. If Saturn is in No.1 and the 7th and 10th houses are vacant, Saturn will not be bad but it will give very good results regarding wealth, property and life etc.

☞ • *If Rahu or Ketu is in No.4 or 10, and Mercury or Venus is in No.7, when Saturn is in No.1 OR Saturn is in no. 7, when the Venus is in no 1, both the houses i.e. 7th & 10th will be considered vacant.*

Man will have a long life like that of a snake or crow; will be a successful Doctor; If under the spell of malefic Saturn in No.1, one is dishonest and liar; If a person has large growth of hair he will be poor and his property may be auctioned because of addiction to vices; absolutely bad for wealth, property lands and career.

☞ • *Saturn in Aries (1st sign) will not show evil results, if Mars is exalted in Capricorn (10th sign). It will be a marriage of convenience, as two enemies occupy each others' houses.*

SATURN IN 1ST HOUSE IN COMBINATION WITH & IN RELATION TO OTHER PLANETS

PLANET	HOUSE NO	EFFECT
Mercury-malefic	Any	Worst fate; everything will be auctioned; all planets bad; but long life.
Sun, Moon, Mars (enemies of Saturn) Sun, Moon, Rahu (enemies of Venus)	4 (except Sun & Jupiter together)	Very bad fate; father's financial condition bad; himself dishonest, thief & cheat.
Sun	10, 11	Unhappy domestic life & ill fated.
Malefic mars	Any	Thief, cheat, dishonest, quarrelsome; sad because of children; less income; bad eye sight.
Sun	7	Liar; ungrateful poor.
Rahu & Ketu— malefic	7 or any planet	Saturn three times malefic; bad for education, wife & wealth.

♦ But Sun's effect will be benefic & good; Sun i.e., father will always help the son (Saturn), howsoever ugly & poisonous he may be.

139

+

REMEDIES
- Donate 'Maash' (Black lentils) for 43 days.
- Bury "Surma" in a deserted place.
- Put a drop of milk on a dot of mud taken from the root of Banyan tree and paste it on the navel and fore-head.
- Donate almonds or coconut or things made of iron.

SATURN HOUSE NO 2

MAASH (BLACK LENTILS); BLACK PEPPERS; AT THE FEET OF THE MASTER.

Here Saturn is in the temple of 'Great Guru'; Very lucky; man of God; comfortable living; a resourceful & intelligent adviser; master of land & property; good health & all comforts; just & fair; will not be cruel. If Mars is benefic, happiness from wife; otherwise sick & ill; will never be poor; will own ancestral lands; will be a leader & of independent thinking.

SATURN IN 2ND HOUSE IN COMBINATION WITH & IN RELATION TO OTHER PLANETS

PLANET	HOUSE NO	EFFECT
Moon-exalted	Any	Long life of mother & self.
Jupiter	4	Most fortunate; though appears simple & naïve, yet very intelligent; can see through the manipulations of others.
Sun	12	Fond of notoriety (bad reputation)
Jupiter -	11	
Malefic mars	Any	Will remain ill from 28 to 39 years.
Rahu	8	Superstitious.
Rahu	9	Fond of remaining alone

SATURN HOUSE NO. 3 (SIGN RESULTS)

IF BAD, TWICE MALEFIC; KETU'S REMEDY FOR LOSS OF WEALTH & SATURN'S REMEDY FOR PROPERTY.

An expert eye-specialist; keep a dog; If Saturn is in 3 or 10, he should deal with machines, Railways, hard-ware, timber, medical profession. If associated with Mercury, good health, but poor; bad relations with brothers.

SATURN IN 3RD HOUSE IN COMBINATION WITH & IN RELATION TO OTHER PLANETS

PLANET	HOUSE NO	EFFECT
Malefic Mars	Any	May create problems for others, but will have a comfortable life.
Moon	10	May die by drowning; thief but bad financial condition.
Sun	5	Unhappy with sons.
Associated with enemies		Loss of money & theft.

SATURN HOUSE NO 4

HOUSE; BLACK INSECTS; SPRINKLING OF A DROP OF MILK WILL BE HELPFUL; WATER SNAKE.

A doctor; Very subtle & shrewd having four eyes; Saturn will never give bad effects, rather it will be beneficial; If the native suffers from rheumatism, snake's sting will cure him instead of killing him. Saturn's profession i.e., Mechanical engineering, medical profession, business in hardware, timber or railways will be beneficial. If some one in the family is a doctor, the native will also be a doctor. Saturn & Moon together will give different results, but moon's results will be bad, i.e., mother will give unhappiness; Donate milk or wash Shiva's snake with milk if Moon's result is malefic or else throw a drop of milk in the well.

SATURN IN 4TH HOUSE IN COMBINATION WITH & IN RELATION TO OTHER PLANETS

PLANET	HOUSE NO	EFFECT
Moon	2,3	Parents will live long; domestic happiness; best for the native.
Jupiter	3	Will become rich after fleecing & duping people.
Moon	10, 4	Mother unhappy; if moon is in no. 10, death by drowning; destruction of wealth & property.

■   The native must not take milk at night.

SATURN HOUSE NO 5

BLACK LEAD (SURMA); SIMPLETON SON; SNAKE - EATING ITS OWN CHILDREN.
Many marriages; but unhappy regarding sons; may appear simple, but will be subtle & clever; will be like a snake eating its own children; may be well-read, but poor; may be a cheat, but still poor. If combined with Jupiter, it will lead to litigation & sickness.

SATURN IN 5TH HOUSE IN COMBINATION WITH & IN RELATION TO OTHER PLANETS

PLANET	HOUSE NO	EFFECT
Benefic Rahu or Ketu	Any	Good life; happy children; will construct houses.
Jupiter	10	Son may steal gold from the house and sell it at the price of iron; very bad indeed.
Vacant	11	Religious minded.
Jupiter	9	Good fortune (5,17,29,45,53,65,77,89th year), but bad for children.
Ketu	4	No bad effect of Saturn on children
Sun, Moon or Mars	7 in annual chart	Bad for health.
Vacant	10	Many marriages, but very late birth of son.
Sun or Saturn	1 in annual chart	May appear simple & foolish, but very clever & shrewd.

✛
REMEDIES • Take a few almonds to the temple ; place half of them there & bring back the other half and keep them at home ; but see that these are not eaten. This should be done when Saturn no. 5 occupies the 5th house in the annual chart. Do it for 43 days.

SATURN HOUSE NO. 6 (SIGN RESULT)

CROW; KEEP A BLACK DOG FOR DISEASES & DIFFICULTIES; REMEDY FOR MERCURY (MOONG) FOR BUSINESS; BLACKNESS OF FATE.
If Saturn in 2nd house is exalted, in 6th sign it is notorious, It is retrograde and adversely aspects the house no 2 & stings it with the poisonous fang, even though it (2nd house) may be occupied by its friend Venus. If Rahu is no. 8, Saturn in no. 6 raises its hood and stings even house no. 2; Saturn in no. 6 will not adversely affect the planet in no. 10. The native

is skillful & intelligent if married after 28 years; otherwise it will destroy mother & children both. Keep a black dog for the sake of sons. If the Saturn occupies exalted houses (reserved for it), even in the annual chart, it will be a benefic snake which will protect the native. Even Mercury will not give bad results; will be blessed with sons; all will be well regarding parents, wealth & intelligence.

When the Saturn is malefic & when it occupies no.6 in the annual chart, it will give worst effects. Such a person will be involved in litigation & police cases. It will be evident when he loses his purse, shoes or cycle, motor-bike, car etc. He should not immediately purchase it, but should throw coconut or almonds in the river at once to ward off the evil results of Saturn no. 6.

SATURN IN 6TH HOUSE IN COMBINATION WITH & IN RELATION TO OTHER PLANETS

PLANET	HOUSE NO	EFFECT
Rahu	3,6 in horoscope or annual chart	After 42 years, best life; even sun in 12th house will not give adverse results.
Ketu	10	A good sportsman.
Venus	2	Saturn will sting the Venus (domestic happiness) with poison.
Mercury	12	Saturn will be destroyed.
Mercury	2	Secretive; wavering mind.
Sun	12	Will not have adverse effect on Venus (wife).
Venus, Mercury or Rahu	4,10	May be beheaded; secretive, ill fated.
Mercury	2	
Or associated with Sun, Moon or Mars		

✚

REMEDIES ◆ Throw coconut or 6 almonds.
◆ Keep a black dog for the welfare of children.
◆ Fill an earthen pot with mustard oil & throw it into the river at night.

SATURN HOUSE NO 7 (EXALTED)

FEROCIOUS ANIMAL; BLACK COW; WHITE LEAD (SURMA); EYE - SIGHT; BLACK CEREALS; EMPLOYMENT.

If Mars is benefic, monthly income will run into thousands; Administrator; wealthy; wise; shrewd; will earn a lot for 24 years; will rise from scratch; If humane, wealthy; otherwise cruel lord; If Mars is malefic, very bad results for 29 years. If malefic, fill up a black flute with sugar & bury it in a deserted place. Wealthy doctor; an expert engineer; an exalted Saturn is as powerful as exalted Jupiter. Very rich; a wealthy landlord; reticent, but selfish; even Mercury is helpful; will travel a lot.

SATURN IN 7TH HOUSE IN COMBINATION WITH & IN RELATION TO OTHER PLANETS

PLANET	HOUSE NO	EFFECT
Mars benefic	Any	Lot of income.
Aspected by Mars & Jupiter		
Or aspected by Mars & Venus		Lot of wealth.
Mars, Moon & Venus-all malefic	Any	Bundle of sorrows.
Malefic Jupiter	Any	Greedy & jealous.
Malefic moon	Any	Diseases of the head.
Enemies	7	Full of diseases.
Sun	4	Night blindness; eunuch; impotent.
Mercury	2	Father's life in danger.
Mercury	1	Will be be-headed.
Mercury	1 in annual chart	Diseased eye.

+
REMEDIES •   If Saturn is malefic, fill a flute with sugar & bury it in a deserted place ; or else bury an earthen pot full of honey.

144

SATURN HOUSE NO. 8 (HEAD QUARTER)

SCORPION; HOUSE OF DEATH; PLACE BELOW THE EARS; DELICATE PORTION OF HEAD.

House no. 8 is the headquarter of Saturn, but is the real house of Mars. If Saturn is alone in 8th house, it is not bad. But if associated with Mars or even Moon, it gives bad results. All types of fear; fear of death; given to self-praise; bad eye sight in old age. If alone, Saturn & Mars are not bad; but if combined, give bad results. If Saturn in no.8 is associated with enemies such as Sun, Moon & Mars in no. 8, Saturn will give worst results and may lead to deaths in the family.

+ Keep a pure silver piece with you.

SATURN HOUSE NO. 9 (SIGN RESULTS)

BLACK & SEASONED WOOD; AAK OR MADAR TREE; HOUSES; REMEDY FOR JUPITER, AS 'THE GREAT GURU'

The native will own at least three houses at the time of death; like a whiff of cool breeze; sympathetic; compassionate & generous; learned; owner of property; comfortable & long life; blessings of parents; will never leave debt for his children; three generations will be comfortable & happy viz., grandfather, father & grandson; Best results for 60 years or even till the end, provided he is humane & generous. If Saturn is exalted in no.9, Venus (goddess of Laxmi) will give the best effect of no. 2, though it may occupy any other house. If Venus is in no. 9, Saturn will automatically give the best effect of no. 9 i.e., it will be nine times beneficial.

SATURN IN 9TH HOUSE IN COMBINATION WITH & IN RELATION TO OTHER PLANETS

PLANET	HOUSE NO	EFFECT
Mercury	6	All the three planets will give best results; wife will be from a rich family. The same results will be obtained for Saturn in 11th house instead of 9th.
Or Venus	7	
Jupiter	5	Nature will be kind enough not to bring any mishap or death.
Mars	3	
Sun, Moon or Mars	3	
Moon	4	Good & noble family; rich parents & rich wife.

Sun	5	No quarrel between Saturn & Sun; rather harmonious relations between son & father; sympathetic nature. The same results will be there, if Saturn is in 11th house instead of 9th .
Jupiter	12	Very rich; but will not care for money.
Ketu	5	No bad effect on children.
Mars	4	Very bad; accursed & diseased life.
Vacant	2	Rich, but cunning & clever; will loot others.
Jupiter	10	Incidence of fire; profit from the business concerning gold & cloth; but losses from machinery etc.

SATURN HOUSE NO. 10 (PERMANENT HOUSE; RESULT OF THE PLANET)

BRINGER OF GOOD LUCK; PERSONAL HOUSE OF SATURN; SNAKE; CROCODILE; EMPTY PAPER.

If Saturn in no. 10 is helpful to the planet in no. 1, it will be twice benefic. If Saturn in no. 10 is the enemy of planet in no. 1, it will be twice harmful. Father will live at least till the native is 48 years old or even more. Saturn will bestow honour, wealth etc., every 7th year i.e., 3, 9, 15, 21, 27, 33, 39, 45, 51, 57, 63, 69, 75, 81, 87, 93, 99th year. Both Saturn & Jupiter will confer good results. The native will own all types of property & will earn great name & fame, but in the fag end of his career he may do something which may bring his downfall especially when he is religious minded. If he is subtle & clever like a snake & cruel towards others, he will dominate others. Even if Ketu is bad, Rahu & Saturn will never be bad.

Father will live at least for 39 to 48 years of his life; his own life span is 90 years; expert in magic; Must not take wine. Benefic Saturn like a black snake confers not only power & wealth, but domination over others. Sun, Moon & Mars will be Saturn's enemies. If wise, resourceful; But if Saturn is malefic, the native will be ill-fated, unfortunate & ill-omened. If house no. 10 is debilitating, it will be a Blind horoscope. The native will lead a wicked & bad life, even if all other planets are good.

SATURN IN 10TH HOUSE IN COMBINATION WITH & IN RELATION TO OTHER PLANETS

PLANET	HOUSE NO	EFFECT
Moon Jupiter	1 4	All comforts; owner of a vehicle.
Mercury	7 in annual chart	Rich in-laws & will help him financially.
Vacant	2	Saturn will be like a sleeping snake, but still good.

If Saturn in 10th house is malefic, it will be like bloody snake. If Sun, Moon, Mars or any other malefic planet is associated with Saturn no. 10, all planets will be Blind i.e., all planets will give adverse results.

Saturn in 10th house with no. 4 malefic or occupied by Sun or Moon or Mars --- Bad for wealth; remedy lies in donating gram dal (yellow Lentil).

SATURN HOUSE NO. 11 (PLANET'S OWN RESULT)

IRON; LUCKY IN-LAWS & SONS; WRITES HIS OWN DESTINY; " ARCHITECT OF HIS OWN FATE".

Saturn's effect, whether good or bad, will be decided by the position of Rahu & Ketu. If Saturn no. 11 is not aspected by any planet in no. 3, it will be dormant & asleep. Fate will be like a pitcher full of wealth, but such a man's fate will ultimately be decided by Jupiter. If Jupiter is bad i.e., if there is no old man (who must bless him) in the family, remedy lies in donating gram dal or any yellow material. Planet in no. 3 will brighten his fate & he will earn a lot through this planet in no. 3. If addicted to bad ways, Saturn's good effect will be nullified. Such a person can become exceedingly rich, if he worships Moon i.e., he must keep a brick of silver with him. Saturn in no. 11 or in association with Jupiter in any house, makes native noble, religious minded & pious; Must keep a pitcher of water while doing auspicious work; must earn a lot of wealth for 24 years. Such a man must have a son, even though all other planets may indicate otherwise; a true man; may inherit property from parents; Whenever Saturn no. 11, occupies the 1st house in the annual chart (Varsh Phal), it brings best results (11,23,36,48,57,72,84,94th year).

SATURN IN 11TH HOUSE IN COMBINATION WITH & IN RELATION TO OTHER PLANETS

PLANET	HOUSE NO	EFFECT
Sun, Mars	10	Very fortunate.
Moon	6	
Sun	1	Exalted status; lot of property & wealth.
Moon	2	
Mercury or	3	All the three will give bad results.
Sun or Jupiter	9	

✛ Throw a few drops of mustard oil on the ground at the Sun-rise (if Saturn is malefic).

SATURN HOUSE NO.12

DOMESTIC LIFE; COMFORTS; ARTIFICIAL COPPER; FISH; THRONE; ALMONDS; BALD HEADED; BURY A RED FLOWER (WHEN SUN IS IN NO.6)

No dearth of food and employment; like lord Shiva's trident over his enemies who will be vanquished; comfortable life, if bald headed; very rich and happy. Rahu and Ketu will not have adverse effect; even Mercury will keep quiet and will not harm. During every 6 - 12 years, of life, he may build a new house. Saturn will be like a protective hood, which will bestow upon the native wealth, property and happiness of the family; but such a person is secretive; nevertheless he cares little for money. Bury 12 almonds in the foundation of the house.

SATURN IN 12TH HOUSE IN COMBINATION WITH & IN RELATION TO OTHER PLANETS

PLANET	HOUSE NO	EFFECT
Sun, Moon, Mars	Not in 2	Comfortable life; happy; architect of his own fate.
Rahu	3,6	Very rich; wealthy, full of comforts.
Ketu	9,12	
Rahu	12	A benefic & helpful snake.
Sun	6	Death of wife (bury a red flower in the earth).
Rahu & Moon	12	Bad for women folk.
Rahu & Jupiter	12	Bad for men folk.

RAHU AND ITS SIGNIFICANCE IN 12 HOUSES

RAHU (GUIDE AND FRIEND OF THE DOWN TRODDEN)

Blue colour; elephant who can touch both the Zenith of the sky and the under world; elephant whose Mahouts are Saturn and Mars. It bedims the moon, but completely eclipses the sun; it is the enemy of Venus; Ketu does its bidding. If benefic and helpful, it commands the whole world.

- In the first house, it eclipses the sun and its throne.
- In second house it loses its sting and bows before the great guru i.e., Jupiter.
- In 3rd house it is exalted and protects wealth and property.
- In 4th it swears by Moon and sheds its evil ways and becomes noble and pious.
- In the 5th house man will get a son.
- It is exalted in 6th; but destroys Venus in the 7th.
- In 8th, it brings death and doom.
- In 9th & 11th, it destroys Jupiter.
- In 12th, it entails a lot of expenditure and becomes debilitating. If Mars is in 12th house, Rahu becomes ineffective.

RAHU'S MAIN FEATURES AND EFFECT

When Mars and Saturn are together (especially when Mars is benefic), Rahu will always be exalted; especially when Moon is exalted in No.4 Mars is in No.12 or Sun and Mercury in No.3 and Rahu alone in No.4 or is associated with Mercury, it will always give good results. When Rahu is malefic, its bad effect will be over after 42nd year and everything will be fine after that. If malefic, it is like a flash of lightning; volcanic lava; very wicked; ring leader of thieves; thugs and the cheat.

If Sun and Venus are together in a horoscope, Rahu will often be bad; and if sun and Saturn are together and malefic, Rahu will be malefic and Mars will also be malefic. In a horoscope if Ketu is in the earlier houses and Rahu in the later, Rahu's effect will be bad and Ketu will be Zero. If Rahu aspects the Sun, Rahu will destroy not only the house occupied by it but also the next house. During the malefic effect of Rahu i.e. loss of wealth and sickness, donate barley or wheat to the poor and keep apiece of silver with you.

It may be noted that if Rahu is exalted, it confers all the blessings and powers; Ketu always looks up to Rahu for orders i.e. Ketu is Rahu's slave and its alter ego.

RAHU HOUSE NO.1 (SIGN RESULTS)

CHIN; MATERNAL GRAND PARENTS; REMEDY FOR SUN; SOLAR ECLIPSE 2 YEARS; MAHADASHA 18 YEARS.

If Mars is in No.12, Rahu will lose its poisonous sting. There is likelihood of change, but not promotion. If Venus or Mercury or both are exalted, man is saved from the destructive effects of Rahu; but still there will be artificial darkness; Rahu in No.1 will be like an elephant climbing up the stairs i.e., man should be rich; will spend a lot on house hold; In the horoscope, Rahu occupying Sun's house, will completely eclipse it as well as the opposite house; fate will not help the man; but eclipse will be on one side and the other part of hemisphere will still be bright i.e. if the man loses one job, another job will be available some where else and after the eclipse the same bright sun will appear on the sky i.e. the man will get back the same employment and splendour.

In no.1 to 6, Rahu will give the same effect as is that of Mercury either in the horoscope or in the Annual Chart. In no. 7 to 12, Rahu's effect will be the same as that of Ketu in the horoscope or Annual Chart. Remedy-Cat's Jhilli or placenta in a copper coloured cloth will be auspicious. Donate wheat, Jaggery and copper.

RAHU IN 1ST HOUSE IN COMBINATION WITH & IN RELATION TO OTHER PLANETS

PLANET	HOUSE NO	EFFECT
Venus	7	Very rich man; but wife's health bad.
Mars	12	Rahu will be ineffective (neither bad nor good)
Sun	7	Sun will be eclipsed by Rahu; bad for career; lack of income; more expenditure; man himself responsible for his downfall.

Rahu's eclipse may last for 2 years; but in the Annual Chart may last for 12 months to the maximum.

Remedy : Cat's (jhilli) or Placenta in a copper coloured cloth will be auspicious. Donate wheat, jaggery and copper.

RAHU IN NO. 1 & SUN IN VARIOUS HOUSES

SUN'S HOUSE NO	EFFECT
1	Bad for career.
2	Irreligious.
3	Troubles for relatives.
4	Problems in one's income.
5	Rahu may now help sun; one will have male child.
6	Defamatory remarks from the sides of the relatives of daughters & sons.
7	Litigation; unhappy domestic life.
8	Unnecessary expenditure.
9	Irreligious.
10	Undependable.
11	Even the just & impartial man will be deserted by his ego.
12	Sleepless nights.

✚ Donate rice or milk or keep silver.

RAHU HOUSE NO.2 (RESULT OF PLANET)

MUD UNDER THE ELEPHANT'S FEET; MUSTARD; IN-LAWS; ARTIFICIAL SMOKE; WHEN OPPOSED TO VENUS, KEEP PURE SILVER; CLOUDS FULL OF RAIN; KING PAYING OBEISANCE TO GURU; FATE LIKE A PENDULUM.

One's financial condition will depend upon Jupiter's position; if Jupiter is exalted, man is rich otherwise bad monetary condition. If benefic Saturn occupies 1st house in the Annual Chart and simultaneously if the Jupiter is benefic, man will earn a lot. Rahu in this house will be like a king who will always pay his regards to Jupiter i.e. the Guru. It will act according to the dictates of "Guru"; there will be no theft or robbery in such a house; such a man will be an administrator; king like position; long life. If he is a sadhu, he will be an eminent one; generous and large hearted; fate will be like a pendulum - rise and fall - sometimes lot of money & sometimes downfall, depending upon the position of Rahu and Ketu in 2 - 8 / 8 - 2 houses; comfortable life; good health; a lot of expenditure but spent on good causes. Venus will confer Wealth for 25 years; will never be arrested, even through Rahu may be malefic; Jupiter, Venus, Moon, Mars, Saturn, Ketu may be malefic but Rahu if exalted will help the native. If Saturn and Rahu, both are malefic, results will be disastrous.

✚

REMEDIES To ward off the evil effect of malefic Rahu :-
- Keep pure solid silver ball with you.
- Keep saffron or gold with you.

RAHU HOUSE NO.3 (EXALTED)

BARLEY; RELATIVES; BLACK COLOUR; IVORY-INAUSPICIOUS; RICH; PROTECTOR OF LIFE AND WEALTH; CONSTABLE WITH A LOADED GUN.

Exalted Rahu will confer all powers and wealth; very rich and owner of property; Rahu alone is like a competent constable with a loaded gun protecting the native; fearless who can tame tigers even, if they are enemies; victorious over enemies; a very sincere friend; and a generous enemy; his dreams will come out true; will have premonition of coming events; Will have male children; long life; promotions; will have the power of crushing enemies; his pen will be mightier than sword; Sun's effect will be twice exalted.

RAHU IN 3RD HOUSE IN COMBINATION WITH & IN RELATION TO OTHER PLANETS

PLANET	HOUSE NO	EFFECT
Mars	3	Eminent personality.
Enemies together (Sun, Venus, Mars)	3	Enemies will not be able to harm Rahu; but happiness from wife & children; very rich.
Sun, Mercury	3	Govt. May bestow some title upon him; honour & comforts at his feet.
Any planet	12	Ketu & Mercury will be bad till 34 years of age i.e., no son till that age.
Any planet (except Mars in no. 2)	3	

✚ Keep pure silver, do not keep ivory.

RAHU HOUSE NO.4

DREAMS; CORIANDER; SLUMBERING BRAIN; RELIGIOUS MINDED; BUT SAD ABOUT WEALTH.

Both Rahu and Ketu in No.4 are afraid of Moon i.e. such a man is noble and pious; wealthy; Intelligent and learned; less of landed property. Now Saturn and Ketu will not aid and abet

Rahu in wicked deeds; even Rahu will bow before Moon, the mother, provided it is alone in No.4; fear of water upto 45 years; after the bad period of Rahu, Moon will again shine with its luster.

RAHU IN 4TH HOUSE IN COMBINATION WITH & IN RELATION TO OTHER PLANETS

PLANET	HOUSE NO	EFFECT
Moon-exalted	Or in 1	Very wealthy.
Exalted Venus	Any	Wealthy in-laws, who will help & enrich the son-in-law.
Sun or Mars or both	2	Good effect of Rahu; Sun & Mars will be helpful.
Exalted Ketu	Any	Good for parents after the birth of the child.
Moon, Sun, Mars, Jupiter	10	Eclipse; but bad days will be over like a nightmare & again there will be happiness & wealth.
Moon	4	
Malefic or debilitating Moon	Any	Bad effect on wealth.

RAHU HOUSE NO.5

ROOF; CHILDREN; HELPS THE SUN; AGE.

Sharp witted; good health; will help the sun; good for Career or Government Service. If mother is alive, she will bless him till the end. If Jupiter and Saturn are together in No.7, son will be born; he will enjoy all comforts and happiness.

RAHU IN 5TH HOUSE IN COMBINATION WITH & IN RELATION TO OTHER PLANETS

PLANET	HOUSE NO	EFFECT
Moon	5	Mystic; fond of occult; Rahu will help moon & sun; will be blessed with a son.
Sun	1,5,11	
Sun, Moon or Mars	4,6	Will be blessed with a son; more prosperous than brothers.
Or Sat & Mars	5	
Together with Jupiter Or adversely aspected		Bad for father's health & fate till 12 years.

Rahu's bad effect in 5th house in the annual chart will be visible on grandson if not on son.

✚
REMEDIES
- Keep pure silver.
- If Rahu's bad effect is discernible on domestic happiness, perform the same marriage ceremony twice with the same woman or man.

RAHU HOUSE NO.6 (EXALTED)

BLACK DOG; BRINGER OF GOOD LUCK; HELPFUL ELEPHANT.

Rahu is exalted in No.6, whereas Ketu is exalted in No.12. The effect of both of them is as exalted as that of Saturn in No.12; will spend on up-bringing and personal comforts; Rahu alone in No.6 is the lord of lightning; has the strength of an elephant; sharp brains; Promotion is always assured but no transfer. Black coloured dog will be helpful; like a Rainbow; Vanquishes enemies; If malefic in No.6, man is a notorious thief and a mad elephant.

RAHU IN 6TH HOUSE IN COMBINATION WITH & IN RELATION TO OTHER PLANETS

PLANET	HOUSE NO	EFFECT
Malefic Mercury & Ketu	Any	Ill health; bad for wealth.
Mars	12	Very bad results, if quarrels with elder brother or sister.
Mercury	12	Bad name; notorious; Rahu's result will be bad; in-laws will see ups & downs; house no. 6,2 & 7 will be bad.
Sun	2	

RAHU HOUSE NO.7 (SIGN RESULT)

BUSINESSMAN DEALING WITH SPECULATIONS; REMEDY LIES IN DONATING CO-CONUT.

Wealthy but cruel and mean Rahu; Bad results regarding parents, wife and domestic comforts;may be issue less. If he is an employee of Police or Electricity Department, it will destroy him. Domestic unhappiness for 26 years; but sun will confer best results i.e. good job and victory over enemies; Unnecessary expenditure; Rahu is Mercury's friend and in its presence its bad effects are nullified to some extent; Such a person saves for others but himself is quite miserly.

Man or Woman with Rahu in No.7 should not marry before 21 years; in that event there is possibility of either death of the partner or divorce. Worst results regarding domestic life.

REMEDIES FOR RAHU NO.7

+

REMEDIES
- At the time of marriage, parents should donate (during Kanya Dan) a solid piece of silver and it should be kept by the girl or boy. Please remember that this silver piece should never be sold.
- Throw coconut in the flowing water i.e. river etc. to ward off the evil effects of Rahu.
- Whenever Rahu occupies 7th house in the Annual Chart or it is in the 7th sign or house in the horoscope , keep a brick of silver and fill a pot with the water of the river and put a silver piece in it and close the lid. This water may be changed off and on.
- All the above remedies will ward off the evil effects of Rahu on the personal and domestic life of the individual.

Rahu in 7th house with Venus in 1st house will result in ill health of wife; she will be physically and mentally sick

RAHU HOUSE NO.8

WICKED MAN IN HIS OFFICE; SMOKE COMING OUT OF THE GRATE; COUCH AND MESSAGE OF DEATH; BITTER SMOKE.

Vicissitudes (ups and downs) of life; himself responsible for bad results; deaths for 5 years. If Mars is in No.12, Rahu will become ineffective. If Mars is malefic, worst results regarding domestic life, loss of money and may incur lot of expenditure; loss for 5 years. Malefic Rahu in No.8 works against Saturn even, howsoever it (Saturn) may be exalted; may lead to litigation and useless expenditure; Sudden accident, illness and loss of money; such a man unnecessarily pokes his nose in others' affairs

+

REMEDIES
- Rahu in No.8 in Annual chart spells doom and destruction. At that time, take 8 almonds to the temple after the commencement of 8th month after birthday and continue this till the next birthday. Leave half of the almonds at the temple daily and bring back the remaining half i.e. 4 almonds back home (10,18,28,44,58,66,73,90th year). Then donate them on the next birthday.
- Counterfeit coins or lead pieces - 8 in no.-may be thrown into the river or one coin every day for 43 days continuously.
- Keep a square piece of silver with you.

RAHU HOUSE NO.9

DEBILITATING; THRESHOLD; BLUE COLOUR; COMPLETE AND BAD SOLAR ECLIPSE; PARTIAL LUNAR ECLIPSE; DISEASES ABOVE THE THROAT; A PSYCHIATRIST CURING THE INSANE AND MAD MEN BUT DISHONEST.

He will be an expert psychiatrist who will cure the insane, but will be dishonest. Jupiter now will be silent and mum, but will not disappear because of fear of Rahu in No.9. Affection and unity with brothers will make him prosperous, otherwise may not have any male issue. If irreligious, children may be good for nothing; but business connected with Saturn (i.e. machinery etc.) will be beneficial; Jupiter and Rahu will be of equal strength and both of them will be opposed to each other. When Rahu starts at 42, it will be beneficial and may entail a lot of expenditure for house-hold purposes. Now Rahu will be 9 times malefic; may also adversely affect house No.5 (Sons) & no. 11 (income); When the planets of house No.4 in the horoscope occupy the 1st house in the Annual Chart (4,16,28,40,52,64,76,88th year), Rahu's adverse effect will be discernible on business etc.

Rahu in the 9th house with Venus in no. 8 or 10, the man will be irreligious & careless.

✚   Keep gold or yellow things on body.

RAHU HOUSE NO.10

SUSPICIOUS; STINKING DRAIN; POND FULL OF DIRTY WATER; IF BENEFIC HELPFUL LIKE THE BRIGHT SAPPHIRE OR SNAKE'S HOOD; AND IF MALEFIC, LIKE SNAKE'S FANG WHICH MAY STING.

Short sighted, or short lived, if not helped by Mars. During bad days, seek Mars' help i.e. donate some red lentils (Masur Daal); if Mars is benefic he will be a successful businessman; if Mars is malefic such a person may involve himself in litigation for 5 years, which may result in loss of face and money. Saturn is Rahu's friend, who will show his result on wealth. Rahu's job is to misguide a man on to evil ways; but Saturn moves both ways - good as well as evil. In other words if Saturn is exalted, Rahu will be doubly blessed and if Saturn is malefic, Rahu will be doubly malefic and harmful. If benefic, Rahu is like Snakes' sapphire, for which everybody aspires and if malefic its sting is poisonous. It may be remembered that the effect of Rahu, Ketu and Mercury in No.10 solely depends upon Saturn.

RAHU IN 10TH HOUSE IN COMBINATION WITH & IN RELATION TO OTHER PLANETS

PLANET	HOUSE NO	EFFECT
Benefic Mars	Any	Rahu will be ineffective.
Moon	4	May break his head.

RAHU HOUSE NO.11

SAPPHIRE

Such a person may lose father and he will be almost Zero in wealth till 36 years; Rahu will adversely affect this house i.e. rich during Jupiter's period, but later hand to mouth living; will be well off during father's life; In a nutshell, man must wear gold chain or any chain made of yellow material or yellow clothes on his person.

RAHU IN 11TH HOUSE IN COMBINATION WITH & IN RELATION TO OTHER PLANETS

PLANET	HOUSE NO	EFFECT
Saturn	3,5	Now Rahu will not adversely effect father's life.
Saturn, Ketu	1,3	Self made rich man; will not demand anything from mother or father; will not cheat people; nor will be wicked.
Ketu	5	Bad for children i.e., Sons.

RAHU HOUSE NO.12 (DEBILITATING; RESULTS OF PERMANENT HOUSE AND PLACEMENT OF PLANET)

Worst; coal; elephant; snow or sea leopard; Don-Quixote (living in a dream land); full of fanciful ideas.

If Rahu in No. 6 was like a Rain-bow, in No.12, it is all stifling smoke; If Venus is in No. 11 or 10, man will be blessed with daughter; the more the number of daughters, the more the wealth. If Mars is also in No.12, Rahu's adverse effect is completely nullified; Mahout (Mars) and elephant (Rahu) work in unison and confer royal comforts. Rahu's effect mostly depends on Mercury; if Mercury is exalted, Rahu's effect will be good and if Mercury is malefic, Rahu will be equally malefic.

Rahu in No.12 will involve unnecessary and useless expenditure; life full of litigation, criminal cases; embezzlement, clashes, bad thoughts etc; bad for family life; loss of wealth and bad relations with friends; but it will not adversely affect his life; such a person is like a Don-Quixote, who is full of fanciful ideas and who dreams of big things, but God has different ideas. If Rahu in No.12 is in exalted sign, the in-laws will be rich and he will be protected from the onslaughts and attacks of enemies. Exalted Saturn's and Jupiter's result may be good, but Rahu's own result will be bad and adverse.

✦   Keel 'Sugar' or 'Saunf' (fennel) in the bed room or take your meals in the kitchen

KETU AND ITS SIGNIFICANCE IN 12 HOUSES

KETU (LORD GANESHA); DERVISH (FAKIR)

Short sighted; Mascot i.e. god of good luck for the family; son; calf; pig; faithful dog leading the people to a temple or 'Dargah' -- the resting place of a sage; Premonition of death; future generation.

KETU'S POSITION IN 12 HOUSES :

KETU'S HOUSE NO	EFFECT
1	Blesses the man with a son; but he is full of imaginary worries.
2	Good administration & benefic travels.
3	Debilitating; ups & downs of life; unhappy with relatives; whining (groaning) dog, but noble fakir; may settle elsewhere.
4	Late birth of a son.
5	Noble sons.
6	Debilitating; lunar eclipse, but victorious over enemies.
7	Brave like a lion.
8	Fills the grave with the children.
9	Bringer of good luck for father.
10	Dependent upon Saturn.
11	Jackal like dog; Saturn totally dependent upon Ketu & vice versa.
12	Very rich; exalted.

KETU'S RELATIONSHIP & ASSOCIATION WITH OTHER PLANETS :

PLANET	EFFECT
JUPITER	Eminent & noble.
SUN	Storm; bad for son & maternal uncles.
MOON	Dog's sweat; both debilitating.
VENUS	Lustful; calf.
MARS	Tiger like dog.
MERCURY	Dog's life in its head; one is good & other is bad.
SATURN	Ears missing; Saturn is dependent upon Ketu.
RAHU	Ketu is Rahu's slave & carries out its wishes & orders.

IMPORTANT FEATURES OF KETU

- Ketu eclipses the Moon, but bedims the sun.
- When Ketu is with Saturn or Mars it is not bad, but if the third planet joins them, the results are absolutely bad.
- Best if it joins the Jupiter, but worst if it joins the Moon.
- With Mercury it is wicked and bad but with Venus it is helpful (to Venus).
- If Ketu is placed in the earlier houses, Jupiter becomes debilitating. If it is reverse, then Moon is debilitating.
- Moon pacifies the Mars, but Ketu makes it malefic.
- Ketu is the angel of goodness; prophet of travels; helpful till the end.

REMEDIES FOR MALEFIC KETU

+
REMEDIES
- During ill health, donate rice or milk and keep silver.
- If Son goes astray, donate blanket.
- During urinary troubles, wear silver rings or silky thread on both the toes of feet.
- If Ketu is malefic (especially when Venus and Moon are together in the Horoscope), and the child's body starts drying up, apply mud paste on the body and allow it to dry up at least for one hour ; then bathe the child; do it for 43 days.

KETU HOUSE NO.1

LEG; MATERNAL GRANDFATHER'S HOUSE; MALEFIC WIND; DISEASES BELOW THE NAVEL.

BENEFIC KETU IN NO.1

One may receive orders for travel and he may be worried but ultimately he may not travel at all. He may lose one job but will get another one immediately. He must not worry on this account. Now Sun will also be exalted although it may be debilitating in No.6 or 7. Whenever Ketu occupies the first house in the Annual Chart, it is a clear indication of the birth of a son or grandson. Even if Ketu is malefic, Jupiter will confer exalted results. Such a person will bring good luck to his farther and boost his sagging finances. If Mars occupies 12th house, Ketu will never be malefic; Ketu in No.1 will never adversely affect sun in No.6 or 7. When Ketu is debilitating after marriage (regarding the birth of a son), Saturn will be helpful. If Ketu is malefic or debilitating, such a person is born outside his ancestral house (away from native land, Inn, Hospital, Maternal Grandfather's house etc.). The place or house of birth will be destroyed.

KETU IN 1ST HOUSE IN COMBINATION WITH & IN RELATION TO OTHER PLANETS

PLANET	HOUSE NO	EFFECT
Mars	12	Ketu's effect will never be bad.
Sun	6, 7	Now sun will not be debilitating & malefic.
Vacant	2 & 6	Bad for mercury (business) & Venus (domestic comforts).

KETU HOUSE NO. 2 (PLANET'S OWN RESULTS)

PROSPEROUS ADMINISTRATOR; TRAVELLER; MOLE; TAMARIND.

Every new travel will be in a different direction i.e., if he first travels to the South, then he will travel to West & later to East; transfer is a must, but promotion can not be assured; Lot of travel on land which may be beneficial; generous & large hearted in good sense; Will earn a lot, but will spend lavishly; May not be beneficial for mother; but will be pride of his wife.

KETU IN 2ND HOUSE IN COMBINATION WITH & IN RELATION TO OTHER PLANETS

PLANET	HOUSE NO	EFFECT
Vacant & Ketu all alone	8 in annual chart	Lot of travel; but prosperous administrator; transfer & promotion will bring prosperity.
Sun	12	Self made rich after 24 years.
Moon or Mars (except Rahu)	8	Bad; short lived.

KETU HOUSE NO 3 (DEBILITATING)

SPINAL CHORD; BANANA; BOILS & WOUNDS; WHINING (GROANING) DOG; BUT NOBLE FAKIR (ASCETIC); WHEN IN TRAVEL, DONATE RICE, JAGGERY OR WHEAT; WHEN SUFFERING FROM BOILS & WOUNDS, DONATE GRAM DAL (YELLOW LENTILS).

A kind hearted man, who remembers the good turn done to him but forgets the evil done to him i.e., he is grateful to the benefactor, but forgives the evil-doer; always helpful to others; a noble fakir or sage; may live away from relatives in distant & foreign lands; always restless for brothers; may be opposed by relatives; may waste his wealth in litigation.

KETU IN 3RD HOUSE IN COMBINATION WITH & IN RELATION TO OTHER PLANETS

PLANET	HOUSE NO	EFFECT
Mars	12	Good luck at 24 or after the birth of a son.
Moon or Mars	3,4	Poor.

+
REMEDIES • If suffering from lung diseases or ill-health, throw yellow lentils (gram dal) in flowing water or put a yellow dot of saffron on fore-head; if suffering from diseases of spinal cord, arthritis, back ache etc.; Wear gold chain & throw 'Til' in the flowing water or donate cow made of silver.
• To ward off harmful travel, throw rice & wheat in the flowing water.

KETU HOUSE NO. 4 (SIGN RESULTS)

HEARING; REMEDY FOR JUPITER; LUNAR ECLIPSE; OCEANIC TIDES; BARKING DOG SCARING THE CHILDREN.

Ketu in no. 4 destroys both the Moon & itself i.e., it destroys mother as well as male child;

should donate "Gram dal" (Yellow lentils) for beneficial & better effects; such a man has more daughters; man of determination; late birth of son; rich; Ketu or Rahu in no. 4 makes the man noble, pious & religious minded. Wicked planets will not exercise bad effect, but all planets will be benefic & good; wise & resourceful; trouble for 6 years; complete lunar eclipse. If malefic & debilitating, person is like a barking dog that scares the children; bad health; diabetic; late birth of a son.

Ketu in 4th house with Moon or Mars in 3rd or 4th house ---- Ketu (son) & Moon (mother), both are debilitating and bad.

KETU HOUSE NO. 5

URINARY TRACT; WATCHMAN (FAITHFUL DOG) OF JUPITER.
Only two sons and that completes the family. If Jupiter is exalted, all is fine. If Jupiter is debilitating, late birth of a son (may be after 45th year) or else the child may suffer from asthma. If Jupiter is exalted, Ketu (son) is equally exalted; but Jupiter's effect will be bad. In short, Ketu in no. 5 will confer monetary benefits.

KETU IN 5TH HOUSE IN COMBINATION WITH & IN RELATION TO OTHER PLANETS

PLANET	HOUSE NO	EFFECT
Saturn	9	Now Saturn will not adversely affect the children, nor will there be domestic clash.
Venus	4	
Jupiter, Sun or Moon	4,6,12	Good financial condition.
Moon or Mars	3,4	Poor; pitiable plight.
Debilitating Jupiter	Any	Will lose health & beauty; child may have asthma.

KETU HOUSE NO. 6 (PERMANENT HOUSE; PLANET'S OWN RESULTS)

DEBILITATING; FULL LUNAR ECLIPSE; RABBIT; MALE SPARROW; FOREIGN LAND; TIGER LIKE DOG; PLACE OF WORSHIP.
Ketu in no. 6 is debilitating. It is an irony of fate that Ketu is debilitating in its own house; Wear gold ring in left hand; can easily come out of enemy's trap through sheer intelligence and grit; very shrewd and clever indeed. If Jupiter is exalted, wealthy; otherwise a mad barking dog. In this house the reverse happens i.e., Ketu helps its enemy, Mercury & destroys its friend, Venus. If both Ketu & Jupiter are malefic in this house, it may lead to meaningless travel; man may have to face enemies for no fault of his. It is bad for maternal uncles. If Jupiter & Ketu are exalted in this house; age 80 years; happy maternal uncles; affectionate; sons; Wealthy & comfortable life in foreign lands.

KETU IN 6TH HOUSE IN COMBINATION WITH & IN RELATION TO OTHER PLANETS

PLANET	HOUSE NO	EFFECT
Mercury	6	Both will be exalted.
Exalted Jupiter	Any	Good sons; shrewd & brave.
Jupiter or Mars	Should not be in 6 or 12	Exalted results of Ketu (son).
Moon	2	Bad for mother & maternal uncles.
Mercury	12	Ketu's effect will be bad & adverse.

KETU HOUSE NO. 7

SECOND SON; PIG; DONKEY; SHEPHERD'S DOG; AS FEROCIOUS AS TIGER; CHILD'S COMPANION.

After 24th year, he will earn money, which may last him till 40th year i.e., he will be a very rich man. He will be victorious over enemies; After the bad period of Mercury i.e., 34th year, he will be a very rich man. All will help him. His enemies will be doomed. Ketu will be like a shepherd's dog which will love its master & flock, but will chase away the enemies. If Ketu is assisted by Mercury, Jupiter or Venus, such a person will not lose his job. Saturn & Venus will never be bad; even enemies (Sun or Moon) will themselves be doomed & destroyed. Of course, Ketu will have adverse effect on the opposite house. Even if Ketu is debilitating, but when it occupies the 1st house, it gives the best results (7,19,31,43,55,67,74,95th year).

KETU HOUSE NO. 8

EARS; POWER OF HEARING; A MIRAGE OR AN ILLUSION; CHEAT; A WHINING (GROANING) DOG, HAVING PREMONITION OF DEATH.

It is house no. 12, which will decide whether Ketu is benefic or malefic. If Mercury is exalted, Ketu cannot be bad. Ketu will be asleep now; but the dog wakes up at the slightest stir; Moon's remedy i.e., donation of rice is recommended; long life more than 80 years. If Jupiter is malefic & in house no. 8 Ketu is associated with another planet, person will remain unhappy with children or may even be deprived of a son till 48th year. Ketu's effect will be bad, if house no. 2 is vacant. Jupiter's remedy (i.e., donation of gram dal or keep saffron) is recommended. If Mars occupies house no. 12, Ketu can never be malefic; if Mars is debilitating, worst results are discernible regarding life & prosperity of children. If Ketu is in house no. 8, Venus & Mercury are usually in bad houses, but if Jupiter or Mars are not in House no. 6 or 12, Ketu's effect will never be debilitating & bad.

KETU IN 8TH HOUSE IN COMBINATION WITH & IN RELATION TO OTHER PLANETS

PLANET	HOUSE NO	EFFECT
Benefic Mars & Jupiter	1,2	Now Ketu (son) is exalted & no remedy is required.
Moon	2	
Malefic Moon	Any	Donate rice, silver or milk.
Jupiter Or Mars	6,12	Bad results regarding son & wealth.
Malefic Mars	4	
Saturn Or Mars	7	Worst results regarding property, houses & children.
Mars	12	His brother may have died a year before his birth.
Saturn	1	

+
REMEDIES • Bury a piece of white & black blanket in a deserted place. If any other planet is associated with Ketu in no. 8, place the things concerning those planets in that blanket also and bury them all.
• Donate a new black & white blanket to the temple or poor man or some voluntary social organisation such as orphanage etc.

KETU HOUSE NO. 9 (EXALTED)

BLACK & WHITE DOG; BITCH WHICH HAS DELIVERED PUPS IS AUSPICIOUS; DOG WHICH UNDERSTANDS MASTER'S COMMAND; OBEDIENT SON.

Bringer of good luck to parents; limited no. of children, but all happy and rich. If Moon & Jupiter are exalted, lucky for the paternal & maternal sides; Promotion is certain, but transfer cannot be assured. The native is brave like a pig & faithful like a dog; May live abroad or a foreign country; away from brothers; self made rich; a square brick of gold in house is auspicious; Ketu in this house is more powerful & exalted than Jupiter; The native believes in the dictum " Let the dead past bury its dead " & be optimistic for the future; inspires others; Ketu is as exalted as Saturn & Venus combined; Beneficial travels. If Ketu & Venus are together in this house, the results are fantastic i.e., he becomes exceedingly rich. If Ketu & Moon are together in the 9th house, it will be bad for mother's relatives.

KETU IN 9TH HOUSE IN COMBINATION WITH & IN RELATION TO OTHER PLANETS

PLANET	HOUSE NO	EFFECT
Exalted moon	Any	Good for mother's relatives.
Exalted Jupiter or Rahu Or exalted house	2	An eminent position & status; adviser; good for father's relatives.
Enemies (Moon or Mars)	3	Death of son.
Malefic Saturn	Any	Thief; dacoit; but financially poor.

KETU HOUSE NO. 10 (SIGN RESULTS)

RAT; FINAL VERDICT LIES WITH SATURN; REMEDY FOR MARS (RED LENTILS OR MASUR DAL); OPPORTUNIST (GOOD OR BAD SENSE); "LONER"

Rich; but may lead a lustful & luxurious life; all will depend upon the position of Saturn; If Saturn is exalted or is in friendly houses, even mud will turn into gold (it will be just like Mida's touch) & if Saturn is malefic or in enemy's house, it may spell financial disaster, loss of health & prosperity. One must be of good character; After 48th year, keep a dog. If Saturn is malefic, the man is an evil genius, lustful, addicted to bad habits; otherwise, Saturn & Jupiter will confer exalted results such as wealth & sons. Such a person is a loner who shuns company.

KETU IN 10TH HOUSE IN COMBINATION WITH & IN RELATION TO OTHER PLANETS

PLANET	HOUSE NO	EFFECT
Saturn	6	A famous sports person.
Saturn	4	Useless sons; remedy lies in donating black & white blanket (see Ketu no. 8).

✚ Keep an utensil of silver filled with honey.

KETU HOUSE NO. 11

PRECIOUS (BLACK & WHITE STONE); BLACK DOG AUSPICIOUS; JACKAL LIKE DOG.

Self made rich man; will create a lot of property; If Saturn is malefic, Ketu's result (regarding house & son) will be malefic & bad; but in a woman's horoscope, it is not so, rather it is reverse. Moon in such a horoscope is malefic & debilitating. Ketu is as powerful as Saturn. If Saturn is exalted, Ketu automatically confers exalted results. Moon is eclipsed, when associated with Ketu. It confers Raj Yoga (exalted status), provided Mercury does not occupy 3rd house.

KETU IN 11TH HOUSE IN COMBINATION WITH & IN RELATION TO OTHER PLANETS

PLANET	HOUSE NO	EFFECT
Saturn	3	Eleven times good; lot of wealth.
Mercury	3	Moon's result is bad (especially the Ketu is in 1st house in the annual chart i.e., 5,11,23,36,48th year).
Debilitating Saturn	Any	Bad for property & son; but not so in a woman's horoscope. First male issue may be born dead. Keep white radish under the woman's pillow & donate it to the temple in the morning. It will protect the woman & the next male issue.
Not occupied by Mercury	3	Raj yoga (eminent position).

KETU HOUSE NO. 12 (EXALTED)

FISH; ADOPTED SON; BRINGER OF GOOD LUCK; LUXURIOUS LIFE; INHERITED PROPERTY.

Promotion is certain, but transfer is not assured. After the birth of a son, one becomes rich; earns name & fame; sucking of thumb is auspicious for family happiness; keep a black & white dog; sons will be helpful & may bring good fortune; Ketu (son) is exalted in this house and confers the best results; but unhappy with brothers; His family members (sons, daughters, brothers etc.) will occupy good positions. In fact, everything will be fine & grand. In such a horoscope, Venus, Saturn & Jupiter will confer good results, but Mars (i.e., elder brother & relatives) will not be helpful.

KETU IN 12TH HOUSE IN COMBINATION WITH & IN RELATION TO OTHER PLANETS

PLANET	HOUSE NO	EFFECT
Vacant (except Rahu)	6	Ketu's exalted result; wealthy, inherits property; all fine & splendid.
Rahu & enemy planet	6	Ketu will be meaningless & will not be exalted because of being aspected by enemies also.

CHAPTER 19

TWO PLANETS IN THE SAME HOUSE

COMBINATION OF TWO PLANETS IN ONE HOUSE

Invariably the planets confer their own individual effect; but sometimes they harmoniously blend & enhance each other's power manifold - benefic or malefic.

1. JUPITER - SUN

Jupiter (father) & Sun (son) confer the most exalted results when they are together in a house. Individually they may not be good, but when they join together, they become beneficial & bestow good results. They become Full Moon (in the best sense); Such a man possesses tiger's strength i.e., he enjoys eminent status, besides a lot of wealth. Here in this case, there is complete blending of both the planets; father & son will help each other.

Such a person is learned, wise, intellectual & eminent; he possesses the virtues of Lord Brahma (the creator) & Lord Vishnu (the supporter).

SUN & JUPITER WITH OTHER COMBINATIONS

COMBINATION	EFFECT
Venus in later houses	Honour, name & fame; noble children.
Both aspect the moon	Exalted moon; eminent status or job; promotion; prosperity; even if moon is harmed by enemies, it will give beneficial results.
Both aspect each other & moon is exalted.	Beneficial travels on govt. duty; lot of income.
Venus in earlier houses.	Bad results.
Both aspected by Saturn or both in no. 4 & Saturn in no. 10.	Both the planets are asleep; loss of wealth & business; but if Saturn is exalted, results are good, otherwise bad.

JUPITER - SUN IN VARIOUS HOUSES

HOUSE NO	EFFECT
1	King like position; an eminent administrator; long life; complete domestic happiness; even though he may be a dunce; sudden death.
2	Resides in an imposing mansion; grand life; bold like a tiger; but cruel.
3	Wealthy, but should not be greedy; otherwise a loser.
4	Splendid life; eminent position in govt.; but all is destroyed if Saturn is in 10th house.
5 & Moon in no. 4	Exalted status; wealthy children; self made rich; victory over enemies; even if Rahu or Ketu or Saturn joins this house, Jupiter - sun will remain benefic & exalted. if Mercury occupies this house, Jupiter will be asleep.
6,7,10,11	Individual effect (whether good or bad); but combined effect is good in old age.
8	Conqueror of death & best fate.
9,12	Complete prosperity & progress; wealthy.

+   REMEDY (IF MALEFIC) : Do not take bribes & keep gold or saffron in the house.

2. JUPITER - MOON COMBINED & THEIR SIGNIFICANCE

INHERITED WEALTH; LAW DEPTT.; BANYAN TREE.

Parents are like huge Banyan tree that will give refreshing & cool shade i.e., he will inherit lot of wealth. Moon (mother) will confer the best results i.e., such a person will be rich; will have mother's blessings; may not be wise, but will have a lot of wealth & property; There is a saying " As the man grows old, he may become infirm, but becomes rich.". So is the case with such a person. When both are exalted, their power becomes manifold. Education for 24 years; travels for 20 years; very wealthy; additional income; comfortable old age.

When Venus - Mars, Venus - Saturn or Mars - Saturn are opposite Jupiter - Moon, best results are conferred.

MOON & JUPITER WITH OTHER COMBINATIONS

COMBINATION	EFFECT
Together with or aspected by Mars	Very wealthy.
Together with or aspected by Sun	Successful businessman; writer.
Together with or aspected by Venus	Decrease in wealth after marriage.
Together with or aspected by Saturn	Others will gain; for friends he is like a philosopher's stone.
Together with or aspected by Mercury	Now Mercury will not oppose; rather it will be helpful.

When Jupiter & Moon are in the earlier houses & Mercury is in later houses, all will be fine & exalted. When both of them occupy good house, they confer best results. Mercury in no. 2 may be bad for father's life & Mercury in no. 4 may be bad for mother. Such a person may be millionaire, but may have to face lot of troubles.

JUPITER - MOON IN VARIOUS HOUSES

HOUSE NO	EFFECT
1	Exalted results of both; must not marry before 28 years; otherwise bad for newly constructed house & male child.
2	Best & exalted results of both; Jupiter will give the exalted effect of no. 4 now; noble & pious; like a huge Banyan tree providing cool shade to many; additional income; but association with Rahu and Mercury will be bad & poisonous.
3	Prosperous; fortunate; exalted position; will be helpful to relatives; but Mercury's association will be bad.
4	Parents will be like a huge Banyan tree providing shade & cool breeze; fountain of wealth right from childhood; exalted results as regards wealth, comforts & peace of mind etc.
5	Sun will confer exalted & best results; wealthy business man; writer etc.
6	The effect of Mercury & Ketu (whether good or bad) will be reflected in these two planets (Jupiter & Moon); providing water (well or hand pump) to hospital & cremation ground will be auspicious.

7	Ill health in childhood; after 24th year, parents unhappy; decrease in wealth after marriage or after the birth of a daughter; but may earn a lot through speculations & investments.
8	Long life; may destroy brothers for the sake of wealth; one brother may be helpful, other may fight & oppose; anyhow he will not lose wealth. malefic Mars.
9	Exalted fate like a tree watered by milk; blessings of parents; may also inherit from mother; beneficial travels for 20 years; the most exalted combination indeed; best results in no. 9 in annual chart; if such a person sells his daughter or takes money from her, he will be doomed & destroyed.
10	Worst results; haughty, audacious & rude even towards father, short-sighted and foolish. Parents may be rich, but the native at the fag end of his life will be poor. Nevertheless he will behave like a true man; (Throw off and on a copper coin in the river).
11	Humanitarian works; will help others; will depend upon the planets of no.3, if that house is vacant. Jupiter - Moon in no. 11 will be meaningless. even planets in no. 5 will be ineffective.
12	Wealthy like a king; but ascetic like Raja Janak; loss of wealth after marriage & birth of a daughter. (Bury a silver cup or vessel in the foundation of the house - it will help).

3. JUPITER - VENUS AND THEIR SIGNIFICANCE

Such a person is a successful lover; women will always help him. If a person is lustful, both the planets (combined) will give bad results. If Jupiter -Venus are in exaltation or in their own sign and free from adverse aspects and occupy a kendra or a trikona, such a person sports with a beautiful damsel, is wealthy, charitable and is the master of horses.

JUPITER - VENUS IN VARIOUS HOUSES

HOUSE NO	EFFECT
1	Like an ill fated sadhu; unhappy family life; will prosper only after the death of father or spouse.
2	Problems in the birth of a son; if a gold-smith, he will be destroyed; but if he deals with mud i.e., agriculture etc. he will prosper i.e., mud will turn into gold and gold into dust.

3	Prosperous and wealthy; woman will be bold like a man; will help brothers financially.
4	Wife may die or leave the husband after the birth of a child; Jupiter no.4 will be good, if the person is not lustful.
5	Will earn a lot through knowledge and education; noble children
6.	Sons may die; even if they survive, may cause loss etc.; he must respect his wife and she should wear a gold pin or clip on the hair.
7	Lucky if deals in a business concerning Mercury i.e., investments & allied business; even if loses money he will not have hand to mouth living; will again become prosperous; adopted child will enjoy at his expense; remedy lies in leading a pure & noble life; if lustful, philanderer & womaniser, he will be unhappy & may lose his wealth; if sun is also malefic, he will be destroyed by his lustful ways.
7 & Mars in no.4	Malefic Jupiter; will be like castrated bull; will not have any issue; adopted child will enjoy.
7 & Mercury in No.7	Mercury will be helpful; such a man will never be short of food, though he may have less of money.
8	For wealth, Jupiter's effects of No.2 is discernible i.e. he will be wealthy, but Venus will give the same effect as of No.8 - which will give comforts and happiness except wealth. In other words, Jupiter and Venus will give different results.
9	Best results of Jupiter no. 9 and Venus No.7 - comfortable life; beneficial travels for 20 years. If malefic, bad domestic life.
10	May destroy ancestral inheritance, but money earned by him will remain intact; If lustful and of bad character, will destroy everything; will turn gold into dust; Paramour or concubine will destroy him physically and financially; unhappy regarding father, children and brothers; will always dream of the "days that are no more".
11	He will be like a pale 'Pandu' (reference to Pandu in Mahabharata) i.e. may even be impotent, fond of masturbation.
12	Comfortable and happy married life, but bad for speculations.

4. JUPITER - MARS AND THEIR SIGNIFICANCE

If Mars is exalted or benefic, such a person is just and fair; will have exalted status; Leader among colleagues; brave; will have God's blessings. If both Mars (benefic) and Jupiter aspect Saturn, such a person will be a terror for enemies and will be rich. If Mars is malefic, the person is ill fated, will bear losses for 5 years and illness & deaths in the family. During Saturn's bad period, Jupiter will be the deciding factor and vice-versa.

JUPITER - MARS IN VARIOUS HOUSES

HOUSE NO	EFFECT
1	Exalted and eminent position; very rich; even Rahu and Ketu will confer best results.
2	Rich affectionate and helpful in-laws. If Mercury is in No.6, person is rich and will earn more; if Mars is malefic, bad results.
3	Will preserve inherited wealth; will not lose even a paisa; will meditate and pray a lot.
4	No dearth of man folk but there may be lack of money.
5	Wealthy for 28 years after the birth of a child; must give something in charity; should not accept charity or bribe.
6	Himself eldest brother, but may be bad for sons (Bad Mercury and Ketu); if Mercury is in No.6, it will have best effect on personal fate and domestic happiness.
7	Such a man will be under debt, even though he is having good income.
8	Both will have their own individual effect.
9	Best results regarding Sons, wealth and domestic happiness.
10	His fate will be decided by house No.4 and 6. If they are vacant, one may have gilded gold instead of Pure gold; nevertheless will become rich by cheating and fleecing others.
11	Will be rich as long as father is alive; thereafter he will be like a bee-hive without honey.
12	Best results regarding children and wife; will bless all.

5. JUPITER - MERCURY AND THEIR SIGNIFICANCE

If both Jupiter and Mercury are together, it is Jupiter who is the loser i.e. Jupiter's effect will be bad, but this bad effect is nullified to a great extent, if
- when Jupiter occupies House No.10,11 (Saturn's House) or No.5 (Sun's House) in the annual Chart, OR
- either Saturn or Sun may occupy House No.2,5,9,12 in the Annual Chart, OR

Saturn may occupy House No.5 and Sun House No.2,5,9,12 in the Annual Chart. If Sun or Moon or Saturn (any one of them) is exalted or benefic, Jupiter's effect will be good. In house No.2 or 4 Mercury will not be bad. If Jupiter is benefic and Mercury is exalted, it confers Raj Yoga (Royal Status); but if both of them are together and fully aspect the Moon, travels will be harmful.

JUPITER - MERCURY IN VARIOUS HOUSES

HOUSE NO	EFFECT
1	If benefic - rich or administrator; but if malefic, foolish Sadhu.
2	Learned; great Preacher.
3	If benefic, brave and contented; otherwise bad for spouse.
4	If benefic, eminent position; otherwise cowardly acts will destroy him and may commit suicide, if addicted to bad ways.
5	Rich and fortunate, provided a son is born on Thursday and the daughter should not be born on Wednesday.
6	If benefic such a person meditates and prays and if malefic he is lustful and given to bad ways.
7	Ups and Downs in life; sometimes rich and sometimes poor. Daughter's Mercury in 7th will be auspicious but bad for son i.e., may have to adopt some one.
8	Always sick.
9	Ill-fated, and short-lived.
10	Prosperous and rich.
11	Rich, when both the planets occupy 1st house in the Annual Chart (11,23,36,48th year) he may become very wealthy; comfortable life; happy domestic life.
12	Good for self; comfortable life; long-lived; but will be an ordinary business-man.

6. JUPITER - SATURN AND THEIR SIGNIFICANCE

VARIOUS COMBINATIONS OF JUPITER & SATURN

COMBINATION	EFFECT
Jupiter and Saturn (combined) when Saturn in malefic house and Jupiter exalted.	Bad for self, but will enrich others.
When Jupiter is malefic and Saturn benefic	Will overcome all impediments
When both are exalted and Sun occupies House No.1	Best results.
When both are malefic and Sun is in No.1	Loss of money and limb.
Saturn exalted and Jupiter malefic and sun in No.1	Loss of money and No loss of limb.
Jupiter exalted and Saturn Malefic and Sun in No.1	Loss of limb only.

When they are together in No.1 (where Saturn is debilitating) or in No.10 (when Jupiter is debilitating) both give good results.

When both of them are aspected by Venus -- such a person shows off; increase in wealth after marriage.

JUPITER - SATURN IN VARIOUS HOUSES

HOUSE NO	EFFECT
1	Poor Sadhu or Teacher.
2	Erudite scholar; intellectual; now Moon will not be debilitating, even though it may be in No.8. Moon's result will be exalted. If one of them is malefic, When Jupiter--Saturn occupy 2nd house in annual chart (9,21,33,45,57,65,74,96th year), bad result on health, money and fathers' life. Remedy lies in placating Saturn i.e. donate coconut or Maash (black lentils) or iron.
3	Rich but ordinary life; comfortable old age; may lose father or wealth at 9 or 18 or 36.
4	Saturn will be helpful; even a snake's sting will cure paralysis and once again man will be fit.

5	Ordinary fate, but honour and name; may be opposed and harmed by Officers or may be involved in litigation (criminal or civil cases), but ultimately will be victorious.
6	If Saturn is exalted and Jupiter is quiet (i.e. Rahu and Ketu in No.2) life will be full of domestic happiness; If Jupiter is benefic and Saturn is debilitating (adversely aspected by No.2), family life will not be happy.
7	Lot of property; good man; may be sick in childhood; Saturn will be exalted; If both of them are benefic, Moon or Venus or Mars are also benefic; best results regarding spouse, mother and elder brothers. If Mars is in No.6 to 12 and exalted, Moon and Venus (mother and Wife) will not be adversely affected; will be rich. When Moon or Venus or Mars is malefic and any of them occupies No.1 in the Annual Chart, adverse results will be discernible and when Sun is in No.1 in Annual Chart, he may face bad financial condition (9,18,36th year)
8	Average wealth, but long life.
9	Very rich; will earn a lot; will be counted among the richest persons; may earn money through fraudulent means.
10	Best for self, may earn great name and fame.
10 and Sun in No.4	Saturn will destroy both the Jupiter and Sun; may be ill-fated and financially bankrupt, but will earn fraudulently for 12 years.
11	His fate will be decided by House No.3; If No.3 is vacant, Saturn will be exalted and will give the effect of No.11. Others may gain through such a person, who will be a sincere friend and lover. If Mercury is malefic in the horoscope, the native may face financial problems.
12	Noble; very rich; now Rahu and Ketu will not have adverse effects. Jupiter and Saturn will confer individual results of house No.12; will earn a lot but will not care for money; lot of wealth after marriage.

7. JUPITER - RAHU & THEIR SIGNIFICANCE

Jupiter moves straight & fast like a tiger, whereas Rahu (elephant) does not move straight; Both are enemies & the results are bad, When Sun or Moon or Mars is benefic & Rahu is exalted. Jupiter will confer exalted results, but when Rahu is in Jupiter's house or is with him, Jupiter will give bad results. Jupiter may be quiet, but not finished. In short, if Jupiter & Rahu are together in no. 1 to 6, Jupiter will be the Master of both the worlds i.e., mundane & spiritual. In 7 to 12, Jupiter will be the master of mundane world. Ketu's remedy is helpful; if Ketu (disobedient son) is also malefic, Moon may be appeased & worshipped i.e., Barley may be washed with milk & thrown into the river for 43 days. These remedies may be adopted when the effect of Jupiter - Rahu is bad.

JUPITER - RAHU IN VARIOUS HOUSES

HOUSE NO	EFFECT
1	Generous & large hearted.
2	Humane; will do good & help the poor; Rahu will be ineffective.
3	Shrewd; bold; If malefic, remedy lies through Ketu (son).
4	Exalted Moon will confer best results.
5	Leader & administrator.
7	Either the father or father-in-law will be alive; If both are alive, one may suffer from asthma; comfortable life in youth.
8	An ordinary & insipid life.
12	Intelligent & skillful; Jupiter & Rahu will not be each other's enemy now.
6,9,10,11	Will give individual effects.

8. JUPITER - KETU & THEIR SIGNIFICANCE

This combination is benefic. Jupiter is the teacher & Ketu is the disciple and Ketu's effect (son) will be exalted.

JUPITER - KETU IN VARIOUS HOUSES

HOUSE NO	EFFECT
1	Comfortable life.
2	Compassionate; exalted status, if no. 8 is vacant; Prosperous administrator, if friendly planets in no. 8.
4	Learned & scholar.
6	If aspected by friendly planets from no. 2 or no. 2 is vacant, good & comfortable life; noble person.
7	Poor Sadhu doing penance.
8	Indolent, lazy & poor.
12	Very rich & prosperous.
3,5,9,10,11	Individual results.

SUN COMBINED WITH ONE MORE PLANET

1. SUN - MOON & THEIR SIGNIFICANCE

Comfortable old age; will inherit ancestral property & happy domestic life.

SUN - MOON IN VARIOUS HOUSES

HOUSE NO	EFFECT
1	King like status; but sudden death.
2	Clash with women, which may be harmful; otherwise good results.
3	Selfish; but lucky for self.
4	Exalted status; very rich, provided no. 10 is vacant. If Saturn is in no. 10, he dies by drowning.
5	Comfortable life.
6	Both the planets will have individual effect, if Rahu or Ketu is also with them; he may die along with the parents, provided no. 2 is vacant. Remedy for Mars (Masur Dal - Red lentils, to be donated).
7,8	Individual effects of the planets.
9	Mother's blessings; beneficial travels for 20 years.
10	Individual result.
11	Life span 9 years only.
12	Individual effect, but Sun will be exalted.

2. SUN - VENUS & THEIR SIGNIFICANCE

Both the planets are enemies and as such only one may give good effect at a time & the other will be malefic. For example if Sun's result is exalted, one may get good job, honour etc., but will have unhappy domestic life at the same time. The reverse is equally true. Such a man is selfish, short-tempered, insolent and hen-pecked. His wife will have bad health & she may have wound marks on her cheeks. In any case father's life is doubtful and even the birth of a son is also doubtful, if both are malefic.

SUN - VENUS IN VARIOUS HOUSES

HOUSE NO	EFFECT
1	Sick wife; bad financial position; insolent, peevish, short-tempered & hen-pecked.
7	Will quarrel with wife, who will have a very bad health; but for self, Sun will give the effect of no. 9 i.e., beneficial travels for 20 years.
9	Bad for wife; sometimes absolutely poor & sometimes very rich; beneficial travels for 20 years.
10	Worst results; "Blind" horoscope; give milk to the snake on Lord Shiva's idol; Saturn will be the most malefic; planets of house no. 4 will be helpful; If no. 4 is vacant, remedy lies in Moon i.e., donation of rice, milk & silver.
2,3,4,5,6,8,11,12	Both the planets will exercise their individual results.

3. SUN - MARS & THEIR SIGNIFICANCE

If both are together, their effect will be benefic, especially that of Sun. The mother of such a person remains ill and sad, after his birth. A house on all the four corners is benefic. Without Sun, Mars is malefic; If both of them are together, Mars is no longer debilitating & malefic. If Sun is light, Mars is its rays and the results are best in all kinds and manner. Both of them (jointly) in any house give exalted results. Now Mars will also give good results. Such a person is noble hearted, pious, fortunate, victorious over enemies & will have exalted status; Age 100 years. If Mars is malefic, person may have to face opposition & cheating in employment & worldly affairs.

SUN - MARS IN VARIOUS HOUSES

HOUSE NO	EFFECT
1,2	Noble; fortunate; age 100 years; victorious over enemies; exalted position; If Mars is malefic, he may die in a battle field; may also see deaths in the family.
9	Exalted status.
10	Problems & clash with relatives over property; If Saturn is in 11th house & moon in 6th, the person will be rich & fortunate.

| 3,4,5,6,7,8,11,12 | Both the planets will exercise their individual results, but sun's effect will be exalted. |

4. SUN - MERCURY & THEIR SIGNIFICANCE

Both will give good results, but sun's effect will be more beneficial. When both are together in a house, Sun will never be malefic i.e., if Sun is malefic or debilitating, Mercury's result will be bad, but it will help the Sun whose effect will never be malefic. In other words, Mercury will be ineffective i.e., person may not rise in his business. If Moon & Jupiter aspect them, results will be bad. If Saturn aspects them, results will be beneficial, but if they aspect Saturn results will be bad & malefic. If both Sun & Mercury are exalted or benefic, such a person rises very high in life and is noble & honest; Good govt. job; If Sun is the holy script, Mercury is the pen of fate. If Sun is the monkey, Mercury is the tail always at the service of the master; long life, but sudden death; Beneficial education & writing.

SUN - MERCURY IN VARIOUS HOUSES

HOUSE NO	EFFECT
1	Exalted position; very fortunate; a minister or officer; very rich; expert mathematician; victorious in all cases, if not adversely aspected by Saturn.
2	Physically & mentally sound, but financially not sound. No. 1 will also aspect it beneficially.
3	Now Rahu will not exercise any malefic effect; exalted results, if sincere lover; But if he is of bad character, results will be bad; even Rahu & Venus will be malefic; He will be selfish, notorious & unfaithful lover; will have to suffer losses for 17 years.
4,5	Individual effect of both the planets. If both of them are in no. 5 & Saturn is in no.9, it will not have bad effect on children & parents; Age 90 years; but sudden death.
6	Mercury benefic & Sun malefic by being adversely aspected by no.2—Ill fated; unfortunate & ominous; will face humiliation. Mercury & Sun benefic & no. 2 vacant ----- Happy regarding children; but short lived. Mercury malefic & Sun benefic, by being beneficially aspected by no. 2— Good results.
7	If Venus is exalted, wife will be from a rich family & will confer all pleasures & comforts upon him. If Venus is malefic or debilitating, everything concerning wife, son, in-laws may be bad; but will have lot of income & will be perfect

	& exalted like Sun; will be full of courage in distress; early life & old age will be splendid; will be an expert mathematician & fond of astrology. Mercury & Ketu will give excellent results after 34th year. If no. 9 is occupied by an enemy of Mercury i.e., Jupiter, Moon or Mars, it will not help Sun any longer; but will oppose it i.e., it will not allow the person with Sun in no. 7, to prosper till the age of 34.
8	Now Mercury will destroy the planet in no. 2; may even adversely effect the sister. Remedy lies in burying a bottle of glass filled with jaggery in the cremation ground; both will have individual effect; if Mars is malefic, the person is quarrelsome, cruel & of bad character & may die while fighting.
9	Bad from 17-27th year; but good for education & service after 24th year & will steadily rise after 34th year; Late birth of son - may be after 34th year; remedy lies in Sun (donation of wheat & jaggery) or Mars (donation of Masur Daal i.e., red lentils).
10	Sun & Mercury will exercise individual effect & the good effect of no. 1 or 2 will also be discernible; but Saturn's effect will be bad. Such a man will, of course, be rich but notorious. If Saturn is malefic, he will have to face humiliation. If no. 1 & 2 are vacant, Sun & Mercury will have good results; but Saturn will still exercise bad influence.
11	It all depends upon the person & family members; If all of them are noble-hearted, everything will be fine and if of bad character & dishonest, everything will be bad & disastrous.
12	Individual results; Mercury, now will destroy the planet in no. 6, but sun (body & employment) will be saved from Mercury's poisonous arrows, provided he wears gold ear-rings or keep gold on the ears; otherwise there will be physical & mental diseases such as hysteria, epilepsy & fits.

5. SUN - SATURN & THEIR SIGNIFICANCE

Saturn is son & is the enemy of sun i.e., father. Sun is all brightness & Saturn is all darkness. Sun bestows life; Saturn in association with Malefic Mars in Scorpio (sign no. 8) kills. When both of them are together, one of the two will give bad results. Even Rahu will be like malefic Mars (22nd year or 36th to 39th year). One's fate will be like that of fight between snake & monkey & in their fight, the woman suffers, but the snake will not sting the son i.e., son will not suffer. Such a person is an unreliable friend like the spinning top. If sun is in the earlier houses & Saturn in the later, Saturn will not be able to adversely effect Sun (i.e., man will have good physique & smiling face); but if otherwise, Sun's energy will be blackened i.e., man will have a weak body & sullen face.

✚   Throw coconut or almonds during solar eclipse.

SUN - SATURN IN VARIOUS HOUSES

HOUSE NO	EFFECT
1	'Kaag rekha & Macch rekha' alternates i.e., rich & poor both. Rahu & Ketu will be malefic; sometimes very poor; Father's wealth will be squandered by son; wife will suffer; If benefic, he will be a man of God.
	With Jupiter or Moon in no. 12 OR Venus & Mercury in no. 2—Bad habits; problems in employment; When in annual chart, they occupy the house where Sun is malefic or bad, he may be imprisoned or sent to mental hospital (31st year).
5	Man of determination; If Saturn is malefic & when it occupies no. 7 in annual chart, worst results for 9 years.
6	If both Mercury & Moon are benefic, Sun will confer good results, but Saturn will be malefic. Keep a black dog for warding off Saturn's adverse effect on Ketu (son) and financial position; Even there will be problems in domestic happiness, if Sun is debilitating & Saturn benefic. Remedy lies in burying blue flower or blue marbles in a crossing in a deserted place in the evening.
7	May be imprisoned, if mercury is in no. 5 & Moon is in earlier houses.
9	Rich, but selfish .
	If aspected by malefic Mars & Mercury in no. 3—House no. 3 & 9 and the planets there-in will be ruined.
10.	May be ruined on account of character - assassination & defamation by others.
11	The same as in no. 9, but in a bad sense.
12	Now both the planets & Venus (spouse) also will have good results.
2,3,4,8	Individual effect of each planet.

6. SUN - RAHU & THEIR SIGNIFICANCE

Complete solar eclipse; Unnecessary expenditure; self created problems; white -black spots on the body (which is not leucoderma); problems in career; (Except in no.5), loss of income; complete solar eclipse, when sun - Rahu are in no. 9 or 12. If Sun - Rahu (combined) are in no. 6, they will destroy not only no. 6, but also no.12 (which they aspect) & no. 7 (the next house); If Rahu is in no.6, and Sun in no.2, Rahu will destroy not only no.12, but also no.2 and no.7. If Rahu aspects Sun, it will be a complete solar eclipse; Bad for children for 21 years; Mars may dominate Rahu; But if Mars is also malefic, man's life is doubtful; prone to allergy (itching, eczema etc.)

✚
REMEDIES • Throw coconut, almonds, mustard & curd in the river during solar eclipse.
- Burn a copper coin & throw it into the river or jungle. But note that no child should be there at that time.
- Rahu is also the master of fire, theft & fever ; At the time of theft, bury barley under some weight.
- At the time of fever, donate barley & jaggery and throw barley washed in milk into the river.

If Moon also joins Sun - Rahu, Rahu's effect is limited to that house only i.e., it will ruin that house only and not others.

SUN - RAHU IN VARIOUS HOUSES

HOUSE NO	EFFECT
5	Till Rahu's period, the person will not be a clerk or an ordinary employee; but will be an adviser or president of an organisation. Bad for children till 21 years, but good for career & employment. **Moon in no. 4**—Poor till the period of Rahu; Poor in-laws & maternal uncles;Just hand to mouth living.
9	Complete solar eclipse.
10,11	Age 22 years, provided not helped by or associated with Male planets; otherwise long life.
12	Complete solar eclipse.
1,2,3,4,6,7,8	Individual effect of each planet.

7. SUN - KETU & THEIR SIGNIFICANCE

Sun will be dim (but not eclipsed); harmful travels; should not take other's advice, which may prove harmful; self created problems; Will be solely responsible for his own down-fall. Ketu & Venus are both Sun's enemies; His son's wife will be fat, stout, out-spoken & will bark like a bitch and she will destroy his son's domestic happiness. Son may ruin his father's wealth; No harm to his life; there will be no solar eclipse, but Sun will just be dim; Prone to allergy on feet i.e., eczema & itching etc.

✚

Throw coconut, almonds, mustard, curd & Til in the river at the time of solar eclipse.

MOON & ANOTHER PLANET (COMBINED)

1. MOON - MARS & THEIR SIGNIFICANCE

When combined both will share their effect equally. When Moon is exalted, Mars will contribute 50% of its effect. But when Mars is exalted, Moon will be twice exalted. When Moon - Mars are in no. 3,4 & 8, Mars will not be malefic (Manglik). Following are the effects of various planets on this combination when aspected :

ASPECT	EFFECT
Both aspected by Jupiter or Jupiter being aspected by them.	Rich.
Both aspected by sun or sun being aspected by them.	Raj-Yoga; exalted status; administrator.
Aspected by Venus Or Venus being aspected by them.	Problems regarding children; will not be able to spend his earned money.
Aspected by Mercury Or Mercury being aspected by them.	Successful businessman; scholar; wise; intellectual.
Aspected by Saturn Or Saturn being aspected by them (except when Saturn is not in 10 or 11).	Saturn's worst effect; death through a snake's sting or poison or with a weapon.
Aspected by Ketu Or Ketu being aspected by them.	Son or nephew in a govt. job; but will not be helpful.

Both Moon - Mars (if benefic) will give exalted results, just like the harmonious blending of milk (Moon) with honey (Mars); Finest results in every sphere; If Mars is malefic, he is an unsuccessful lover.

MOON - MARS IN VARIOUS HOUSES

HOUSE NO	EFFECT
1	Individual effect of both the houses.
2	Rich man.
3	Wise; resourceful; exalted status; name & fame; comfortable life; fabulously rich, but haughty.
4	Will spend a lot; very rich, provided Mercury & Saturn are not in no. 4 or 10.
7	A very wealthy man; but will die in an accident.
9	Rich, but haughty; rich sons; but will die of a shock.
10	Tragic death in an accident.
11	Superstitious; greedy; If Saturn is exalted, wealthy, otherwise not.
12	Comfortable & peaceful life, like the blending of milk with honey.
1,5,6,8	Individual effect of both the planets.

2. MOON - VENUS & THEIR SIGNIFICANCE

WEAR SILVER CHAIN.

Both the planets will give combined effect upto 37th year; life will be just like muddy milk. The houses which are occupied by Moon - Venus, become malefic i.e., there will be quarrels and clashes between mother-in-law & daughter-in-law. It is the Moon (mother) who opposes Venus (wife). If Moon is malefic, mother-in-law will harass the daughter-in-law & if Venus is malefic, the daughter-in-law will harass the mother-in-law. But if both of them are exalted, it is a drawn game. If Moon is harassing the Venus, take the help of Mercury i.e., If water is to be taken out of curd, put cloth over the curd & a little ash on the cloth. If Venus is harassing the Moon, take the help of Mars (donate Masur Daal).

MOON - VENUS IN VARIOUS HOUSES

HOUSE NO	EFFECT
1	Sick wife; she may be mad even or may lose memory.
2	A successful pharmacist; a successful lover; but muddy (bad) fate; even Jupiter will be malefic.
4	An eminent ascetic & sage; a thorough gentleman (especially when it is not

	aspected).
	If Saturn is in no. 4, he will have blessings of mother.
	If Sun is in no. 3, he will have blessings of father.
	If Sun is in no. 5, he will be effeminate (bashful like a girl); but will not be stupid.
	If Moon is in no.4 & Venus in no.7 & not being aspected from no. 10, he will be a perfect gentleman. If both are malefic, the person is drug-addict; always tipsy with wine & drugs.
7	Teetotaller; Man of god. If he utilises his wealth for a noble cause, it will confer all comforts; otherwise he may squander his wealth in evil ways; mother may lose eye-sight.

If Sun is in no.1, he will have blessings of father. |
| 8 | Impotent; coward; may squander all his wealth & destroy his family life & health by his lustful ways. For better results, he must donate something & serve his old mother. |
| 3,5,6,9,10,11,12 | Individual effects. |

3. MOON - MERCURY & THEIR SIGNIFICANCE

If benefic, one may go abroad on business after 34th year. If Mercury is exalted, Moon will give exalted results. If both of them are not in their houses i.e., no. 4 & no. 7 and are not aspected, person enjoys exalted status & lot of wealth, but he will be a coward & chicken-hearted. If they are aspected by Sun, Jupiter or Saturn, results will be beneficial. If both of them are in debilitating houses or are malefic, person will be ruined by his lustful habits. To ward off the evil effect of Mercury, donate fennel (saunf) or Masoor Daal (Red lentils).

MOON - MERCURY IN VARIOUS HOUSES

HOUSE NO	EFFECT
2	Father's long life; Father's wealth will not be ruined. Mercury will be helpful.
4	If exalted, very wealthy; otherwise worst worldly affairs; will give the effect of debilitating Saturn; will ruin himself by unnecessarily inviting troubles; mental & nervous weakness; imaginary fears & superstitions; may even commit suicide.
6	If exalted, will earn as a cloth merchant; intelligent; blessings of the parents; But if malefic, he will be a murderer (as Moon is Mercury's enemy).

7	Rich but unhappy; mother may be blind.
8	The same bad results as given in Moon - Mercury no. 4.
10	Worst life; If no. 8 is vacant, tragic death.
11	Like a pearl in a shell; best results after daughter's marriage or own marriage.
12	Now Saturn's effect will be poisonous, even though it may be exalted.
1,3,5,9	Individual effect of both the planets.

4. MOON—SATURN & THEIR SIGNIFICANCE

Results of both the planets will be bad & will give the combined effect till the age of 44. If both are malefic, his wealth is enjoyed & used by in-laws or relatives or friends. Whenever, Moon's enemies such as Ketu, Rahu, Saturn, Mercury or Venus are in house no. 1 in the annual chart, it may lead to loss of wealth or theft or bad name.

MOON - SATURN IN VARIOUS HOUSES

HOUSE NO	EFFECT
1	The same results (good or bad) as explained in Sun - Saturn combination.
2	For better results, one must do humanitarian deeds, such as digging of well or providing water to thirsty people; may meet with an accident or may be killed with a weapon.
3	Lot of property; Thieves may commit theft, coffers without money; Remedy of Saturn for wealth & remedy of Ketu for son; If Ketu is malefic, bury red alum.
4	May die by drowning at night, when Sun is not in no. 1,7 or 10. If Sun is in no. 1,7 or 10, he may die by drowning during the day. Others including his wife or beloved will enjoy his wealth. Remedy lies in offering milk to a snake. If Sun helps Moon - Saturn combination, the results are good; but still the person may meet his watery grave during the day time; may even lose eyesight and suffer from cataract of the eyes.
5	The same effect as mentioned in Sun - Saturn in no.1; bad for wealth or children; Life full of troubles like a volcanic mountain. Keep dry dates in the house.
6	Proverbial three dogs which may cause utter ruin & destruction e.g., a parasite brother in a sister's house, a parasite grandson in the maternal

	uncle's house or a parasite son-in-law in the in-law's house --- all are looked upon & hated. Both Moon & Saturn will give worst results. Ancestral property may be destroyed, but such a man will have his own income & houses.
7	Diseases of the eye; may be blind man; bad family life.
8	Diseases of the eye in the old age; stung by a snake at 9,18,36th years.
9	Wealthy; but bad effects of Moon; Wound marks on the body; Even 'Divine Amrita' will be poisoned by Moon.
10,11	May lose wealth, because of lustful ways & bad character.
12	Unhappy married life; will not care for money.

✛
REMEDIES
- Take water with lemon or sugar cube for 43 days.
- Give milk to snake in Lord Shiva's phallus (Shivling).
- Throw coconut, almonds, mustard & til during lunar eclipse.
- Keep a plate of silver full of water in an iron box (except in the case where Moon - Saturn are in no. 5.

5. MOON—RAHU & THEIR SIGNIFICANCE

Fear of water during half the life span; Throw coconut, almonds & mustard during lunar eclipse; white & black spots on the body (which is not leucoderma). Moon controls Rahu's tremors; In-laws will be financially ruined; Imaginary fears & superstitions may make a man temporarily behaving like a mad man. If they are in no. 1 to 6, mother may die during those years. If they are in no. 7 to 12, mother will not die; but both these planets will adversely affect the house in which they are placed. Rahu's adverse effect will be removed by Ketu only. If Ketu is also malefic, remedy lies in Jupiter, otherwise in Moon.

If Rahu & Ketu are together with moon in any house or are in no. 4, such a horoscope is that of a noble & pious man and all the planets will become good & noble.

MOON - RAHU IN VARIOUS HOUSES

HOUSE NO	EFFECT
9	Partial lunar eclipse.
All other houses.	Individual effect of these two planets.

6. MOON—KETU & THEIR SIGNIFICANCE

In such a horoscope, all male planets such as Jupiter, Sun, Mars will be exalted or benefic;

otherwise man will not be able to fulfill his domestic responsibilities; complete lunar eclipse. If Moon is malefic & in no. 6, mother & son may die. Remedy lies in keeping black & white and red coloured things or their donation to a voluntary oganisation or poor persons.

Throw coconut, til, almonds & mustard during lunar eclipse in a river. Both, if combined or aspecting each other, will give bad results. Suppose one is in no. 3 & the other is in no. 11, mother may die; child may die during sea journey.

MOON - KETU IN VARIOUS HOUSES

HOUSE NO	EFFECT
4	Such a man is noble & pious; In fact all planets will become noble & pious.
6	Lunar eclipse; mother & son will be destroyed.
9	Combined results of both the planets will be bad; but individually both will confer good results.
12	May earn a lot, but will have little in the long run; Bad for Moon (mind & mother) & Venus (wife).
1,2,3,5,7,8,10,11	Individual effects of both the planets; but also see Moon --- Rahu for results.

VENUS & ANOTHER PLANET (COMBINED)

1. VENUS—MARS & THEIR SIGNIFICANCE

Wealthy himself & in-laws; Their combined effect will be discernible till 36th year; Like a sweet Pomegranate i.e., rich & sweet life; travels for 20 years; comforts for 7 years & exalted; If both are aspected by Jupiter, very wealthy; If both are aspected by Moon, every thing exalted and a perfect gentleman; If both are aspected by Saturn or Rahu or Ketu, life full of difficulties, sorrows & sufferings.

RELATIONSHIP BETWEEN VENUS & MALEFIC MARS (MANGLIK)

Bad; Malefic Mars destroys Venus (woman); may cause tragic death even; Fear of fire for 17 years & sickness for 9 years.

VENUS -- MARS IN VARIOUS HOUSES

HOUSE NO	EFFECT
2	Wife may bring hefty dowry i.e., great wealth; may live even with in-laws, who will be very rich.
3	His wealth will be utilised by his brothers & sisters; but himself will be a womaniser & lustful.
4	Maternal uncles will themselves be ruined & will also ruin him. Death by drowning; Malefic Mars will be doubly malefic.
7	Very rich; comfortable life; Happy family members of four generations.
8	Himself prosperous; but a bad critic & back-biter; will have courage to fight enemies.
10	May fight for a trifle or involve himself in litigation over a small piece of land; may desert even brothers at the instigation of wife; poor and quarrelsome;

	his wife may be of dark complexion; his brothers-in-law will be very rich. If his in-laws are of dark complexion and his wife fair coloured and noble hearted, he will be very rich and will have exalted status.
1,5,6,9,11&12	Individual effect of each planet.

2. VENUS - MERCURY AND THEIR SIGNIFICANCE

Both the planets are equally powerful and are also powerful like the sun and will confer their combined effect from 22nd year to 48th year; happy domestic life for 37 years and a lot of wealth. If they are malefic, person is a womaniser and leads a lustful life.

Both the planets, when together make a man rich; even Saturn gives an exalted effect (except in No.4 where their result will be bad); Semi-Government or Public service employment.

VENUS—MERCURY IN VARIOUS HOUSES

HOUSE NO	EFFECT
1	Fortunate; Semi-Government Job; but short lived.
2	Womaniser; if of good character all fine.
3	When moon is malefic, all from mothers' side will help, except step mother; people from among in-laws will destroy him in partnership in business
4	Maternal uncles and in-laws will be ruined and are not helpful; his own character is doubtful. Mothers' relatives will create problems. If Moon is exalted or benefic, everything will be fine.
5	Will not exercise bad effect on children, but bad for wife.
6	Rich; Raj Yoga for self; but may not have Sons; but daughters will be as bright as Sun; Comfortable family life; If sun is in No.2 such a person earns from writing and printing books. If Saturn is in No.2, the native will earn more and more and it will be an honest income.
7	Exalted results; best domestic life; if moon is being adversely affected or eclipsed by Ketu and Rahu, problems in marriage and birth of a son. A bowl of brass (Kansa) will be helpful.
8	Worst family life; both sickly; problems in marriage and birth of a son; wife may do foolish things; Mercury being malefic will bring ruin on sisters and maternal uncles; in short worst results.
9	After the birth of a daughter (or after 17th year), worst results will follow; both the planets will be as malefic as debilitating Mars.

10	Wise, intelligent and good health, unless No.2 is not bad.
11	Separation from the near and dear ones.
12	Both the planets are responsible for bad health (provided Saturn or Jupiter are not in No.2 or 12 or 3). Like a mad goat and mad dog; bad domestic life like Sugar mixed with sand; bad health of wife, but his own life will be upto 100 years.

3. VENUS - SATURN AND THEIR SIGNIFICANCE

Both the planets will give combined effect till 52nd year; Saturn will always help Venus; even Mercury will not be malefic, Rahu and Ketu will also be benefic.

If both aspect Jupiter, both will be exalted and father will always bless the person. If both are aspected by Mercury, his relatives will cheat him and squander his wealth and if both are aspected by sun, the person will meet a tragic death.

VENUS—SATURN IN VARIOUS HOUSES

HOUSE NO	EFFECT
1	Mars in no.4, Sun in no.2, Moon in no.12 --- 'Kaag Rekha'; womaniser; lazy; life full of troubles; poor; bundle of sorrows.
	With Rahu or Ketu in no.1, Sun in no.7 --- Worst results; bad health, may be suffering from T.B.; life full of sufferings.
3	Others will enjoy his wealth.
4	Individual results.
	Sun in no.10—Tragic and heart rending death.
7	Relatives will cheat him and squander his wealth.
	Moon in no.1, Sun in no.4—Impotent; coward; a good for nothing man.
9	Exalted results; now Venus will not be malefic like Mars; even a prostitute will have a good and comfortable domestic life; best results of Venus.
9 or 12	Jupiter in no.5,6 or 10 --- Will have a lot of property, best domestic life.
10	Both will have good individual results. Romantic youth and preacher in old age; lot of property and wealth.
	Sun in no.4 --- Will create property; death will not be tragic, but long lived.
12	Exalted results; comfortable family life.

	Mercury in no.6 --- womaniser.
	Jupiter in no.5 or 9 --- Rich man; comfortable domestic life; lot of property; will loot others.
Other Houses	Individual result of both the planets.

4. VENUS - RAHU AND THEIR SIGNIFICANCE

Without Mercury, Venus will be mad. Both Venus and Rahu will behave like enemies and Venus will be destroyed. There will be problems in the birth of a Son and domestic peace will be destroyed. Not only will the spouse have bad health but there will be problems in the birth of children (Son). Their malefic effect will be visible when the person will suffer from piles. Both of them in all the houses, including No.2, will be malefic.

✚
REMEDIES   • Keep silver in the house.
          • Donate coconut or white butter in milk for 43 days.
          • Silver ring or bangle on the right arm of the woman.

VENUS -- RAHU IN VARIOUS HOUSES

HOUSE NO	EFFECT
1	Wife may be mentally unsound; bad health.
3	Malefic results of both till 34th year.
7	Now both Venus and Mercury will be destroyed; Even Ketu will also be malefic in No.1 which will destroy Moon.
12	Though Venus is exalted, yet wife's health will be bad; husband may lose wealth. Bury a Blue Flower in the evening to ward off bad days.
In all other houses	Individual results.

5. VENUS - KETU AND THEIR SIGNIFICANCE

Enemies 40 years; In exalted houses both are exalted, and in debilitating houses both are malefic.

VENUS - KETU IN VARIOUS HOUSES

HOUSE NO	EFFECT
1	Problems in birth of children; may be issueless even.
	Mars in no.4—Unhappy because of death of children and other friends.
6	Most malefic; worst results; unfortunate; barren wife.
9	Most exalted results, of both the planets; Venus in conjunction with Ketu in this house will no longer be malefic.
12	Wife will be like a Sow (female Pig) in boldness and giving birth to children who are equally bold, and healthy.
In other houses	Individual results of each planet.

CHAPTER 23

MARS AND ANOTHER PLANET (COMBINED)

1. MARS-MERCURY AND THEIR SIGNIFICANCE

If Mars is benefic, both the planets will confer good results. If Mars is malefic, Mercury will be doubly bad and malefic Jupiter's position (whether benefic or debilitating) in the horoscope will determine the effect of both Mars and Mercury. When both of them are before Venus in the horoscope, Venus's effect will be exalted; sons 24 years; noble and good; wife intelligent and wise, her utterances are the words of God, as if god were speaking through her; Must have a Son.

If Mars is malefic, fear of fire; bad for children. Unhappy because of fear of death, humiliation, and worries. Remedy in this case is the same as that of Debilitating Mars.

MARS - MERCURY IN VARIOUS HOUSES

HOUSE NO	EFFECT
1	Sturdy body; healthy; will spend on wife's kith and kin. In case of malefic Mars, bury a decanter filled with honey in a deserted place.
2	Rich; wealthy in-laws; may also help him financially or may inherit property from them.
3	Thieves may commit theft in his house and he may lose wealth. Mind will be full of bad thoughts; but if elder brother is alive and helpful he may lead a better life; blessings of parents. Venus in no.9 --- Will have a son although Venus in No.9 is malefic.
4	There will be no problem or trouble for him; may create problems for others, unknowingly.
6	Now Mars and Mercury will not be enemies; good results as per No.3 above (in good sense)

7	Family life will be ruined; Unnecessary litigation, quarrelsome, foul tongue and full of dirty and mean thoughts.
8	Usually Mars in Scorpio is debilitating, but now it will no longer be malefic in conjunction with Mercury. Of course, it is bad for maternal uncle who may renounce the world; Loss in business or dismissal from service.
11	If addicted to wine, he may have squint in the eye; bad for house, gold and father; Remedy of Jupiter and Moon, will be helpful.
Other Houses	Individual effect of each planet.

2. MARS - SATURN AND THEIR SIGNIFICANCE

Rahu gives exalted results; Jupiter in no.2,5,9,12 also gives exalted results and makes family life comfortable. Both the planets will remain together till 40th year. Their malefic or benefic results will depend upon Rahu i.e., if Rahu is benefic, both will be exalted; otherwise malefic. Exalted Mars & Saturn will make the man victorious. Malefic Mars along with·Saturn, confers worst results. If Mars aspects Saturn, one is deprived of son. Mars, if alone, occupies 10th house, it is exalted; whereas Saturn in no.3 will make a man poor (he may have property but not ready cash).

Mars & Saturn are like two dacoits, who will lead a comfortable life in old age; Bold, good health, terror for others; may get the share of his brothers; will have the qualities of both snake & tiger i.e., will pardon the meek & humble, but will destroy the cruel person, Dacoits may loot & rob his house, because of lot of property & wealth.

If malefic, he may lose wealth & ready cash; may be sickly, but will have a long life; he must obtain receipt before lending money. Keep the milk of mare which has just conceived in a bottle of glass. It will help. For health, remedy lies through 'Malefic Mars' (See Malefic Mars no.4). Keep the milk of mare which has just conceived in a bottle of glass, it will help.

The following chart will indicate as to how the various planets affect this combination :

HOUSE NO	SIGNS	PLANET'S EFFECT
1	Government service	Mars
2	Marriage and in-laws	Venus
3	Daughter's marriage	Mercury
4	Agricultural land	Moon
5	Birth of a son	Sun
6	Bitch's pups	Ketu
7	Romantic association with woman	Venus

8	Death trap	Mars (malefic)
9	Ancestral wealth & blessings	Jupiter
10	Snake's presence in the house during day time (Do not kill it)	Saturn
11	Self made rich	Saturn
12	Ancestral wealth	Jupiter

MARS - SATURN IN VARIOUS HOUSES

HOUSE NO	EFFECT
1	'Kaag Rekha' - both the planets will give good results from the day he joins service. If Mercury is malefic, he may ruin everything; may suffer from blood related diseases. Nevertheless, In-laws will be rich. A dark-eyed woman will cause ruin and a grey-eyed woman whether wife or beloved, usually becomes his associate and the results are bad.
2	Will be rich after marriage; rich in-laws & may get wealth & property from them; Even Jupiter will confer best results. Moon, Rahu in no.12—may meet with an accident or undergo loss if he visits temple in the evening with mother or father-in-law.
3	Will be opposed by his own relatives; unhappy family life; Loss of wealth; unhappy with uncle or younger brother or sons; In-laws may even poison him; But he himself will be bold and will be rich after daughter's marriage.
4	Remedy through Moon; Purchase of agriculture land will confer good results; Otherwise both will give malefic results as mentioned in Moon - Saturn no.10. If malefic, both the planets will give malefic & bad results --- which may lead to death and accident even.
5	Good fortune after the birth of a son.
6	Selfish and ungrateful; may suffer from disease of a stomach; Donate sweets; good luck after the bitch gives birth to pups either in the house or in front of the house.
7	Relatives & sons will be benefitted through him; Rich; complete happiness from wife & children; diseases of the eye in the old age.
8	Trap of death; incidence of fire; deaths, mournings & life full of troubles; house is like a cremation ground or grave yard. Keep, water from a well or

	a hand pump in the cremation ground, in the house, otherwise worst results; everything will be ruined.
9	If associated with Mercury, worst results - 'kaag Rekha' since birth - Otherwise (without Mercury) exalted position; Royal upbringing; Very rich; This happy condition will continue till 60th year. In short, very comfortable and exalted life.
10	Administrator; Lot of property; rich; Mars if alone in this house, is the most exalted planet (it should not be aspected by any other planet); Lucky wife; exalted results after marriage. Moon in no.4—Rich; best luck; dominating personality; good position in government. Both in no.10 & 11 are exalted; confer wealth, happiness & best status (provided they are not in malefic houses).
11	Will be lucky after he creates his own property; good income, but still under debt.
12	Individual and best results of each planet. Now Rahu & Ketu will be good.

3. MARS - RAHU AND THEIR SIGNIFICANCE

If Mars is the Mahout, Rahu is the elephant. When both of them are together, Rahu becomes ineffective. In other words, Mars will fully control the elephant (Rahu). If both of them are in a house where Rahu is exalted (house no. 3 & 6) and is aspected by friends, such a man is like a king riding an elephant. If one of them is in a malefic house (there must be a white & reddish spot on the body), Rahu is like an elephant which has run amuck (mad).

MARS - RAHU IN VARIOUS HOUSES

HOUSE NO	EFFECT
10	Ketu in no.4, sun in no.6—Urinary troubles; Ketu (son) malefic; Remedy :Throw an earthen pot filled with barley & mustard into the river or in flowing water.
All other Houses	Individual result of each planet. Remedy : Take your meals in the kitchen.

4. MARS - KETU & THEIR SIGNIFICANCE

Two Ketus (one real & the other artificial, but exalted Ketu) i.e., if Venus & Saturn are together or in each others' aspect, Mars is doubly benefic. Even if Mars is malefic, Ketu will destroy the malicious Mars and will make it doubly noble. When both of them clash, keep a black & white dog and bitch.

MARS - KETU IN VARIOUS HOUSES

HOUSE NO	EFFECT
2	Prosperous and rich officer; individual result of both the planets.
6	Bad effect of both.
9	Changes will be visible after 28th year; No.3 & 5 will be the deciding factor. If no.10 is exalted, everything will be fine. Rainy water will be helpful. Ketu (son) will be good. The same remedy as in no.10 below.
10	Bad fate after 28th year; Malefic Mars; even son will be ruined. Will remain bad till 45th year. Bury a silver cup filled with pure honey and rainy water under the foundation of the house.
11	Both will give the same effect as is in No.10, provided Mars is not malefic.
In all other houses	Individual effect of each planet. Mars—Ketu in No.8, the same bad result as in Malefic Mars No.4, Ketu No.8 and Mars - Ketu in No.4).

MERCURY AND ANOTHER PLANET (COMBINED)

1. MERCURY - SATURN AND THEIR SIGNIFICANCE

Wealth for 45 years; troubles for 10 years; sons for 24 years and protection from enemies for 42 years. Such a person is powerful like a hawk; eagle-eyed (who can clearly see his prey and pounce upon it) and poisonous like a flying snake; but will be fortunate and will have the blessing of parents who will live long.

MERCURY - SATURN IN VARIOUS HOUSES

HOUSE NO	EFFECT
2	Good health; sympathetic; fortunate; happy and long lived parents.
4	If both of them are associated with moon or both of them are in house No.4, they will be like a poisonous snake for others; Moons' effect will be malefic, but Mercury's results will not be bad.
7	Will be addicted to wine; lustful; ungrateful; but very rich and comfortable life.
9	Bad till 34th year (Kaag Rekha during Mercury's period); thereafter exalted result of Saturn No.9. Blessings of parents who will be noble and long-lived.
11	Richest man of the area, provided Rahu or Ketu are on their left or right and Saturn is not adversely affected by enemies from No.3; wealth for 45 years. If Saturn is adversely aspected by No.3, all will depend upon Saturn (bad or good).
In all other Houses	Individual effect of each planet.

2. MERCURY - RAHU AND THEIR SIGNIFICANCE

Both benefic; Rahu is elephant and Mercury is its trunk; when in the first six houses (1-6), the results are good and if in the remaining houses i.e., 7 - 12 (except House No.11), both will give bad results.

MERCURY - RAHU IN VARIOUS HOUSES

HOUSE NO	EFFECT
2,3,5,6 (own signs or friendly signs)	Noble, Honest i.e. good for all.
7,10,11	Dirty hawk i.e. good for self but bad for others.
1,4,8,9	Very bad for self.
12	Worst for self and others; malefic results for in-laws; everything will be destroyed; life full of sorrows and sufferings; will shout like a mad man in the mental hospital or a prisoner in the jail. **REMEDY: Make 100 marbles (Golis) of mud and take one daily to the temple for 100 days continuously.**
1	Problems in the birth of a son.
3	Sister though rich, will soon become a widow.
11	Sister may become widow or may be divorced 7 days, 7 months or 7 years after marriage.
In all other Houses	Individual results of each planet.

3. MERCURY - KETU AND THEIR SIGNIFICANCE(SIGN RESULT)

Ketu is dog and Mercury is its tail, both enemies; mad dog; result of both is malefic. If both are together, Ketu will be debilitating; ups and downs in life; Remedy through Mars; If both aspect each other i.e. (one is in No.3 and the other in No.11), fate like that of a mad dog.

MERCURY - KETU IN VARIOUS HOUSES

HOUSE NO	EFFECT
6	If Ketu is malefic because of adverse aspect from No.2, it will be bad only for things connected with Ketu, but will not be bad for others. If Mercury is malefic, it will be bad for all. If both not adversely aspected by No.2, all is fine.
12	There may be problems in the leg, urinary tract, waist, feet, spinal cord etc. between 17 to 34th year. Remedy is the same as per Mercury No.12.
In other houses	Individual result of each planet.

CHAPTER 25

SATURN AND OTHER PLANETS (COMBINED)

1. SATURN—RAHU AND THEIR SIGNIFICANCE

Rahu or Ketu with Saturn in No.9 is exalted. Saturn is the god of death who rides the elephant(Rahu). Saturn is the snake and Rahu is the precious sapphire on its hood. When both are combined they will be like a benevolent snake i.e., such a snake who is not poisonous, but helpful to all.

If there is an ordinary black spot just bigger than a mole, one may lead an ordinary life; if it is a big black mole which can be covered by the thumb, it will be 'Padam' and one will lead a good life, and if it is a very big black spot i.e. Lahsun, it will eclipse other planets i.e. one may lead a bad and poor life and may be short lived even.

If 'Padam' (big black spot which can be covered under the thumb) is on the right side of the body and is not visible, the results will be exalted. When Saturn - Rahu are combined and are not aspected by any planet (friend or foe), and nor there is any other planet with them and both of them are in No.1 to 6, they will be considered to be on the right side and will be exalted. If they are on the left side i.e. from No.7 to 12, 'Padam' may not be very exalted.

If 'Padam' on the right side of the body, as stated above, is from house No.1 to 4, the person is like a King; from House No.5 to 8, the person is like an emperor and if from House No.9 to 12, the person is a mystic and spiritualist.

If there is 'Lahsun' i.e., very big black spot on the body, all planets will be eclipsed and the worst results will be visible till 39 years of age. If this big black spot is above the naval towards the head, men will be destroyed and if it is below the naval towards the feet wealth will be destroyed., In both the cases, the person will be poor (beggar like) and sickly.

If Rahu aspects Saturn, Saturn is destroyed and if Saturn aspects Rahu, Rahu is destroyed i.e. Malefic.

SATURN - RAHU IN VARIOUS HOUSES

HOUSE NO	EFFECT
2	If there is a black spot resembling a snake on the left hand, results will be exalted.
7	Bad domestic life (even if Saturn is benefic). If Venus is malefic in 8,9,or 4, unhappy family life and problems in the birth of a male child
9	Very exalted and beneficial.
12	Serpent like black spot on the right hand, exalted results.
In all other Houses	Individual result of each planet.

2. SATURN - KETU AND THEIR SIGNIFICANCE

Both exalted but good results are available after 40; will be blessed with sons, if a third planet joins them; all the three will be bad and malefic.

SATURN—KETU IN VARIOUS HOUSES

HOUSE NO	EFFECT
6	There will be a line starting from neck upto the anus; age 70 years
8	Protection from death; haughty.
9	Most exalted; Rich, long comfortable life; life full of pleasures.
In all other Houses	Individual result of each planet.

202

RAHU - KETU AND THEIR RELATIONSHIP

According to the ancient astrology, Rahu and Ketu cannot be together. Their position is just opposite to each other i.e., 180°. If Rahu is head, Ketu is body. Rahu represents the portion of the body above the navel and Ketu below the navel. Although both of them are opposite to each other i.e., 180° in the horoscope, yet from the point of view of aspect, they will be considered together. The node in the earlier houses will be considered together with the node in the later houses. For example, if Rahu is in no.1 & Ketu is in no.7, both of them will be considered together in no.7. In other words, Rahu or Ketu in no. 1 to 6 will merge its effect and result in no.7 to 12 & the node occupying a later house will give better effect (except house no.5 & 11, where individual node will have its own effect confined to that house only).

Rahu-Ketu relationship has been interpreted differently by different astrologers. Some are of the opinion that Rahu is an Earthquake tremor and Ketu is the accompanying storm; others think that they are angels writing the Book of Fate (good as well as evil deeds). Still there are others who regard them as symbols of Day and Night. The traditional astrologers regard Rahu as Saturn's (snake's) head and Ketu as its tail. But the most authentic opinion is that Rahu is the mad elephant and Ketu is the naughty pig or dog. Never-the-less, both are considered evil planets which mislead the man towards evil and wicked ways. Rahu eclipses Sun but its tremors are checked by Moon; whereas Ketu eclipses Moon.

Both Rahu & Ketu revolve round the Mercury. Their effect (good or bad) is determined by the position of Mercury. If Rahu & Ketu are in no.4 or are with Moon, such a horoscope is noble & good and there will be no evil effect of wicked & malefic planets on the horoscope; Rather all other planets will become noble.

If either Rahu or Ketu is in no.8, Saturn may be deemed to be in no.8 also, though it may be occupying some other house. The result will depend upon Saturn (whether good or bad).

When the positioning of Rahu & Ketu is together in a house, as explained earlier (no.1 merging into no.7 and so on & so forth), the house in which they are deemed to be together, becomes malefic & is destroyed. This condition is not applicable to no.6 &12, where individual effect (whether good or bad) is visible.

Rahu's bad effect lasts for one year & Ketu's for two years, thus making a total of 3 years.

If both Rahu & Ketu become malefic, Rahu's bad effect will last till 42nd year and combined bad effect will be upto 45th year. There-after everything will be fine & beautiful.

It may, however, be mentioned that Ketu always follows Rahu's commands. Ketu is always at Rahu's behest & willingly submits to the master's will.

✚
REMEDIES • To ward off Rahu's evil effects, remedy lies in Moon i.e., Keep a pure silver piece with you and also throw rice, silver piece etc. in the flowing water.
 • To ward off Ketu's evil effects, remedy lies in Sun i.e., Keep a copper piece with you and also throw copper, jaggery & wheat in the flowing water.
 • If Rahu or Ketu is in House no.1 - The remedy lies in Sun i.e., keep a copper piece and also throw copper, jaggery & wheat in flowing water.

✚
REMEDIES • If Rahu or Ketu is in House no.4 - Remedy lies in Jupiter i.e., keep gold piece and also throw gram daal, saffron etc. in the flowing water.
 • If Rahu or Ketu is in House no.7 --- Remedy lies in Saturn i.e., keep an iron piece with you and throw Maash (black lentils) and iron piece in the flowing water.
 • If Rahu or Ketu is in House no.10 --- Remedy lies in Mars i.e., keep red handkerchief with you and throw Masur daal (Red lentils) in the flowing water.

RAHU & KETU AND THEIR MUTUAL RELATIONSHIP

RAHU'S HOUSE	KETU'S HOUSE	EFFECT
1	7	Storm at birth; Bad results till 40th year regarding 1st house (self).
2	8	Ketu's result good till 25 years; after 26th year, bad results.
3	9	Exalted sign (Raashi) results.
4	10	24th & 28th years - Moon's results bad; later exalted.
5	11	Both are enemies and bad results.
6	12	Exalted sign results.

7	1	Bad results of both regarding 7th house (spouse).
8	2	Ketu exalted; But Rahu's effect is bad.
9	3	Debilitating; unhappy with brothers & relatives; Bad for father & in-laws.
10	4	Good for father; Bad for mother; bad health.
11	5	Good for self; bad for sons.
12	6	Both debilitating and malefic; bad results.

THREE PLANETS COMBINED

1. JUPITER - SUN - MOON

If benefic, exalted results; a successful businessman & a famous writer.

2. JUPITER - SUN - VENUS

Good luck after marriage; noble & well-mannered wife.

3. JUPITER - SUN - MARS

Most exalted; will have the power & strength to tame three lions; Most fortunate; the whole family i.e., grand father, father, uncles & elder brothers will be powerful & dominating. Such a person will occupy an exalted position; may be that of a judge having power of life & death over people. In fact the best combination in the horoscope.

4. JUPITER - SUN - MERCURY

Jupiter & Sun will be exalted; Raj Yoga; If all the three are in no.5, the result may not be exalted financially, but still there will be no dearth of money. Such a person, even if imprisoned, will be like a 'Royal Prisoner'. If they are in no.2, such a person may not marry his beloved.

5. JUPITER - SUN - SATURN

Honour and fame, when they are in no.6.

6. JUPITER - SUN - RAHU

Even if the person is a king, people may not respect him; Bad effect (except in no.5).

7. JUPITER - SUN - KETU

Sun's results will be very bad (except in no.5).

8. JUPITER - MOON - MARS

Best results of all the three planets.

9. JUPITER - MOON - MERCURY

Profits from business; best results except in no.2,3,4; may have to face troubles, even though rich. If all the three planets are in no.2, father's life may be in danger; In no.3, bad results of all the three; In no.4, bad for mother, remedy lies through Jupiter.

10. JUPITER - MOON - VENUS

May see many ups & downs in life; sometimes rich & sometimes poor; When benefic (except in no.7), they will confer exalted results. But after marriage, there may be loss of wealth. If they are in no.7, man is like a moth or butterfly running after a woman. If Sun is malefic, man is a frustrated lover.

   When all the three in no.2 and Mars is debilitating & combust, the native may be deprived of children.

   In such a case, Moon will be Venus's enemy i.e., it will not be a sacred love, but lust. One may be a womaniser & may spend his wealth on other women i.e., keeps & prostitutes.

   If all the three are in no.2 and Mars is exalted - successful in love and exalted results.

11. JUPITER - MOON - SATURN

Jupiter & Saturn will give exalted results; a very sincere friend (except in no.9).

   If all the three are in no.9, Moon's result will be malefic; fate like an eddy or whirlpool in the river i.e., bad.

12. JUPITER - MOON - RAHU

Jupiter may now be quiet, but will not disappear. Jupiter & Moon will not give bad result except in no.12, where both of them will be malefic & bad.

13. JUPITER - MOON - KETU

Very bad results of all the three planets.

14. JUPITER - VENUS - MARS

Deprived of children; luxurious but troublesome life.

15. JUPITER - VENUS - MERCURY

Problems in marriage & domestic life.

16. JUPITER - VENUS - SATURN

Exalted especially in no.9. His wife will be outwardly humble & full of smiles, but will precipitate quarrels, clashes & divisions in the family; just like a Shakespearean villain— "Man may smile & smile & yet be a villain".

17. JUPITER - MARS -- MERCURY

If Jupiter - Mars - Mercury are in no.8, Rahu in no.11 & Ketu in no.5 ---- Sons may suffer from asthma & diseases of legs. Remedy lies in wearing gold on your person.

Malefic results, especially if aspected by Rahu. Remedy lies in worshipping virgins (who have not attained puberty) and donating almonds at their feet.

18. JUPITER - MARS -- SATURN

All the three (except in no.2) will be malefic; dearth of men in the family; even Jupiter is malefic. Such a man is like 'Dr Jeykel & Mr. Hyde'. He will run with the hare & hunt with the hound; leader among thieves; Mean thoughts & diseases will bring disaster.

If all the three are in no.2 --- Though he may be a leader among thieves, yet rich.

19. JUPITER - MARS -- KETU

Bad luck till 45th year, but a lame brother will help him. Remedy lies in putting yellow flowers on a black stone.

20. JUPITER - MERCURY -- SATURN

All the three (except in no.12), if Mercury is malefic, troubles, poverty, sorrows & sufferings are in store for him (especially in no.7); But if Mercury is exalted, life full of comforts & riches.

When all in no.12 --- Most exalted; like Divine Amrita (divine elixir of life).

21. JUPITER - MERCURY -- RAHU

Miserly and close-fisted, though very rich.

22. JUPITER - MERCURY -- KETU

Helpful and benevolent destiny (especially in no.2); rich & comfortable life.

23. JUPITER - SATURN -- RAHU

Worst results especially in no.12; Jupiter will be a thief, Rahu a cheat and Saturn a poisonous snake i.e., all the three will spread poison and malice all-around.

When all the three are in no.2 --- Father, grand father or uncle may commit suicide.

24. JUPITER - SATURN -- KETU

Very bad for children.

25. JUPITER - RAHU -- KETU

Bad luck; may have to face problems; may suffer because of vagaries of fate (how-so-ever clever & on his guards he may be).

26. SUN - MOON -- VENUS

Sometimes exceedingly rich, but sometimes poor, especially in no.9; But will be a thorough gentleman and full of human kindness.

27. SUN - MOON -- MERCURY

At 17 or 34 years of age, father's wealth may be destroyed and his mother or grand-mother might have died of a snake bite, provided Jupiter, Saturn, Rahu (either all the three or any two) are in no.3. In no.1,7,10 & 2, they give benefic effects.

28. SUN - MOON -- RAHU

Bad results regarding mother and wealth - both will be ruined. If all the three are in no.5, Sun's effect will be exalted but will be bad regarding children. Remedy lies through Mercury.

29. SUN - MOON -- KETU

Uncomfortable life, though rich.

If all the three are in no.5, Sun's effect will be exalted; But bad in respect of sons; will not be issue-less.

30. SUN - VENUS -- MERCURY

Now Venus (spouse) will be destroyed; Ketu will be the deciding factor regarding domestic life; If Ketu is exalted and is helped by Mercury (Ketu in no.12 & Mercury in no.3), results will be good. If Ketu is malefic or debilitating, one will have no son or the birth of the son may be delayed till the old age.

If all the three are in no.3, with Saturn in no.12 --- Bury a few almonds under some dark room in the house; It will be good for male issues.

+
REMEDIES • Wear a silver ring.
- If there is a bundle of 'Nawar' in the house, it may be removed.
- At the time of marriage of son or daughter -- take a pot of copper, fill it with 'moong' (Green lentils) and put a copper lid on it & throw it gently into the river.

31. SUN - VENUS -- SATURN

Separation and divorce because of some misunderstanding; Red colour floor is inauspicious. Remedy lies in burying an earthen pot filled with pieces of red stone washed in milk, in a deserted place.

32. SUN - VENUS - RAHU

Sickly and unhappy wife especially in no.1.

33. SUN - VENUS -- KETU

Bad in respect of wife & son especially when in no.1; wife sickly, unhappy and depressed.

34. SUN - MARS -- MERCURY

He has the strength to fight against enemies; Man of determination.

35. SUN - MARS -- SATURN

Wealthy, but when these are in no.11, person is unlucky and obstinate.

36. SUN - MERCURY -- SATURN

No quarrel between son and father; good results even if they are in malefic houses; But Jupiter is bad especially if these three planets are in no.2,5,9,& 12. If Sun or Saturn are in good houses, results will be beneficial regarding business and wealth.

37. SUN - MERCURY -- RAHU

More than one marriages; bad in respect of children; provided Venus is not associated with any other planet; but there will be no bad effect on native's job & wealth. Remedy lies through Moon.

38. SUN - MERCURY -- KETU

His relatives will squander his wealth, but they will be selfish and ungrateful.

39. MOON - VENUS -- MERCURY

Malefic results of Sun & Venus; but there will be no problem in employment; Life span 85 years.

If all the three are in no.4—Long life.

If all the three are in no.5—Life span two years.

If all the three are in no.7—problems in marriage and in respect of children. Worst results in domestic life, employment & business.

✦ Remedy lies in feeding the fish for 40 weeks every week-end.

40. MOON - VENUS -- SATURN

Bad for self; he must act upon the dictum, " God helps those who help themselves ". His wealth will be enjoyed by his children; He may die in a foreign land.

41. MOON - MARS -- MERCURY

Good health and wealth, if in no.1,4,5; but bad for health and wealth if in no.10 & 11.

42. MOON - MARS -- SATURN

Except in no.11, all the three will confer bad results in respect of wealth, which may be ultimately used by relatives; may have leucoderma and black & white spots on the body. Short-tempered, but a domineering officer.

If all the three planets are in no.11— Very good in respect of employment & job.

If all the three planets are in no.3,4,8—losses; unhappy domestic life.

43. MOON - MARS -- RAHU

If the child is born upside-down, bad for father's life and may even be a posthumous child. Remedy lies in preparing the pudding (Halwa) in milk and serving it to the needy & poor.

44. MOON - MARS -- KETU

Moon and Ketu will be malefic; Bad results in respect of sons, who may be born after 48th years of age.

45. MOON - MERCURY -- SATURN

Except in no.4, it is the horoscope of a murderer; but such a person is wealthy and dare-devil.

If all the three are in no.4—Maternal uncles will be ruined.

Such a person may suffer from hysteria, depression and swoons. Remedy lies in watering the mango tree with milk.

46. MOON - MERCURY -- RAHU

Father may die by drowning; but there will be no bad effect on mother.

47. MOON - SATURN -- RAHU

Saturn may be malefic during 33rd to 36th year; may lose son.

48. VENUS - MARS -- MERCURY

All the three malefic in respect of marriage and sons, especially when they are in no.3.

49. VENUS - MARS -- SATURN

Exalted in every respect; will get pleasures of long domestic life; rich; will receive Divine help when surrounded by enemies. In fact, it is the most beneficial combination.

50. VENUS - MERCURY -- SATURN

Complete happiness in respect of domestic life and sons; rich; happy long life. He should give a piece of bread to black cow, black dog and crow; should not have sky-lights (ventilators) in his house; should not allow his own domestic black dog to eat from others.

51. VENUS - MERCURY -- RAHU

Though there may be more than one marriage, yet unhappy family life especially when all the three are in no.7.

52. VENUS - MERCURY -- KETU

Problems in respect of marriage and sons, especially in no.7.

53. VENUS - SATURN -- KETU

May have two living women or wives.

54. MARS - MERCURY -- SATURN

Saturn is doubly malefic; bad health; loss of wealth; diseases of eye & blood; maternal uncles will be ruined.

+

When in no.6, give milk in a temple. When in no.2 or 12, give sweets in a temple.

55. MARS - SATURN -- KETU

Most malefic and debilitating Mars. House will be partly cemented and partly of mud; With a 'Neem tree' and a black dog.

56. MARS - SATURN - ANY OTHER PLANET

All the three malefic and poisonous.

57. MERCURY - SATURN -- RAHU

The same as mentioned in Venus - Mercury - Rahu.

58. MERCURY - RAHU - KETU*

Worst in no.1; will be the cause of ruin of all the blood relations; will have no son and may die a miserable death himself. If Saturn is also in no.8, all the three planets will give individual results.

59. SATURN - RAHU - KETU*

Three dare-devils or three wicked musketeers; all the three are wicked planets; Rahu and Ketu being agents of Saturn, have the same wicked properties or inclinations, but do not have the power and strength of Saturn. House no.8 is their head-quarter.

* Refer para 1 of Chapter 26.

THEIR NATURE - SATURN, RAHU-KETU AS WICKED PLANETS :

- Whenever an enemy planet (alone) is occupying a house opposite to them, that planet is destroyed.

- Whenever two or more enemies are opposite to them, their wickedness is doubled.
- Whenever an enemy planet along with a friend of these wicked planets is opposite to them, that friendly planet is also completely destroyed.
- If a benefic planet (e.g., Jupiter, Moon or Mercury) joins Saturn - Rahu or Saturn - Ketu, all the three will become malefic and bad.
- When two wicked planets (e.g., Saturn - Rahu or Saturn - Ketu) are together in a house, the results will be beneficial for the native.
- When their result is malefic, even Jupiter becomes malefic.

MORE THAN THREE PLANETS COMBINED

1. JUPITER - SUN - MOON - MARS

Will earn international name and fame; If in no.2, they are the most exalted.

2. JUPITER - SUN - VENUS - MARS

Most exalted and royal status; very wealthy, fortunate with Royal blood; bold and magnanimous like a king; strength of three tigers.

3. JUPITER - SUN - VENUS - MERCURY

If all the four are in no.3 and no.11 is vacant --- worship the rising Sun for better luck in career.

4. JUPITER - MOON - MERCURY -- SATURN

If all the four are in no.2 -- bad health and wicked conduct.
If all the four are in no.6 -- good health, wealth and name.

5. JUPITER - MERCURY - MOON - RAHU

Bad till 42 years in respect of the house in which they are placed or else all the four will be ineffective in that house. But after 42nd year all will combine together to confer exalted results.

6. SUN - MOON - MARS -- SATURN

Good results if in no.8,2,6,12.

7. SUN - MOON - MERCURY -- KETU

Father may die by drowning or as a very poor man.

8. SUN - MOON - VENUS -- MERCURY

Exalted status of parents; a thorough gentleman doing good to all.

9. JUPITER - MERCURY - SATURN - RAHU

Loss in business, if all in no.12; but benefic results if financially helped by father-in-law & uncle.

10. SUN - VENUS - MERCURY -- SATURN

If in no.4, he will earn for others; He may have two living wives, but both are issue-less and of bad character; Useless life.

11. SUN - MARS - MERCURY -- SATURN

Like a damaged kite; bad results concerning the house which they occupy; If all are combust, such a man is bold and courageous; If all are benefic, such a man becomes rich by looting others.

12. MOON - VENUS - MARS - MERCURY

All the four malefic; will be benefic only after daughter's marriage.

13. MOON - VENUS - MARS - SATURN

Comfortable life and good position in a government job, especially when they are in no.2.

14. MOON - VENUS - MERCURY -- SATURN

Deaths and births will alternatively take place in the family.

15. VENUS - MARS - MERCURY - RAHU/ KETU

People will oppose the marriage; and loss of money especially when they are in no.7.

16. MARS - MERCURY - SATURN -- RAHU

No bad effect on the house in which they are placed. If Sun occupies the adjoining house, one of his brothers may be rich and the other may be without a son.

PANCHAYAT OF FIVE PLANETS

Panchayat without Mercury but with Rahu or Ketu is the most exalted and best.

- If Panchayat consists of male, female and wicked planets (but without Mercury), such a person is fortunate, enjoys exalted position, comfortable domestic life, long lived and noble children. In short, all pleasures of world will be at his command, although he may be a dunce and duffer.
- If Panchayat comprises Jupiter, Sun, Venus, Mercury & Saturn and all are in no.1 to 6, results will be exalted. If they are in no.7 to 12, he will be a self-made rich, besides having all other comforts.
- A Panchayat of any five planets will confer best results in all respects. Even if such a person is devil-like, he will be better than others.
- A Panchayat without wicked planets (Saturn, Rahu or Ketu) becomes meaningless and useless, if that person is noble and good. A man with such a panchayat must be wicked and devil-like, so that people may respect him out of fear. In that case, Panchayat will confer exalted results. If such a person is a gentleman, he will be robbed by the people i.e., others will exploit him. In that case, he should distribute coconut, banana and almonds among the needy and the poor.

ALL PLANETS TOGETHER

Although Rahu and Ketu cannot be together, yet one merges its effect into the other (i.e., Rahu in no.1 will merge into Ketu in no.7 and will himself become zero).

- All planets combined in house no.2 - Most exalted status.
- All planets combined in house no.3 - King-like.
- All planets combined in house no.8 - Exalted status but egoist.
- All planets combined in house no.9 - Exalted status; will help others also.

PROFESSIONS CONNECTED WITH PLANETS

S.NO.	PLANET	PROFESSION / DEPARTMENT
1	JUPITER	Aviation; Preaching; Teaching; Law & allied professions.
2	SUN	Government officer; Writing; Audit & accounts; Business; Armed forces.
3	MOON	Education; Treasury; Navy; Sea travels.
4	VENUS	Agriculture; Veterinary; House-hold.
5	MARS	Army; Administration; Public works; Butcher (if malefic).
6	MERCURY	Business; speculation; Investment.
7	SATURN	Timber; Machinery; Medical; Railways; Iron merchant.
8	RAHU	Electricity; Police; Spying; Jails:
9	KETU	Children; Tourism & counselling.

CHAPTER 31

TRAVELS AND TRANSFERS

Moon is the planet of sea travels, whereas Jupiter is the planet of air travels. But Ketu is the lord of transfers and travels. While predicting the transfer and travel to be undertaken by an individual, Ketu's position in the annual chart may be determined as under :

KETU IN ANNUAL CHART	RESULT
HOUSE NO 1	Be prepared for travel; Order for transfer may be issued. You may be ready to undertake the journey, bag & baggage, but ultimately you will not travel. Even if you have already left, you may have to return after 100 days, provided House no.7 is vacant.
HOUSE NO 2	Transfer with promotion or gain, provided house no.8 is not malefic.
HOUSE NO 3	Travel away from kith and kin.
HOUSE NO 4	Probably there will be no transfer or travel; If ever it takes place, it will be to a place where mother resides, provided house no.10 is not malefic.
HOUSE NO 5	No transfer; At the most there may be a change of room or inter-departmental change. Even if it does take place, it will be beneficial provided Jupiter is exalted.
HOUSE NO 6	Orders for transfer outside city, once issued will be cancelled provided Ketu is awake.
HOUSE NO 7	Certain transfer to the native place, provided house no.1 is not malefic and Ketu is awake.
HOUSE NO 8	Transfer against one's will and choice, provided Mars or Moon is not in house no.11. It is likely that one may suffer ailments pertaining to ears, spinal cord, arthritis etc.

HOUSE NO 9	Promotion is certain, but not transfer; Travel to the native place willingly and happily, provided house no.3 is not adversely aspecting it.
HOUSE NO 10	Doubtful; If Saturn is exalted, transfer is doubly beneficial. If Saturn is malefic, transfer will be doubly malefic. Only house no.2 will be helpful. Remedy lies in gently offering milk and water (Argh) to Sun in the morning.
HOUSE NO 11	Orders for transfer will of course be issued, but will never reach the individual. Transfer will only be on paper. In case transfer is affected, it will be eleven times beneficial, provided it is not adversely aspected by house no.3.
HOUSE NO 12	Happy times indeed with family members; Promotion is certain, but not transfer. If travel is involved, it will be advantageous, provided house no.2 or 6 are benefic.

MARRIAGE AND CHILDREN

A. MARRIAGE YOGA

Before predicting about engagement or marriage, all aspects, whether friendly or adverse should be taken into consideration in the annual chart. Venus, Saturn, Mercury & Ketu are friends and when they favourably aspect each other in the annual chart, marriage yoga is formed.

- If in the annual chart, Venus or Mercury is favourably aspected by Saturn or Saturn occupies the 1st house, marriage may be predicted.
- If Venus and Mercury are separately positioned and if Mercury is favourably aspecting Venus, marriage yoga is formed (except Mercury in no.12).
- If Venus or Mercury is malefic or debilitating in the horoscope, and Jupiter, Sunrn or Mars are favourably combined or associated with Venus or Moon, marriage yoga is formed in the year Saturn helps Venus or Saturn is in the 1st house in the annual chart.
- If according to the annual chart, if Venus or Mercury occupies the 1st house OR house no,2,10 to 12 (except Mercury in no.12), OR house no.7 (but Moon, Sun or Rahu should not be in no.3 or 11) OR the same house in which they are placed in the horoscope, marriage yoga is formed.

BIRTH CHART

```
JUP  MER          2        1                   12
SUN  RAHU

VENUS
                          ASCENDING SIGN            11   SATURN
  3
           4

                                    7        10
      5                                            8
  6                                                    9
   MARS

     MOON                                   KETU
```

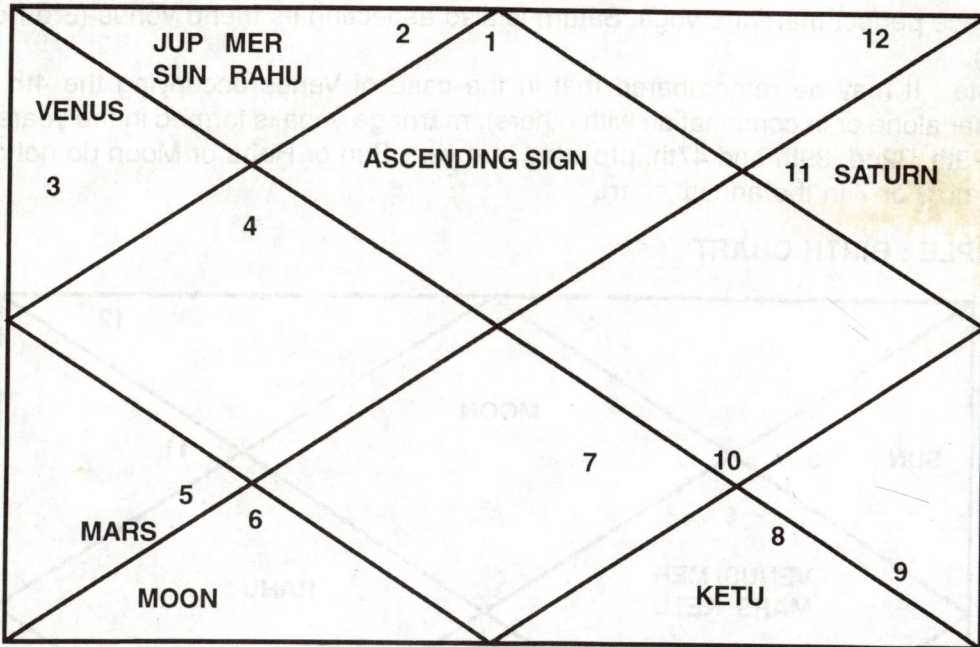

ANNUAL CHART (29TH YEAR)

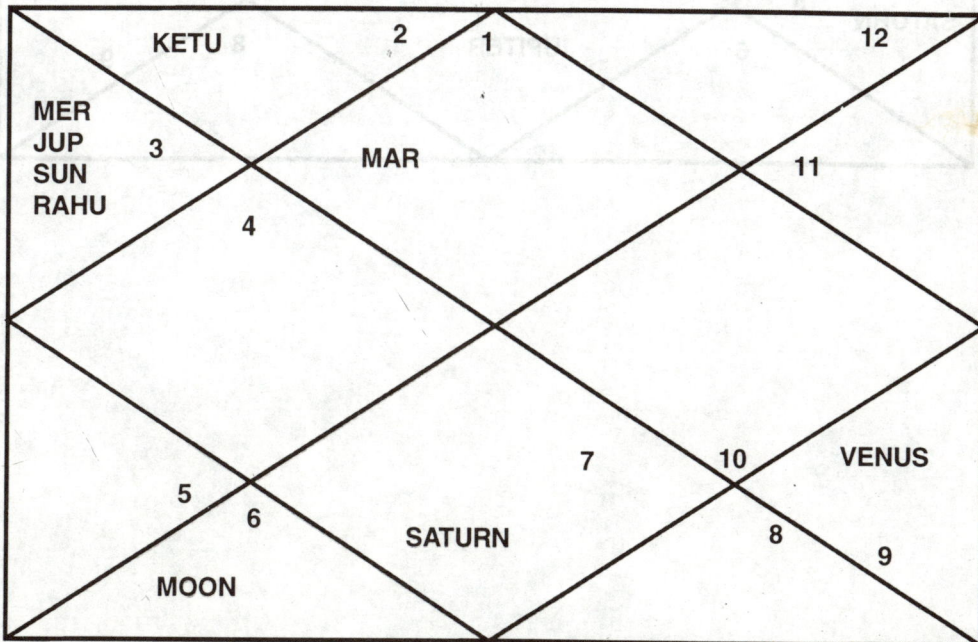

```
        KETU          2        1                   12
MER
JUP      3                  MAR                        11
SUN
RAHU
           4

                                    7        10     VENUS
      5                                            8
  6                                                    9
            SATURN

     MOON
```

Engagement must have been solemnised this year, as Mercury is favourably aspecting (50 %) the 7th house occupied by another friend Saturn and Venus in the 9th house (100 %); hence perfect marriage yoga. Saturn is also aspecting its friend Venus (3rd from 7th house).

Note : It may be remembered that in the case of Venus occupying the 4th house (whether alone or in combination with others), marriage yoga is formed in the years 22nd, 24th, 29th, 32nd, 39th and 47th, provided that year Sun or Rahu or Moon do not occupy house no.2 or 7 in the annual chart.

EXAMPLE : BIRTH CHART

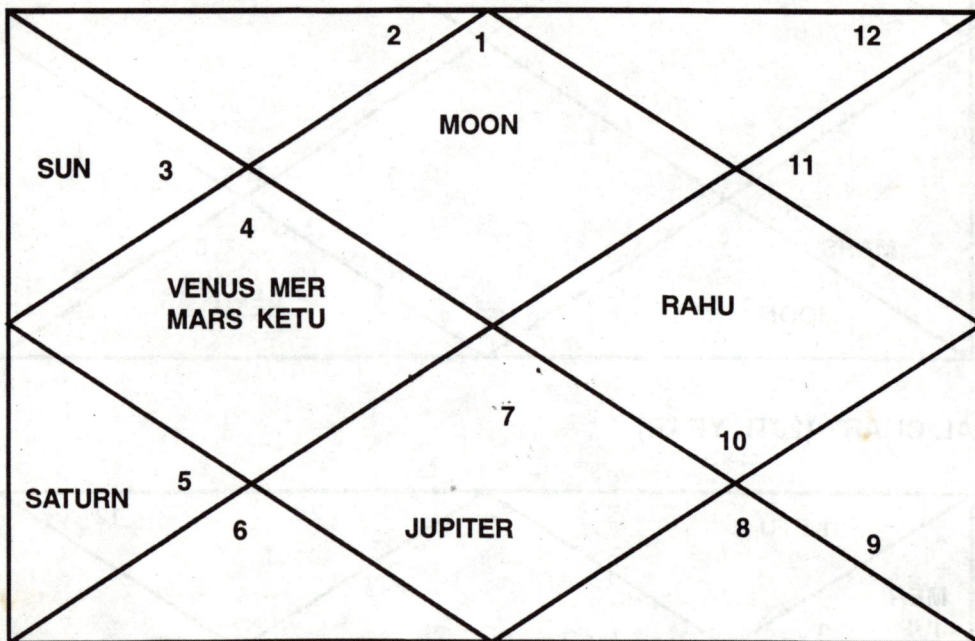

2	1	12
SUN 3	MOON	11
4		
VENUS MER MARS KETU		RAHU
5	7	10
SATURN		8
6	JUPITER	9

SATURN	2	1	12
3	4 (JUPITER)		VEN MER MARS KETU (11)
	7		
5 / 6 (MOON)	SUN	10 (RAHU)	8 / 9

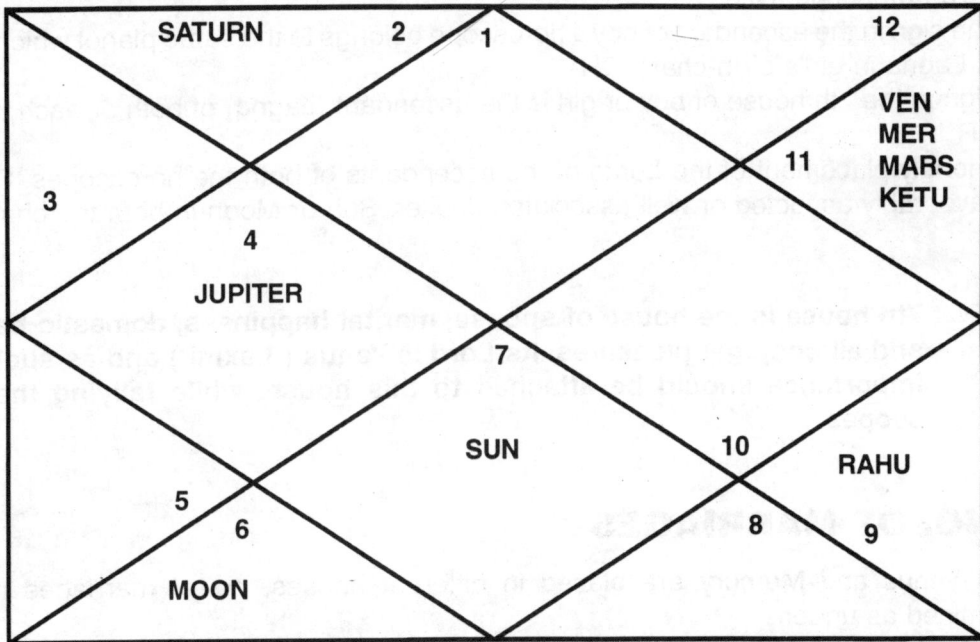

As Sun (Venus' enemy) occupies house no.7 in the annual chart, marriage will not be performed. In this case, when Venus occupies house no.4 (the house of the horoscope) or house no.7 (the house of Venus) in the annual chart, marriage yoga is formed.

B. MARRIAGE AGREEMENT (TALLYING OF HOROSCOPE)

Before finalising a marriage, the parents of the girl and the boy approach an astrologer to tally the horoscopes. If the horoscopes are compatible, parents give their consent and the marriage is solemnised. The traditional astrologer gives importance to Nakshtras, signs and 'Gunas'. A ready-reckoner is available in all the Panchangs and almanacs (Jantris) based on Nakshtras and Gunas. But the modern astrologers also attach equal importance to the placement of planets in the horoscopes.

The following rules may be observed while tallying the horoscopes :

☞ Marriage will be cordial, sweet and harmonious, if

* In the boy's horoscope, the sign of debilitation of the Lord of the 7th house is the Raashi of the girl. OR
* The Raashi of the girl is the exaltation sign of the Lord of the 7th house of the boy's horoscope. OR
* Venus (Lord of 7th house) in the boy's horoscope occupies the sign that is the Raashi i.e., Ascendant of girl's horoscope. OR

- The sign occupied by Venus in the boy's horoscope happens to be the ascendant in the girl's horoscope. OR
- The sign in the ascendant of boy's horoscope belongs to the same planet which is Lord of Lagna in girl's birth-chart. OR
- Sign in the 7th house of boy or girl is the ascendant (Lagna) of both or each of them. OR
- Friendly placement of the Lords of the ascendants of both the horoscopes. OR
- Favourably aspected or well associated Jupiter, Sun or Moon in both the charts.

☞

NOTE   **7th house is the house of spouse, marital happiness, domestic harmony and all conjugal pleasures. Its Lord is Venus (Laxmi) and as such great importance should be attached to this house, while tallying the horoscopes.**

C. NO. OF MARRIAGES

When Venus and Mercury are placed in different houses, no. of marriages may be determined as under :
- If Venus alone is in house no.2,4 & 7, there will be only one man or woman.
- If Mercury alone is in the house no.1,5,9 &12, there will be only one man or woman.

D. NO. OF WOMEN OR MEN

- If Venus is exalted or benefic in the horoscope or it is combined with or helped or aspected by its friends, Mercury, Saturn, Ketu ---- there will be one wife only.
- If Venus is made malefic or debilitated, no. of marriages will be more than one.
- If Sun, Mercury and Rahu are together, there will be more than one marriages.
- If Mercury is in no.8, no. of women will be more but all will be alive.
- If Sun aspects Saturn (i.e., Sun in no.6 & Saturn in no.12) in the annual chart, wife will die OR whenever Sun destroys or is in collision with Saturn in the annual chart, spouse will die. See chart of aspects at page 31(Enmity).
- When Jupiter is debilitating in no.10 and Sun is in no.5, there will be more than one marriage.

E. CHILDREN

Man will have children if :
- Jupiter, Sun, Venus, Mercury and Saturn are all benefic or exalted OR
- Jupiter or Sun or both are benefic or exalted. OR
- Mars is in the permanent houses assigned to Venus or Mercury (7th house) or in their signs (i.e., 2,3,6,7th) and are not adversely affected by enemies. OR

- Mars is benefic or exalted. OR
- Mars is with Mercury, Venus, Rahu in their permanent houses (i.e., 7th, 12th) or in their signs (i.e., 2,3,6,7,12th). OR
- Saturn is with Sun, Moon, Jupiter in their permanent houses (i.e., 1,2,4,5,9,11th) or in their signs (i.e., 4,5,9,12th). OR
- Mars and Saturn are combined.

F. SPOUSE'S NATURE

Relationship between Sun and Mercury reveals the nature of the wife.

➢ When Sun and Mercury are separately placed :

POSITION OF SUN	POSITION OF MERCURY	EFFECT
Earlier houses	Later houses	Wife will be good-natured, provided it is not adversely aspected by Saturn.
Later houses	Earlier houses	Wife will not be good-natured.

➢ When Sun and Mercury are combined :
- When Sun and Mercury are together in an exalted or benefic house, and are not adversely aspected by or associated with Saturn or enemies, family life will be happy and wife will be well-natured.
- But when Sun-Mercury (combined) are adversely aspected or associated with Saturn or enemies, wife will be subtle and cunning like Saturn i.e., Snake.

G. ONE WIFE / HUSBAND ALIVE

One will have one wife or husband, if in the horoscope :-
- Mercury or Venus or both are exalted & benefic and are helped & aspected by friends.
- Saturn aspects the Sun.
- Saturn & Venus Help each other & are not associated with Male or enemy planets.
- Mercury is either in the 1st house or 6th, and Venus is not malefic.

Such a person has one living wife or husband and enjoys all domestic comforts & pleasures.

H. DEATH OF HUSBAND

Wife loses her husband if Venus & Mercury are adversely aspected by enemies or if Sun & Ketu are melefically associated with or adversely aspect Mercury.

I. ISSUE-LESS COUPLE

- When Mercury-Mars or Venus-Ketu are in the 1st house, and Venus or Mars or

225

Mercury are malefic or debilitating.
- When Venus-Jupiter are in 7th house.
- When Moon is in 8th house.
- When Moon & Ketu are in the 11th house.
- When Moon and Venus are directly aspecting each other & are combined with enemies or malefic planets.

Such a person is not blessed with children.

Further if Venus & Rahu are in 5th house, man may have one living daughter.

J. IMPOTENT MAN

Such a man is impotent, if
- Saturn is in no.7 and Moon is in no.1.
- Venus is in no.5 and Sun is in no.4.

K. INFERTILE WOMAN (INCAPABLE OF PRODUCING A CHILD)

When Venus is in no. 2 or 6, and is without any aspect or combination i.e., Venus is all alone in no.2 or 6, such a woman will be incapable of producing a child, although she may be blessed with all womanly virtues and is an incarnation of Laxmi.

L. COUPLE WILL NEVER BE ISSUE-LESS

- When Venus is exalted in no.2 or 6 and is helped by Jupiter or Sun. OR
- When Sun is in no.6 and no.12 is occupied by friends. OR
- Rahu is in no.3.

Such a person will never be issue-less.

M. AGES OF HUSBAND & WIFE

If Venus is aspected by a friend.	Both will live long.
If Venus is aspected by an enemy.	Wife will die earlier than the husband.
If Mercury is aspected by a friend.	Husband will live longer.
If Mercury is aspected by an enemy.	Husband will die earlier than the wife.
If Venus-Mercury (combined) are aspected by a friend.	Both will live long.
If Venus-Mercury (combined) are aspected by an enemy.	Both will die early.

If Venus is aspected by Saturn (Friend) and Mercury is aspected by Moon (Enemy).	Wife will live long; Husband will die earlier than wife.
If Mercury is aspected by Sun or Rahu (Friend) and Venus is aspected by Sun, Moon or Rahu (enemy).	Man will live longer. Wife will die earlier than her husband or wife may be short-lived.
If Mercury is aspected by Moon (Enemy) and Venus is aspected by Sun, Moon or Rahu (Enemies).	Wife will live longer; Husband may be short-lived.
If Sun is in no.6 and Saturn is in no.12.	Wife will be short-lived.

If Venus is exalted or benefic, there will be one wife and both will live long.

N. CERTAIN COMBINATIONS (GOOD OR BAD) REGARDING CHILDREN

- Male planets alongwith Moon, if benefically placed confer long life on children.
- Ketu or wicked planets in house no.5, destroy male child; But the planet in no.9 protects the child even though house no.5 is occupied by wicked planets (e.g., if Saturn is in no.5 and Mars is in no.9, Mars will confer long life on child born on Tuesday).
- If Ketu is in no.9 and Rahu is in no.5, the child born on Sunday morning will have long life.
- If Venus or Mercury or both combined are in house no.5, there will be no adverse effect on the child's life, but if either of the two occupies no.9, there will be adverse effect on male child.
- If Venus, Mars and Mercury (all the three) are in house no.3 and are not aspected from house no.11, there will be problems in respect of marriage and children.
- If Venus, Mercury and Rahu (or Ketu) are in house no.7, there will be problems regarding marriage and children.
- IF Venus & Mercury are in no.5, it will not have any bad effect on children.
- If Sun is in no.6 and Mars is in no.10 or 11, the son will die.

➤ All the following combinations are bad for children :-
- Wicked planets are in no.5 or 9; 3 or 9; and Mars is in no.4. OR
- Jupiter's or Sun's enemies (i.e., Rahu, Venus, Mercury, Saturn) occupy no.5 or 9; or 3 or 9. OR
- Mars occupies no.4. OR
- Wicked planets are in no.9. OR
- Rahu-Mercury (combined) in no.1. OR
- Rahu alone in no.9. OR
- Venus-Ketu (combined) in no.1 and Mars in no.4.

O. TIME OF BIRTH OF A CHILD

If Mars or Venus or Ketu or Mercury occupies the 1st house in the annual chart (provided 5th house is not occupied by malefic and debilitating planets --- in that case child will die) or Moon or male planet occupies the 1st or 5th house or Ketu alone is in 11th house or Mars or Venus or Ketu or Mercury is in no.2 in the annual chart, man will be blessed with a son. Further if Ketu is exalted in the annual chart, son will be born; and if Mercury is exalted, daughter will be born.

✚

REMEDIES If there are problems or belated conception—

- Tie a red thread on the woman's wrist (40-43 days before child's birth) and then tie it on child's wrist at his birth ; woman should wear a new thread.
- Just before the birth of the child, ask the woman to touch milk & sugar (contained separately in separate new cups or glasses) and then donate them to a temple ; but do not bring back those cups and glasses. This will facilitate easy delivery.

PLANETARY INFLUENCE ON HUMAN DISEASES

There's a divinity that shapes our ends' says Shakespeare. Stars do exercise a lot of influence not only on our destiny, but also on human ailments and diseases. When Pandora's box was foolishly opened, all the ills were let loose upon mankind, but hope alone remained. Obviously planets which exercise evil influence upon human mind and body are counter-acted by other benefic planets. There are remedies for all such ailments.

Here is a list of diseases and the malefic planets which cause the diseases and their remedies. In the case of combined planets, remedy regarding the malefic planets be resorted to, e.g., in case of Jupiter - Rahu, during bad period, Rahu's remedy be adopted during sickness.

If there are persistent cases of sickness and ailments in the house, following remedies may be adopted :

+
REMEDIES • Donate ripe yellow pumpkin to the temple off and on.
• Keep two copper coins under the pillow and throw them into the cremation ground off and on.

S.NO.	NAME OF THE MALEFIC PLANET	NAME OF THE DISEASE	REMEDIES
1	**Jupiter** 7th, 10th house. Taurus, Libra and Capricorn i.e. 2nd, 7th, 10th Raashis, especially Libra.	Asthma, Diseases of the lung.	• Donate gram Dal for 43 days. • Throw copper coin into the flowing water for 43 days. • Wear gold chain or yellow thread and preferably yellow clothes etc. • Keep saffron in your pocket. • Paste saffron on the navel.

			• At the time of marriage or wedding anniversary, take two pieces of gold of equal weight - throw one into the river and keep the other. If one can not afford the gold, he can use turmeric for the purpose. Note that the weight should be minimum, but must be equal.
2	**Sun** (Virgo, Libra, Capricorn) i.e., 6th, 7th, 10th Raashi, especially Libra.	Irregular heart-beat (when not helped by Moon); Insanity, epilepsy (froth at the mouth); Loss of sensation of the limbs.	• Donate wheat or jaggery and copper piece for 43 days. • Throw jaggery or copper piece into the flowing water. • Keep a copper square piece in your pocket. • Bury a copper square piece in a deserted place. • Take some sweet before doing auspicious work. • At the time of marriage or during the wedding anniversary, take two pieces of copper of equal weight (weight is immaterial); throw one into the river and keep the other with you.
3	**Moon** Libra, Scorpio, Capricorn and Aquarius i.e., 7th, 8th, 10th and 11th Raashis, especially Scorpio.	Heart problem, irregular beating of heart; restlessness; epilepsy; Fits, depression, insanity; eye-ailments of cornea.	• Donate rice or milk for 43 days. • Keep silver in the house. • Keep a square piece of silver in your pocket and one under your pillow. If one can not afford silver, a piece of rice may be kept. • Do not take silver as a gift. • Do not take milk in a glass tumbler, but take it in a silver or steel glass.

			• Bury milk and silver in the foundation of the house.
			• Fix four copper pieces in the four legs of your cot for sound sleep and piece of mind.
			• For Moon in Aquarius (11th sign), donate sweets made of milk (Khoya) for 43 days and heat a thin wire of gold and put it into milk 11 times before taking milk (for potency and virility).
			At the time of marriage or wedding anniversary, take two pieces of silver of equal weight (weight is immaterial) - throw one into the river and keep the other with you.
4	**Mars** Cancer & Scorpio i.e., 4th and 8th Raashis and 8th house.	Ulcer, diseases of the uterus & womb; Diseases of Stomach and intestines; Cholera, liver troubles; boils, wounds and burn marks.	• Donate rice, milk or silver for 43 days. • Fill an earthen pot with honey and bury it in a deserted place. • Put some milk in the mud taken from the roots of Banyan tree and put a dot of such mud on the fore-head and navel. • Throw a few crumbs of sweet bread to birds. • Throw 'Revaris' (made of jaggery & Til) into the river. • At the time of marriage or during the wedding anniversary, take two red stones (but not bright) of equal weight; throw one into the river and keep the other with you. • Wash barley in milk and throw it into the river.

			• For fever, wash barley in the urine of the cow; tie it in a red cloth and then throw it into the river.
5	**Venus** Aries, Cancer, Virgo, Scorpio i.e., 1st, 4th, 6th and 8th Raashis, especially Virgo.	Skin diseases; eczema; Ring-worm; Dermatitis etc. Boils, itching etc.	• Pierce the nose (for women only). • Donate seven cereals i.e., Barley, wheat, rice, maize, moong, gram dal, mustard etc. for 43 days. • When Venus is in Cancer (4th Raashi), throw rice or gram dal in flowing water for 43 days or else donate it. If Venus is associated with any other planet in Cancer sign, bury a kernel of peach stuffed with lead (surma) in a deserted place. • If Venus is in Sagittarius (9th sign), bury a square piece of silver under a Neem tree and also bury silver & honey under the foundation of the house. • Always wash your private parts with curd or milk OR else put a few drops of curd or milk in the bathing water. • At the time of marriage or during the wedding anniversary, take two pearls(white curd like); throw one into the river and keep the other with you. Wife must wear some gold ornament on the head off & on.
6	**Mercury** Scorpio, Gemini, Sagittarius and Pisces i.e., 3rd, 8th, 9th and 12th Raashis, especially Sagittarius and	Small pox; diseases concerning brain; insensitive to smell; disease of the teeth, mouth (tongue) and veins.	• Donate Moong for 43 days. • Avoid green colour. • Pierce the nose and wear nose ring of gold and silver (for women only). • If Mercury is in Gemini (3rd sign),

	Pisces.		wash Moong at night and throw them to birds in the morning for 43 days.
			• Take a few leaves of 'Pallah' or 'Dhak'; wash them with milk and bury them in a deserted place. Cover them with a black stone and mud. Do not bring back the shovel or pot of milk.
			• Take three cowries of yellow colour; burn them and throw the ash into river.
			• Clean your teeth with alum (Phatkari).
			• If Mercury is in Scorpio (8th sign), bury an earthen pot filled with honey in a deserted place.
			• If Mercury is in Sagittarius (9th sign), avoid green colour; keep silver; wash the new yellow and white clothes before wearing them; keep a small ball of iron and paint it red. Donate mushroom and put into an earthen pot.
			• If Mercury is in Pisces (12th sign), wear yellow thread around your neck; avoid green colour and gently throw a new pitcher into the river.
			• At the time of marriage or during the wedding anniversary, take two diamonds of equal weight (weight is immaterial); throw one into the river and keep the other with you. If you can not afford diamond, use shell (seep in Hindi).
7	**Saturn** Aries, Gemini i.e., 1st and 3rd Raashis, especially Aries.	Eye-ailments; cough (all types); asthma connected with malefic Jupiter.	• Donate Maash (black lentils) for 43 days. • Throw coconut into the river or flowing water for 43 days.

			• Donate mustard oil.
			• Bury Surma in a deserted place.
			• Put a drop of milk on a dot of mud taken from the Banyan tree and paste it on navel or fore-head.
			• If Saturn of Aries (1st sign) occupies the 7th house, bury a black flute filled with sugar in a deserted place.
			• At the time of marriage or during the wedding anniversary, take two iron pieces of equal weight; throw one into the river and keep the other with you.
8	**Rahu** Scorpio, Pisces, Sagittarius i.e., 8th, 9th and 12th Rashis especially Pisces and Sagittarius.	Fever; Brain diseases; plague; accidents; sudden loss or injury.	• Donate mustard for 43 days. • Throw coconut into the river for 43 days, if Rahu is in Libra (7th sign). • Keep a square piece of silver. • Wash barley with milk and add jaggery into it and throw it into the river (against fever and theft). • At the time of marriage or during the wedding anniversary, take two square pieces of silver of equal weight (weight is immaterial); throw one into the river and keep the other with you. Do not use 'Neelam' in the ring, when Rahu is malefic. • If Rahu is in Scorpio (8th sign), throw 8 lead pieces and 8 almonds. • When Malefic Rahu occupies 8th house in the annual chart, take 8 almonds every day (starting from the 8th month after birthday till the next

			birthday) to the temple; leave four there and bring back the other four. Then donate them on the next birthday.
9	**Ketu** Gemini, Virgo, Scorpio i.e., 3rd, 6th and 8th Raashis, especially Virgo.	Diseases of the limbs; sciatica; Arthritis; Rheumatism; ulcer; venereal diseases; boils; cancer; urinary troubles; ear ailments; spinal cord; Hernia; dislocation of limbs; Vericose veins.	• Donate and throw 'Til' (sesame) into the flowing water for 43 days. • Donate a cow made of silver and paint a few streaks of black colour on it (black and white). • Donate a white and black blanket. OR bury a piece of black & white blanket in the cremation ground (when Ketu is in Scorpio i.e., 8th sign). • At the time of marriage or during the wedding anniversary, take two black and white stones of equal weight; throw one into the river and keep the other with you.
10	**Jupiter-Rahu**	Asthma; Respiratory troubles.	As suggested for Rahu.
11	**Jupiter-Mercury**	Asthma; Respiratory troubles.	As suggested for Mercury.
12	**Sun-Venus**	Asthma; T.B.	As suggested for Rahu.
13	**Moon-Rahu**	Pneumonia; Madness depression.	As suggested for Rahu.
14	**Mars-Saturn**	Leprosy; Bursting of skin; impure blood.	As suggested for Saturn.
15	**Venus-Rahu**	Impotence.	As suggested for Rahu. Throw coconut or donate white butter and milk.
16	**Jupiter - Mars** (Debilitating)	Jaundice	As suggested for Mars (malefic).
17	**Moon-Mercury** (adversely aspected by Mars)	Glands.	As suggested for Mercury and Moon both.

18	**Rahu-Ketu**	diabetes	As suggested for Rahu.
19	**Venus-Ketu**	Diseases concerning Ketu	As suggested for Ketu.
20	**Sun-Rahu**	Fever; loss of wealth; itching; useless expenditure, theft etc.	• Heat a copper coin; throw it into the jungle at night (Note that no child should be present at that time). • Wash barley with milk; put jaggery into it and throw it into flowing water for 43 days.

These remedies are not to be taken in the clinical sense. Doctor must be consulted to cure the disease. These remedies are meant to boost the sagging morale of the patient who may donate to the poor.

☞

NOTE
- Remedies may be adopted in respect of Raashis (signs) only and not in respect of houses.
- Remedies for all planets may be adopted from Morning till Sun-set ; but in case of Saturn it should be adopted during evening.
- All remedies should be adopted for 43 days continuously without break. Failure even for a day is not permissible. One has to restart for another 43 days.
- Mother or any nearest blood relation can also do it, but it is just an exception and not a rule.
- Detailed remedies are also mentioned in the chapters of various planets.

DISEASES

- If house no.3 or 9 are malefic and debilitating, house no.5 will obviously be malefic and bad. If sun or Moon occupies house no.9, no.5 will be good and benefic.
- For no.10, no.5 and 6 will be like poisonous arrows and will be malefic.
- According to horoscope, if sun or moon is associated or is combined with Venus, Mercury or any wicked planet (e.g., Saturn, Rahu or Ketu) and if they occupy no.1,6,7,8,10 in the annual chart, there will be health problems.
- If no.3 is occupied by malefic or wicked planets, there will be health problems; and if no.3 is vacant, malefic no.8 will create health problems; and if no.8 is vacant, then malefic 5th house will signal bad health.
- House no.8 will indicate sickness and disease and house no.2 or 4 will be the pretext for that ailment; and house no.10 will be the worst.

For which house	Responsible for clashes or diseases or accident	The house responsible for this	House no which will help
NO.3	Sudden accident & loss	House no.1	Will be helped by no.11
NO.3	Will deceive	House no.6	Will be helped by no.7
NO.3	Will maliciously clash & collide.	House no.8	Common wall of assistance - no.2
NO.5	Sudden accident or loss.	House no.7	Will be helped by no.1
NO.5	Will deceive.	House no.8	Will be helped by no.1
NO.5	Will maliciously clash & collide with.	House no.10	Common wall of assistance - no.4

The above houses are according to annual chart.

☞ The above remedies are not to be taken in the clinical sense. Doctor must be consulted to cure the disease These remedies are meant to boost the sagging morale of the patient who may donate to the poor.

HOUSE, PROPERTY, INCOME, EXPENDITURE, MONETARY DEALINGS ETC.

1. HOUSE

If Saturn is benefic according to the annual chart or it favourably aspects or is aspected by Rahu / Ketu or is associated with Rahu / Ketu, one will build houses; but if Saturn, in the annual chart is not favourably aspected by or associated with Rahu / Ketu, one will sell or destroy the houses. House no.2 will reveal the condition of the house and House no.7 will indicate the happiness or otherwise connected with the house.

☞

NOTE   • One must donate something to the poor or temple or voluntary organisation etc., before entering the house on an auspicious day.
            • Bury a piece of pure silver with honey in the foundation of the house for prosperity of self and children.

2. INCOME

It depends upon the exalted planets in their own houses or exalted planets in friendly houses or planets of fate. For example Jupiter in cancer in 4th house is exalted and confers a lot of income & comforts upon man. If the planet of fate or any other planet is malefic it may cause loss.

House no.4 is the outlet for wealth. If house no.4 is vacant, Moon will be deemed to have occupied house no.4.

COMPUTATION OF WEALTH, WHEN TWO PLANETS ARE COMBINED

COMBINATION	EFFECT
MOON-MARS	Lot of wealth (especially in no.3); if both these planets are in no.10 or 11, the person will be greedy.
MOON-JUPITER	The native may get buried treasure; lot of gold and silver; Parents will be like a shady Banyan tree.
MOON-SATURN	Lot of wealth, if both are with Jupiter or placed in the houses whose lord is Jupiter; otherwise bad for wealth; like a Lemur or black faced monkey.
MARS-VENUS	Wealth controlled by wife and in-laws.
SATURN-JUPITER	Wealth connected with goodness and teaching, which may increase after marriage.
MARS-JUPITER	Lot of wealth.
MARS-SATURN	Wealth of a dacoit.
MARS-SUN	Royal inheritance;Land-lord and administrator.
VENUS-JUPITER	Wealth for show-off (empty from within); just like laddoos made of Bundi.
SUN-JUPITER	Most exalted; royal like wealth.

- Whenever the enemy planets in house no.2 occupy the 1st house in the annual chart, it may result in theft, loss of wealth, unnecessary expenditure etc.
- House no.11 is the house of income, and house no.12 is the house of expenditure and house no.3 is the outlet.

The planets occupying house no.3,5,9 or 11 indicate the position of relatives.

- If house no.1,4,7 and 10 are vacant, such a person has not brought anything with him; it is just like keeping the luggage in the cloak-room.
- If the house no.9 is vacant, person gets inherited property.
- If the house no.11 is vacant, person gets inherited property as well as self earned wealth.

3. EXPENDITURE AND SAVING

Moon is wealth and Saturn is the treasurer. Their placement will reveal the monetary condition of the individual. Saturn and Mars are the lords of property. Moon and Jupiter are the lords of gold and silver. House no.11 is the house of income. House no.12 is the house of expenditure and house no.9 is the house of saving (concerning ancestors). House no.2 indicates personal saving and house no.5 reveals savings from children. Consequently income, expenditure and savings will depend upon the positions of the planets in these houses. If benefic, results will be good and if malefic, results will be bad.

4. HOW TO CONTROL EXPENDITURE

The savings will be automatic in the following cases :-
- Jupiter-Sun combined, Both exalted in their own houses or in friendly houses or both exalted individually in own houses or in friendly houses.
- Sun-Mercury - combined or individually as in case of Jupiter-Sun combination.
- Jupiter-Saturn-combined or individually as in case of Jupiter-Sun.
- Mercury - Saturn - combined or individually as in case of Jupiter-Sun.

If Mercury-Jupiter, Venus-Jupiter, Saturn-Sun are combined but not associated with others, there will be unnecessary and useless expenditure, whether there is income or not. If Jupiter is not associated with either Sun or Saturn i.e., either Sun or Saturn is not in Jupiter's sign (Raashi) or is not favourably aspected by Jupiter, income and expenditure will be limited i.e., if a person controls his expenditure, his income will decrease.

A person with planets in no.1,4,7,10 or with a male planet in no.11 will spend and save from his personal savings only.

5. ANCESTRAL PROPERTY AND DEBT

Average life will be the result of the subtraction of house no.11 and house no.12. Out of the nine planets, exalted planets will confer benefic results; whereas the malefic ones will confer bad results.

Example : Suppose there are five benefic planets and four malefic planets.

9 planets + 5 good planets	14
9 planets -- 4 bad planets	5
Total	19
Divide by 2	19/2
Divide by 12	19/24

Result : **If a person inherits 24 shares of property at the time of birth, he will leave only 19 shares for his children. Results of ancestral property will be indicated in the 35 years cycle.**

☞ **NOTE** The planets of house no.9 are the 'gifts', which a man brings for others at the time of birth and the planets of house no.2 are the 'treasure', which a man carries with him at the time of death.

6. MONETARY TRANSACTIONS

Four Kendras (no.1,4,7,10) determine one's fate as under :-

1st house	Body	Profession, relatives business concerning exalted Sun.
4th house	Wealth	Profession, relatives business concerning exalted Jupiter.
7th house	Property	Profession, relatives business concerning exalted Saturn.
10th house	Food	Profession, relatives business concerning exalted Mars.

- House no.3 (Brothers and blood relatives like uncles etc.); House no.5 (children); House no.9 (ancestors and parents) and house no.11 (personal income) ----- all these houses will determine what one gets from blood relations, as mentioned in the brackets.
- House no.2 (in-laws, temple); House no.6 (living compatriots, colleagues, relatives of sons & daughters or maternal uncles); and house no.12 (inanimate worldly things, godly help or good fortune) ---- will determine what one gets from the sources mentioned in brackets.
- House no.6 determines the monetary dealings of the individuals. Friendly planets in this house will benefit the person and the enemy planets will harm him.

PRECIOUS STONES AND MALEFIC PLANETS

In order to ward off and nullify the evil effects of malefic planets, astrologers recommend the wearing of certain types of precious stones. It should be remembered that these stones must be worn on the advice of a specialist having knowledge of gems and not semi-literate professional astrologers whose aim is to dupe the customers and make a fast buck. Injudicious wearing of such stones may cause more harm than good. Here is the list of precious stones related to various planets.

PLANET	COLOUR	STONE	TIME	REMARKS
Malefic Sun	Copper	Ruby	Sunday between 8am to 10 am.	Studded in a copper or a gold ring in the Ring finger.
Malefic Jupiter	Gold like	Topaz	Thursday between 6 am to 8 am.	Studded in a gold ring in the index finger
Malefic Moon	White	White pearl	Monday- Moonlit fortnight or Pooranmashi day between 10am to 11am	Studded in a pure silver ring in the ring or index finger
Malefic Venus	Curd like	White pearl or white diamond	Friday- dark fortnight or Amavas between 1 pm to 3 pm	Studded in a gold ring in the middle finger.
Malefic Mars	Red	Red coral or red ruby but not bright.	Tuesday between 11 am to 1 pm.	Studded in a gold or copper ring in the index or ring finger
Malefic Mercury	Green	Emerald	Wednesday between 4 pm to 6 pm.	Studded in a gold ring in the little finger.

Malefic Saturn	Black	sapphire	Saturday night just after the appearance of stars.	Ordinarily Sapphire should not be worn. Donate only iron articles.
Malefic Rahu	Blue	sapphire	Thursday evening twilight	Sapphire should not be worn. Donate only sarson, barley and coconut.
Malefic Ketu	Black and white	Black and white stone (cat eye)	2 hours before rising of Sun on Sunday	Do not wear any stone. Donate black & white blanket, bananas and seasame.

WARNING

Precious stones should be of purest ray serene. A defective stone may cause harm. Make sure the planet for which the precious stone is being worn is malefic, after taking into consideration not only the house in which it is placed but also the Raashi and adverse aspects.

CHAPTER 36

AGE OF A PERSON

AGE	PLANETARY POSITION
12 Days	Moon No.6 - Sun No.10 - Moon-Ketu No.6
One year	Sun-Saturn combined in Jupiter's Permanent house, when male planets are not in association with or helpful.
9 years	Sun-Moon combined in no.11.
10 Years	Moon-Ketu in no.1
12 years	Moon no.5, Sun no.11, when Male planets are not in association with or helpful. If Saturn is in no.5, he will have a long life, as Sun & Saturn will be friends now.
15 years	Moon-Rahu in no.1.
20 years	Jupiter-Rahu in no.2 OR Jupiter-Mercury in no.6.
22 years	Sun-Rahu no.10 or 11, when no.8 is occupied by malefic (leading to death) planets and simultaneously Sun-Rahu are jointly placed in no.10 and Saturn alongwith a female planet in no.2 OR Sun-Rahu jointly in no.11 and Saturn is malefic in house of death; Person will have a long life if Saturn is in no. 3, 5 or 6.
25 years	Moon-Rahu in no.6 OR malefic Mars (Mars-Mercury no.6, or Venus and Ketu are both debilitating).
30 years	Mercury-Jupiter no.2 OR Jupiter-Rahu no,3.
35 years	Moon-Mercury-Rahu jointly placed.
40 years	Jupiter-Rahu no.9 or 12 or a lot of hair on fore-head.
45 years	Mercury-Ketu no.12 OR Rahu-Jupiter no.6.
50 years	Moon-Rahu no.5, provided both of them are not aspected by any planet OR malefic planets in no.2 or 7.

AGE	PLANETARY POSITION
56 years	Moon-Rahu-Mercury jointly in no.2 or 5.
60 years	Moon-Mercury no.2.
70 years	Jupiter-Ketu no.9 OR Saturn-Ketu no.6 OR Moon-Saturn no.7.
75 years	Moon-Rahu no. 9 OR Moon no.9.
80 years	Moon-Jupiter no.4 OR Moon 3 -- 6 will leave lot of wealth.
85 years	Exalted Moon in no.7.
90 years	Exalted Moon in no. 1, 8 10, 11.
96 years	Exalted Moon in no.2 or 4.
100 years	Jupiter-Ketu no.12 and exalted Moon OR Moon-Jupiter in no5, OR Mars in no. 1, 2, 7 and Sun in no.4, OR exalted Male planets or helpful to Moon OR exalted Moon, Sun and Jupiter.
120 years	Moon-Jupiter in no.12.

CAUSE OF DEATH

PLANETARY POSITION	CLAUSE OF DEATH
Moon, Saturn, Mars in no.5 or 8; malefic Mars and Venus in no.5 or 8 - but not associated with or aspected by Sun or Moon.	May die in the battle-field.
Saturn-Venus combined in no.10 and Sun in no.4.	Heart rending death.
Exalted Sun in no.1 alone and not associated with or aspected by any other planet.	Natural but sudden death.
Moon-Mercury jointly in no.3 or 6. OR Moon-Saturn jointly in no.7 OR Moon-Malefic Mars jointly in no.7 or 10.	Death by shock.
Mercury in no.12, Saturn in no.7 OR Moon-Mercury combined and debilitating Sun OR Moon-Mercury jointly in no.4	May commit suicide.
Mercury in conjunction with Rahu or Ketu and aspected by or associated with Saturn	May die of snake-sting or electrocution.

Mercury-Saturn jointly in no.4 OR Mercury-Moon-Saturn jointly and malefic Sun.	Murderer.
Saturn in no.3; mercury in no.11 OR Saturn-Sun in no.10, Mercury no.8.	May die in a jail.
Venus no.1, Sun no.7 alongwith enemy planets or wicked planets OR Sun-Venus combined in no.3 in birth chart or annual chart.	May die of Tuberculosis.
Sun-Mercury-Moon combined in no.4	Death by a fall from the horse.
Moon-Rahu in no.4	Death by drowning OR strangulation or by hanging.
Sun-Saturn in no.7 OR Sun-Saturn-Mercury in no7.	May be assassinated.
Mercury-Jupiter in mutual aspect	Paralysis

SHORT - LIVED

8 X 8 = 64 is the maximum age i.e., 8th day or 8th month or 8th year - is malefic, danger to life.
- If Jupiter is surrounded by many enemy planets.
- Jupiter, Mercury and Venus in No.9.
- No.9 is occupied by many enemies of Jupiter i.e., Mercury, Venus and Rahu.
- Moon and Rahu in No.7 or No.8
- Mercury in No.9
Such a person's life will be in danger during 8th, 16th, 32nd, 40th, 48th, 56th and 64th year.

MOONS' POSITION IN ITS SIGNS AND ITS LIFE SPAN :

DAY OF DEATH	SIGN	LORD OF THE HOUSE	AGE
Wednesday	1 (Aries)	Mars	90 years
Friday	2(Taurus)	Venus	96 years
Wednesday	3(Gemini)	Mercury	80 years
Friday	4(Cancer)	Moon	85 or 96 years
Tuesday	5(Leo)	Sun	100 years
Sunday	6(Virgo)	Ketu and Mercury	80 years

Friday	7(Libra)	Venus	85 years
Wednesday	8(Scorpio)	Mars	90 years
Thursday	9(Sagittarius)	Jupiter	75 years
Tuesday	10(Capricorn)	Saturn	90 years
Saturday	11(Aquarius)	Saturn	90 years
Thursday	12(Pisces)	Rahu-Jupiter	90 years

FINAL HOUR I.E. DEATH

Final day or year of life is determined by Moon's Position and the planets in No.8 - 12 i.e., Moon's position in the horoscope is known and a malefic planet in No.8, if adversely aspected by No.12, that will mark the end of one's life.

Before making predictions about death House No.6 (underworld and compassion), House No.8 (death and Justice) and House No.12 (Sky and Justice) may be thoroughly examined.

THE FINAL ANNUAL CHART

- Venus and Wicked planets become the most debilitating and malefic.
- Mercury, Rahu and Ketu combine together some how or the other.
- House No.3 is occupied by malefic planets or is vacant and No.8 or 6 or both are occupied by malefic planets or are made malefic.
- Nos.1,7,4,10 are vacant or are not occupied by planets of Birth chart in these houses.
- Moon becomes debilitating.
- No.4 is poisoning No.8 through No.2.
- Mercury occupies No.3,8,9 and 12.
- Saturn is destroying Moon through Ketu.

☠ WARNING

Don't predict death; Time and date will not invariably be correct. Only God knows when a person is to die. Such a prediction may lead to demoralization of patient. Remember "God is great and all compassion". On death, no one can issue a final verdict as it is solely in the hands of the great Master. Pope has rightly said, "God in His mercy hides the Book of Fate". Man may die many deaths before the actual death, if he has a pre-knowledge of it. Let me close the book with the following couplet in Urdu and with a prayer for the Lord in my heart :

> *"Parrhe bhatakte hain lakhon daana, kroron pandit,*
> *Hazaron sayane,*
> *Jo khub dekha to yar aakhir-*
> *Khuda ki baaten Khuda hi jaane"*

"Millions of sages, pandits and Scholars wander about in search of the ultimate reality, but ultimately they come to the conclusion - Mysterious are the ways of god !"

"I beseech God's blessings on all human beings."

Amen !

Uttam Chand

PRACTICAL PALMISTRY

—Dr. Narayan Dutt Shrimali

The Dawn of Self-knowledge

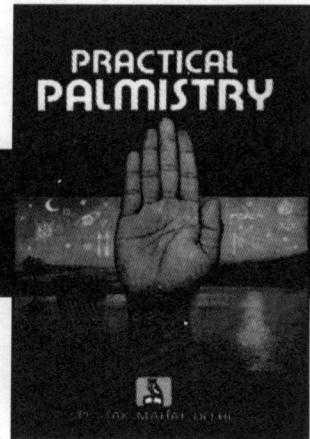

Palmistry is an important organ of the science of astrology, which can forecast the future of an individual authentically. Human existence confronts many hurdles and uncertainties. Hence, man suffers from indecision and is unable to concentrate on his goals.

Of all the sciences of the world, Palmistry has come to the rescue of modern man because it cannot only tell us about the past, but can also predict the future. A palm is a treasure of vitality and working power of a human being from the materialistic point of view and is the source of all activities of life from the astrological point of view. By means of our palm, we know our past and believe it, we understand the present and try to mould ourselves by acquainting ourselves with the future, so that we may remain constantly active.

Practical Palmistry, by Dr. Narayan Dutt Shrimali, is an endeavour to introduce the vast knowledge of Palmistry for the readers' benefit. It contains all the aspects of Palmistry with illustrations and complete information. The vast knowledge of palmistry is encapsulated in this book, but the language is kept simple, which enhances its readability and wider acceptance.

Demy Size • Pages: 365
Price: Rs. 80/- • Postage: Rs. 15/-

NUMEROLOGY
Key to Your Inner Self

—Hans Decoz with Tom Monte

NUMEROLOGY

A Complete Guide to Understanding and Using Your Numbers of Destiny

KEY TO YOUR INNER SELF

PUSTAK MAHAL

Understand Your Life Better

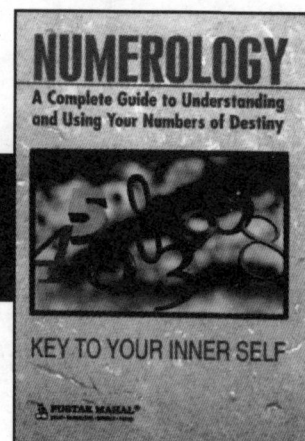

Before the development of verbal communication, ancient man only had the most simple and basic thoughts, most of which were confined to survival. But with language, our spiritual horizon expanded, relationships became complex and the going got tougher.

This book, **Numerology: Key to Your Inner Self,** will help you to understand your life better. When one is introduced to the language of numbers, the universe seems far greater and more complex, yet easier to grasp.

World-renowned numerologist, Hans Decoz and accomplished writer, Tom Monte have teamed up together to produce an easy-to-understand guide that introduces the reader to the basic concepts and applications of numerology. The book begins with a fascinating explanation of what numerology is and gives an intriguing look at the philosophy that lies behind it. Included is a step-by-step guide to calculate your own numbers and to interpret them in a chart form.

Demy Size • Pages: 272
Price: Rs. 88/- • Postage: Rs. 15/-

Instant Handwriting Analysis

—Ruth Gardner

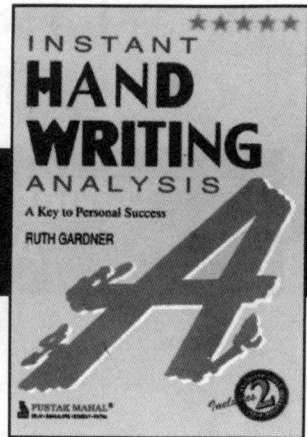

Do your 'Gs' divulge a sensitive nature? Does your writing slant show you to be impulsive? Find out with Ruth Gardner's *Instant Handwriting Analysis*.

Handwriting patterns signal elements of your unconscious, and reveal your desires, fears, weaknesses, strengths, attitudes and more! With this book, someone who doesn't even know you could learn all about you in just a few moments!

This work covers some of the most important and basic factors of handwriting analysis for the explorer of Graphology — a scientific study on the field.

Now you can analyse your own handwriting and that of friends and family with this easy-to-use book. In just a few moments, you will know what the slant, stroke, word-spacing, margins, size and pressure, letter formations and signature reveal about your personality. You can even learn to change certain aspects of yourself by changing the way you write!

Compare your writing with the samples in this book — it's that simple! There is even a section on doodles. You may find that graphology is your next career or hobby!

Demy Size • Pages: 152
Price: Rs. 80/- • Postage: Rs. 15/-

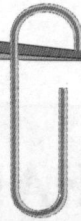

Marriage-Matching Astrologically

—*T.M. Rao*

- *'Marriages are made in Heaven' —discover its true essence*
- *How stars influence your marriage*
- *Find the 'made-for-each other' partners through horoscope matching*

There have been many astrological books on marriage-matching available in the market—but most of them deal only with certain aaspects and not all the essential information are available at one place.

The aim of this book is to put in a concise form all the essential principles of 'Marriage-Matching' so that the readers can have their satisfaction of getting all the information at one place. This book tells us how to dispel the unnecessary and unknown fears that may crop up in the selection of *bride* or *groom*. It also tells us how the Divine approval and blessings of heavenly stars play the role on the search for perfect combination.

❖ Know how stars influence the marriage

❖ Find the right partner through correct horoscope matching

❖ Ensure remedial measures to pacify conflicting *Nakshatras* and *Rashis* in the event of mismatch

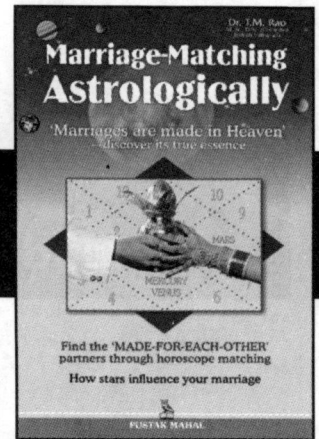

Demy Size • Pages: 142
Price: Rs. 80/- • Postage: Rs. 15/-

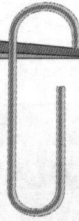

Astrology for Layman

—*Dr. T.M. Rao*

The most comprehensible book to learn Astrology

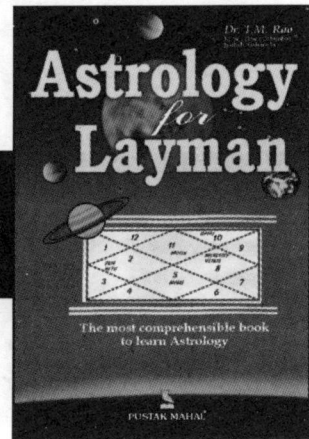

Astrology today is universally recognised to be a 'science', based on sound mathematical principles and calculations. But while it is easy to agree with this promise, it is difficult to find a well-researched comprehensible book to guide the general reader. Answering this need, 'Astrology for Layman' is designed to bring home to the reader the fundamentals of the discipline along with the predictive aspect. One who reads this book will not only be able to make fairly correct predictions, but will also be encouraged to take to the study of more advanced works.

The book is a complete astrological guide that begins from the basic fundamentals viz. how 12 *rashis* have been formulated, the basic principles of casting a horoscope, what are the qualities ascribed to people born under different signs (for instance, people born under Aries are of independent view), what's the meaning of *Bhavas* (viz. what does a planet indicate in a specific house), what do the *Mahadashas* of different planets mean, what are *'yogas'* (for instance, *'Sakaka yoga'* makes a person stubborn and hated by relatives and *'Parvata yoga'*, makes a person passionate) – besides offering special section on the subjects of matrimony, compatibility along with case studies predicting major events of a person's life like career-change, gain or loss of fortune, etc.

Demy Size • Pages: 184
Price: Rs. 80/- • Postage: Rs. 15/-

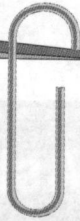

Explore the Power of ASTROLOGY

—Dr. A.P. Parashar
Dr. V.K. Parashar

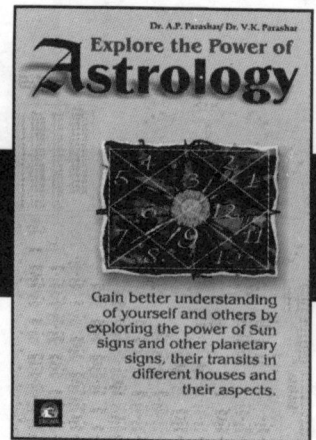

Backed by years of astrological experience, Dr Ambika Prasad Parashar and his son Dr Vinod Kumar Parashar offer a fresh perspective on each Sun sign and the signs of other planets when they transit different houses in a chart (*kundali*). Examining the main areas of life – relationships, finances, family, career, health, love and personal characteristics – the authors probe the gifts of the Sun signs interwoven with the influence of other planets' aspects and transits in the houses. The book tells readers how things operate in life due to astrological influences, so that they can approach life from a new perspective to discover the right vocation and attain great success, happiness, love and peace. Case studies of prominent persons are dealt with extensively to help readers understand the planetary influences and other signs that indicate foreign travel, property, love, money, position, luck and other factors in life. The book also throws ample light on how to compute one's own *lagna* (rising sign) and make one's own chart, if required.

Demy Size • Pages: 200
Price: Rs. 96/- • Postage: Rs. 15/-

भृगु संहिता फलित प्रकाश

ज्योतिष शास्त्र का कालजयी ग्रंथ
महान् ऋषि भृगु महाराज की अमर रचना

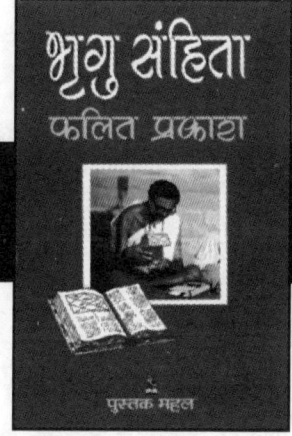

❑ **पुस्तक की विशेषताएं :**

✦ असीम ज्ञान एवं पाण्डित्य से ओत-प्रोत हज़ारों वर्ष पूर्व रचा गया फलित ज्योतिष का अभूतपूर्व ग्रंथ, जो आज भी प्रासंगिक है और आने वाली पीढ़ियों के लिए लाभकारी है।

✦ इसमें केवल फलित अंग हैं। इससे संसार के किसी भी स्त्री-पुरुष की जन्मकुंडली में स्थित विभिन्न ग्रहों के शुभाशुभ प्रभावों की जानकारी आसानी से प्राप्त की जा सकती है।

✦ फलित ज्योतिष का सबसे बड़ा लाभ यही है कि जन्मकुंडली द्वारा जीवन में घटने वाली तमाम तरह की घटनाओं का पता चल जाता है।

✦ शुभ फलों से उत्साहवर्धन होता है और जीवन सही रास्ते पर गतिशील रहता है। अशुभ फलों का विचार हमें सतर्क कर देता है, ताकि विपत्तियों से बचने के उपाय किए जा सकें। यही सब इस ग्रंथ में दिया गया है।

डिमाई आकार • पृष्ठ : 800 (सजिल्द)
मूल्य : 225/- • डाकखर्च : 20/-